THE AGE OF SEPARATION

A Holistic Framework to Reclaim
Our Power and Save Our Planet

RYAN J. KEMP

Printed in the United States of America
First Printing, 2020

ISBN 978-1-73538-184-8 (Paperback)
ISBN 978-1-73538-180-0 (eBook)
Library of Congress Control Number: 2020914665

Cover and book design by Susan Malikowski
Printed in the U.S.A.

ryankemp888@gmail.com
www.ryanjkemp.com

This book is dedicated to all the guides in the world who help shine a light on the path toward peace. Thank you.

Walking towards the light,
Forever towards our own sun,
A candle in time

No matter what, burn.
Illuminate your darkness,
Torch your deepest fears.

Shed your rays on all,
No walls between the other;
The light permeates.

Through the cracks it comes,
And the fog it does lifteth,
Warming frozen Hearts.

Three hundred sixty
Back towards the horizon point,
Where our refuge lives.

Contents

Preface

Alōha, and thank you for your interest in this book. I want to extend my gratitude to everyone who is keen enough in the current state of their individual world and own collective external states to make the decision to become more informed beyond polarizations. Our viewpoints have long been fragmented through the commoditization of knowledge and the specialization of interest. We are taught to standardize and to focus on what will help us climb the ladder of society. We ignore histories and balk at alternative viewpoints if they don't fit in with the consensus medium or with our own ambitions, which are not inherent, but rather, have been drilled into us.

While I wrote this book based on my own life's journey, I hope that my words can help us all integrate ourselves into the multi-dimensional world in which we belong. By embracing the movement toward holistic models and ways of being, we will create a happier, more peaceful world for ourselves and for our children. After all, this planet is the only one we have. We are all in this together, despite any differences in our beliefs.

The aim of this book is to provide a glimpse into a holistic framework for readers to utilize ancient wisdom to shift into a new paradigm of value. This value system counterbalances the current economic model of accumulation, exploitation and the extreme polarizations of duality, all of which are the drivers of violence, war, poverty, and separateness. When catapulted by multi-faceted global issues, we can look deeply within ourselves to see what we value, and can be guided in this return to the root of our beings by the experiential pathways that our ancestors have trodden. Eastern practices such as Yoga, Buddhism and Ayurveda, as well as our planet's indigenous belief systems all connect at the source—the worldview of non- separateness.

From disciplines like the *Yamas* (the first limb of Ashtanga Yoga) and the path of *vairagya* (non-attachment), to Ayurvedic medicine, to our food supply, to psychedelics, our journey will allow us to return to our roots and reclaiming our responsibility as sovereign human beings. We do this by reclaiming the things that make us human and re-avowing fragmented parts of ourselves, thereby healing the levels of disconnection that run rampant in our modern world. We begin to take responsibility for the reclamation of our own power.

To achieve true non-dual peace—that is, peace without the relative necessity of war—we must reach a point where we are no longer attached and reactionary to the constant changing of external stimuli. Once we reach this equanimity, we begin to experience interconnectedness and non-dual states of being that cultivate compassion and togetherness out of understanding, acceptance and love. These principles run parallel to the worldviews of many indigenous cultures, are achieved by psychedelics, and are the ultimate state of Yoga.

This book will explore *sattvic* (peaceful) living principles, Yogic experiential science, Buddhist discoveries that mirror quantum physics, indigenous worldviews, and the evolving psychedelic boom to assist us in deconstructing the paradigm of accumulation as the inherent disease- inducing mechanism of an individual organism and the planetary body. By halting consumption and the accumulation of various physical and non-physical objects, we can heal ourselves, humanity, and the planet, thereby creating non-dual peace.

Before we delve into the narrative, I would like to articulate its main principles, so that they may be considered in context. These are as follows:

- **These words are universal to the human condition.** This is a book of applied experiential truths rendered from ancient and modern masters, indigenous groups, and personal experience. These truths are not subjective or sectarian, but rather, are time-tested and universal to the human condition. However, it is worth bearing in mind that we can only derive real subjective truth from our own experiential wisdom and that although we can express truth in words, the ultimate truth cannot be spoken or relayed in form, language or any other medium of expression.

- **Knowledge is different from wisdom.** Wisdom can rarely if ever be derived from simply reading something. If you read about water, can it quench your thirst? Can it tell you how it feels to find a river with a cold, fresh flow and letting the water slip down your throat? By like token, this book is for authentic truth-seekers, ones willing to do the experiential work themselves. These truth-seekers, who are intrinsically motivated to learn and grow, will experience incremental change as they patiently absorb countless years of wisdom into their energetic systems, and begin the journey back to themselves.

- **Experiential testing is necessary for any 'progress.'** As stated above, we derive truths from our own experiential wisdom. This book features specific prompts, questions, activities (internal as well as external), with which you can engage so that reading it is a transformative experience.

- **We move from superficial to deep, gross to subtle.** As you progress on this reading journey, some information or realities, once you experience them may prove at first to appear quite disheartening, nihilist and difficult to bear. These are normal shifts that happen as you begin to uncover layers that have been suppressed beneath the superficial parts of the mind, and are a key part of the journey. Vulnerability is not always easy. Imagine silt being stirred up in a riverbed from a storm; the water at first becomes cloudy. A very important aspect as these deeper layers arise is to keep in mind the goal of equanimity, or non-reactivity. Reactivity can be defensiveness, denial, escapism, any of da kine. Equanimity or non-reactivity to your own progress and the changing external reality is one of the 'checkpoints' towards extricating yourself from the dualistic system of language, and moving toward freedom, which is the inclusion of everything without the attachment to the aversion or craving of any of it.

- **These are not mainstream views.** Most of what you read here will not be seen in most mainstream contexts, because it counteracts our current economic system; an exploitative one that forces us to work in order to live, and commoditizes practical wisdom. This is how Yoga became exercise, shamanism became a trend, and sacred practices and principles like asana and ahimsa lent their names to brands. The only real reason we need money is to meet our basic needs—food, water, and shelter. Everything else is superfluous. As we begin to minimize our lives with an effortless ceasing of accumulation, the simplicity and presence becomes paramount.

To conclude, this book lays bare some of the reasons for our distraction from what truly matters and in doing so, can bring us back towards the origin of personal responsibility and the reclamation of our power as sovereign human beings. My hope is that these words may help guide us to a path of non-violence, honesty, generosity, and community that has been pointed at for many for thousands of years. Thank you for joining me on this journey. May you get from it what you will.

Ryan Kemp
Kaukapakapa, New Zealand,
February 22, 2020

Introduction

It is great to be a generalist—to be curious about everything, but not to be an expert at anything. Specialization only leads to fragmentation. To be a jack of all trades, to me, has always seemed more well rounded. As we have no original thoughts in the first place, since all thoughts are derived from the languages, communities and cultures of which we are a part, our individual responsibility only has meaning in terms of our relationship to our planet, cultures and languages as a whole; to the trees, to your mother, to your dog, to the air we breathe. Without relationship and the platform for which this relationship unfolds, we would be unable to return to ourselves.

To that regard, I would like to start by giving you a brief synopsis of where these words are coming from, so that you understand the evolution of consciousness that 'I', the writer has experienced, which gives some context to the unfolding book.

The first time I experienced another reality was at the age of 17, with the assistance of a substance called *salvia divonorum*, or 'the diviner's sage.' It was legal at the time in New Hampshire, and my friends and I purchased a bag of the 120x concentration. When I say another reality, these are the only words I have to describe another realm/dimension/plane of existence where the rules of this reality that we normally function upon did not apply. A lifetime passed through my consciousness in about five minutes of Earth time, and the space that I was in was unlike any landscape I have yet to see on Earth. A bridge of eyes led me down into underground tunnels and kingdoms, where the directions were all switched around; left was up, right was northeast. There was a magnetism of some sort that is hard to describe in words, but my physical body was unable to sit up. These five minutes of transportation, I was told later by a kahuna on the island of O'ahu, was the initial crack where the light began to come in.

The next morning after the salvia experience, I remember trying to function in high school baseball practice. When the coach hit me a ground ball, I just let it roll right through my legs, still not accepting the fact that this was my body. It was as if I was witnessing Ryan at baseball practice rather than truly being there to participate in it. After all, I had just spent a lifetime in a completely different reality, as vivid and tangible as this one. The other place and time in which I found myself the night before was so real that it took me about a week or two to finally re-assimilate back into the understanding that this so-called Ryan was in fact my life in this time-space locus. If I knew what I know now, I perhaps would've sought out the council of elders who could have helped me digest these realizations and integrate them into an aligned life that can merge with societal constructs. However, with no eldering process around, I was thrust back into a society where I was only more and more confused.

A few years later, I enrolled at Northeastern University in Boston. I was very talented at baseball, so I first started out on the varsity baseball team with an academic scholarship. That only lasted a year or so, and then I quit, not wanting to succumb to, what I viewed at the time, the ego of an oppressive coach who monopolized all of my free time on the weekends and gave me little time in the field in return. In 2011, the summer after I quit the baseball team is when I began traveling. I studied Chinese Philosophy in Hong Kong for a summer term, and then studied in Valencia, Spain soon thereafter. My exchange credits allowed me to graduate from Northeastern University in the summer of 2012.

After finishing university in Valencia, Spain in the summer of 2012, at ESIC Business School, I moved to Bali-Nyonga, Cameroon, a small farming village in the Northwest (Anglophone) region of the country close to the border of Nigeria, to begin working on a project called Jola Venture. The goal of this project was to find a collaborative way to cut down on the food spoilage rates of farming confederations, which were hovering close to 50% in the area surrounding Bamenda. As a 22-year old from an upper-middle class family living in suburban Boston, being catapulted into a Sub-Saharan African farming village was quite the trip! There was no running water, we often had to kill our own chickens if we wanted to eat them and everyone around me was the opposite skin color. Talk about reverse conditioning; it was definitely a wake-up call. A few other graduates of Northeastern and I lived in a small house there for about seven months. We had two goats named Gatsby and Grimsby, a trifecta of chickens, and a small garden out back where we grew tomatoes and peppers.

Our average day in the village was normally research-based. We would hop on the backs of motorbikes, which in pidgin is called okada, to visit small farming communities about 10 miles out of the main village of Bali-Nyonga. We would ride down bumpy, pothole-ridden dirt and mud roads, with farming tools and cook-stoves on the backs of the *okada*. We would chat with the village leaders, learn about their culture and worldviews, share some of our own, and learn about their specific farms and varietals. We would hear about the roots of their struggles, their desires and their proposed solutions. We would share lunch and fresh palm wine, and return home around sunset, after having eaten delicious foods, chatted, drunk, danced and delved into the depths of the day.

Meeting and connecting with the Cameroonian people simultaneously connected me to my own being, by casting a light on how limited my worldview was. I often wondered how I was being perceived by them, or thought I was being perceived, through my small understanding of neo-imperialism and the atrocities brought on by colonists in prior centuries. Here is where my entitlement and privilege began its disintegration process. All of these parts of my so-called personality and essence that I had accepted as concrete parts of myself were now under a magnifying glass for the first time in my life. And similar to when a magnifying glass starts to focus light on an object, it begins to melt away. This was the beginning of the journey chronicled in this book.

After leaving Cameroon, given that I was a recent graduate, I found a job that fit roughly with my university's major's focus. I had less than $10 left in my bank account, and some parental pressures to do something with my life, so I began to look for a job. I was blessed to still be able to live with my parents in the suburbs of Boston before I found the job, which was at a software company somewhere south of the city. It was one of the most sterile, boring and lifeless office environments and companies I have ever witnessed or been a part of to this very day. By mid-summer, about four months into the job, I was ready to be done.

In the mid-summer of this year I then traveled to Israel on birthright, or Taglit, where I had a few very intense experiences. One such experience was at Kotel, which is often referred to as the Western/Wailing/Buraq Wall, which I will describe here.

I had wrapped *tefillin*, a set of small black leather boxes containing scrolls of parchment inscribed with verses from the

Torah, around my arm and head. This *tefillin*, I was told by a Jewish man at the wall, is utilized by people of the Judaic faith as a direct antenna to Elohim, or Adonai. Once tuned in with the *tefillin*, I walked up to the wall with written prayers of well-wishes for loved ones and planted them in the wall. Then, I began to chant in Hebrew.

Within fifteen seconds of beginning the chanting, my body was taken over by something. It blew through and into the top of my head like a cool wind and I was taken over by intense bodily spasms, shakes, and profuse sweating. This left me feeling shell-shocked and quite confused, and after completing the chant I staggered over to a bench somewhere far from the wall and just sat for a while and cried. When I described this to woman I met in Mt. Ida, Arkansas who lived on a quartz mine years later, she said it was a spiritual initiation. Whether or not I was primed for this by a salvia trip of 120x concentration when I was 17 is another question to which I will never know the answer. Frankly it doesn't matter because it happened. As we learn to release our storylines and the continuity of our identity, we begin to realize that everything is perfect just as it is.

This experience in Israel was profound enough to reawaken me from the spiritual nap that I had fallen into at my job and the consensus reality that was preached surrounding it. I began again to seek answers more fervently, and looked for external stimulation from my direct environment to attempt to find those answers. This mostly manifested itself through experimentation with various types of entheogens; psychedelics.

A few months later, I quit the lifeless software job and ended up on the Hawai'ian islands, on a small artists' village on the west side of O'ahu in Waia'nae. By this time, I was ingesting entheogens in large doses and on an intensive basis. There were times where visually, literal veils were falling from my eyes, most prominently on a trip to Montreal with a dear old friend of mine, where the entire visual depth field of energies changed. In this period, plants and I communicated for the first time and many of these things that I viewed as impossibilities began to enter the realm of the possible, or at least, potentialities of existence that I had never had imagined even in my dreams. Specific things and people that once mattered to me no longer mattered. I began to view everything that had been happening around me and within me as conditioning, or as an energetic pattern formation, a neural pathway, to the extent that I had no idea what I actually even liked to do or who I was. Put briefly, I was now lost in a vast world of endless possibility and interconnectivity, one in which the truths that I thought that I had known vanished.

For the next seven years, I lived on three different Hawai'ian islands for around three months at a time as well as traveling back and forth through the U.S.A., the Caribbean, Central America, Australia, Africa, Europe, and Asia. The longest I spent in one location was five months in San Francisco in 2016 while working for a start-up in the healthcare field.

For this entire time, I dipped into roles as varied as: permaculture farmer in the Dominican Republic, primal skills trainer in Texas, shoeless beach poet on various Central American shores, horse and pig caretaker in the West Maui mountains, veggie burger fry cook in Massachusetts, sustainable development consultant for the government of Cameroon trying to introduce recycled polymers to prevent the erosion of rural farming roads (where we were approved for a $150 million dollar loan from the Development Bank of Southern Africa, yet the corruption of the government foiled our plans), dishwasher at a tapas restaurant in Darwin, Northern Territory, Australia, children's book author, start-up employee in San Francisco for a venture funded company, solar micro-grid energy entrepreneur in Myanmar, mangrove forest tree-planter on the banks of the Bay of Bengal, camper van bum in Tasmania, intentional community apprentice in a food forest in Ka'ū, Big Island, Mahayana Buddhist student and meditator in a monastery in Nepal, Burning Man build-crew member, and finally, project engineer for a large scale solar EPC company based out of New Jersey. I was fired from the solar company this past year, February 2019, and embarked to Italy, Ghana, and Romania for further exploration.

Having visited more than 45 countries over the course of the past eight years, and never having spent more than five months in the same location, I have experienced countless life-paths, cultures and worldviews, and my identity has evolved. Put another way, we could also say that my identity has begun to dissolve.

All of this traveling did have an escapist quality towards it in the beginning, nudging me to move from a conditioned way of life toward a more open one where I questioned what was actually going on in the world and within myself. I became averse to cities. I was craving adventure and connection with the land. It had come to my attention that every single thing that I had accepted as factual, necessary, or true to me was actually false, unproven or just someone else's conditioned opinion. The only aspect of truth that I could truly touch was from my own personal experience and I was looking to rack up as many as possible.

The more I began to look at the ways of life of most of my peers and family within 'the system' or consensus reality, the more it looked like the game of *Life* that we all used to play as kids. We go to school, get a job, get married, have kids, retire, die. Yet not everyone I saw was happy. In fact, very few were. There seemed to be more jealousy, questioning and skepticism, harboring resentments and feeling disillusioned and disconnected in these environments. Anger and irritability was rampant. Many members of my family who were retiring couldn't use their bodies anymore to do the things they wanted to do because of toxic stress levels, unhealthy eating habits and the loss of wonder and desire to pursue habits outside of consumerist lifestyles. What's the point of all of this, I thought? We work until we can no longer function outside of work. We become bored easily, our physical bodies decay, and we become accustomed to the comfortable beige of a modern-lifestyle. Therefore, I sought a new way to relate to what was going on within myself from a cultural, global, and cosmic viewpoint. Is the world in fact a mirror? Am I in fact a bi-product of every culture within my DNA? What is it to be human?

Now, as I write this in early 2020, I have been submerged into many different states of being, including non-dual states. A non-dual state means that there was no do-er essentially; there was simply a witness to an objective unfolding, a happening. These states first came about in form during many psychedelic experiences, but during my recent time in Mysuru, India, as I was becoming a certified Ashtanga Yoga teacher, were the deepest, most profound experiences that I have had to date. While in Kerala, India, I also became certified as an Ayurvedic masseur and dietitian, and continued to experience these phenomena.

At this point, I have experienced and intuitively understand and grasp the principles of what I am writing about. For example, what is Yoga, and why are non-attachment and selfless service routes to true peace in ourselves and on the planet? My desires and ambitions have been reallocated into the concept of *sādhanā*, which is to assist and guide myself through writing about my experiences, and in turn, share them. I feel a *kuleana*, or a responsibility to share, and if others resonate with what I share or create then that is great, if not, that's alright as well. I am not trying to convince anyone of anything here. Ultimately I am writing to myself. The goal for me in writing is to put down the weight of everything I continually carry in a way that is truly going to lead me back towards a level of constant wonder and self-awareness. It is cathartic and effortless. This level of self-awareness catalyzes my movement towards realization and internal peace, which in turn trickles out to our collective, external habitat.

As in my journey, every spiritual journey must begin with a shift of vantage point. This catalyzes a deconstruction process. Normally this begins to occur when we experience something that enables us to relinquish some level of control. From near-death experiences to entheogens to other spiritual practices, our identified realities begin to be peeled away from the framework that we view as stable and safe. We begin, as we deconstruct our mechanisms of security and identification, to see that all of it is a complete illusion.

In order to rebuild anything into something unshakeable, if the framework is shaky, you have to burn it down to the nails. Like the lava on the Big Island of Hawai'i, destroying existing land but building new Earth, we start from an internal process of demolition. From here, we can start to dive into our current value system and the origination of our core wounds which protect the treasure of our Hearts. See you on the other side, 'ohana—alōha.

CHAPTER ONE

Enlightenment is a Demolition Process

"Asking, 'What is the Truth?' is a demolition project. Most of spirituality is a construction project . . . It just keeps building, and a person feels, 'I'm getting better and better.' But enlightenment is a demolition project. It simply shows you that everything you have ever believed was true isn't . . . It's a removal project. What does it remove? Everything. And unless it's a removal of everything, it's not ultimately liberating."
—Adyashanti, Emptiness Dancing

"Enlightenment is ego's ultimate disappointment."
—Chögyam Trungpa

The beginning of the journey towards awakening lies in the realization that we do not really know anything. The majority if not all of what we have been told is not the truth. Anything that is not the truth we can consider as a lie. Why are we being lied to? Lies hide the truth. Truth is power. When you find truth, nobody can take it away from you. You cannot charge for Truth because a person does not need another person to obtain it. When you have found it, you no longer need to relinquish your own power. Whether or not this is intentional or not, we can never know. Even building conspiracy theories around it will lead us to relinquish more control to the ones we blame. With this framing of the enemy, we continue the cycle of us and them thereby trapping ourselves in the polarities we wish to ameliorate.

These lies, or omissions of truth can be structured in many ways. To name a few, they can be motivated or accidental methods of misinformation, manipulation of truths, alteration of key facts that would sway opinion, or the complete ignoring of histories and cultures that represent opposite world-views of the established narrative. Most of the established narratives we are told are some form of propaganda that helps manage and herd the consensus. If we look to establish a consensus reality agreement of functionality, then we become dependent on that mode of operation; especially as other modes of operation or world-views are destroyed.

Let's take a look back at Nazi Germany and their Minister of Propaganda from 1933-1945, Joseph Goebbels. He states,

> "If you tell a lie big enough and keep repeating it, people will eventually come to believe it. The lie can be maintained only for such time as the State can shield the people from the political, economic and/or military consequences of the lie. It thus becomes vitally important for the State to use all of its powers to repress dissent, for the truth is the mortal enemy of the lie, and thus by extension, the truth is the greatest enemy of the State." [1]

The Truth becomes the enemy to a consensus reality. The Truth can topple the entire structure of the elaborate building being constructed upon dependency. This is because it aligns people with their true power. Like Jenga, when you pull out the pillars of a building, which in this case are resting on the backs of the people, the building collapses. To this regard, when we truly see our complicit nature in the structural integrity of something we do not align with, we have but no choice to change.

As we stay trapped in the existing constructs we begin to forget the subtleties of the subjectivities of truth. We utilize science and proof in order to believe something which casts out our own intuitive processes and things that are hard to explain in words. We begin to dismiss experiences if they do not align with something that is stated in science. If we cannot quantitatively define something, we don't believe it to be real. This limits us deeply as we mostly operate in terms of the visible world. We cling to the physical world, the world of form, and are fearful or skeptical of the invisible. We are trained out of our intuition, as we are told knowledge is more important than imagination. And, we are told that the more knowledge the better, which is why we continually look to obtain more and more of it. Einstein states the opposite—that imagination is far more important than knowledge. Moreover, even this knowledge, that we have the desire to accumulate to increase our value to a societal model, is knowledge that is formulated and labeled as academic for the seamless continuation of our current exploitative operating system (OS) that we function within. Therefore, knowledge becomes hypocritical and fragmented in the scheme of our extractive economic model of accumulation. It is being pegged specifically to the proliferation of a system in which corporate desire and the maximization of profit lead to the oppression of people, animals and the environment, and the disconnection of humans and Nature. Knowledge alone does not create wisdom, and our desire to obtain as much of it as possible renders the subtleties from which it is acquired numbed.

On a practical level, as of today, to compensate for the lack of integrity in the economic structure, the government is buying shares of ETFs, bailing banks out, and helping large-scale corporations so that they do not fail. Why? Because if they did, the entire operating system would fail. We print trillions of dollars based on fractional reserve lending that is no longer pegged to anything real. Monopoly money is real. From the lobbying grounds to biased interest representation, we are allowing the allegedly legal framework of deception and bribery to justify our way of life. Just take a quick look at interconnection between the food and pharmaceutical industries and their relation to legislation.

Only since the advent of the internet, which puts endless information at our fingertips, have we had the chance to really delve into the depths of research, opinions, and experience from around the world in seconds. Yet most people are not using this amazing tool for these things due to the distraction capabilities programmed into our biology so that we become addicted to the feedback loop of social stimulation. If our brain's biological mechanisms attempt to battle the YouTube super-computer, I doubt we will win. The mind-numbing channels of sponsored news, social media and consumption continue to keep us in their grasp and drained of personal and financial resources. I mean, it's called a television program for a reason! We are now constantly in a state of either being distracted or being the distractor. This mantra of multitasking is in the name of efficiency and productivity, and thrives on the lack of our attention spans caused by instant gratification. Our ability to concentrate is being whittled away at such a clip that the average attention span now of a human is 8 seconds.[2] I think a goldfish's is 5 seconds; not good company to be in. If we cannot allocate attention to any visible facts, of course we don't see what is happening right in front of our faces. If we cannot even focus on average more than eight seconds on what is in front of our faces, we have no chance to tap into the subtleties of intuition while bombarded with stimulation. Without this attention to detail, there is a lack of intention, and without intention, we are flags in a windstorm.

We are kept busy and compartmentalized to reduce our holistic ability for critical thinking. Many jobs want you to be keeping busy in business even if there is no work to be done. We are becoming more and more specialized in specific things, creating more and more fragmentation in the world, and essentially, more and more fragmented within ourselves. Being busy and biased has become the norm. We attach to our opinions like they are our own and consume other's to back them up and defend our stance. This inevitably creates unrest and violence because of the disconnection of a shared stance behind the superficial opinion structures that are rooted in our own desire to be right.

This compartmentalization has rendered us into a hyperconsumerist society that seeks external validation for internal feelings of inadequacy. To paraphrase George Carlin, the American pastime changed from baseball to consumption long ago. This includes not only the consumption of material goods, but also the consumption of ideas, ideologies, beliefs, fandoms, information, identifications, and more, which separate us from each other by forming strongholds of collective identity that make us feel right. Self-righteousness stands at the gate with shield and sword, preventing us from entering into the deep inner worlds of purpose and meaning for which we long.

We can only be right if someone else is wrong. As we become so enamored with this collective consumption, people can hardly sit still anymore and look at a tree, or listen to the wind. The only antidote to all of these woes is stillness and presence. Along with it comes the depth that has been supplemented with superficiality and efficiency, and with that depth comes the subtlety of experience and interconnectedness.

LANGUAGE AND CONDITIONED SUPERFICIALITY

No wonder people feel that they are lacking purpose and depth in their lives. After all, purpose stems from experiencing and witnessing the depth, the nuances of multi-dimensionality within the lives that we live. We live in the delicate nature of life in balance with death. Purpose is witnessing the sacred in the profane.

Most of us skim the surface of our relationships, romantic and non, never asking deep questions for fear of not being respectable or for fear of being vulnerable. And then we allow ourselves to feign contentment at the lack of connectedness that stems from it, meanwhile feeling hollow and lonely. We're trapped in a catch-22, between craving to be seen yet being afraid to be. Trust is lacking. We are defending ourselves because we have the illusion of something to protect. If we don't need to protect our fragile little egos, what would we defend? Who would we be if no one was home?

Loneliness in itself is one of the main insecurities that drives dependency on a centralized system. If you recognize your interconnectedness with all things, loneliness cannot exist. You can be alone yet not lonely. Language, specifically the English language, is one aspect of this equation that I feel leads to our inbred division, and hence loneliness.

We often think about language in pretty superficial terms. Yes, it is absolutely necessary for the relaying of ideas and communication, yet we remain trapped in its labels. Unless you begin to really delve into phonetics, that is.

While sitting in Wailuku River State Park in Hilo, as I watched the river water flow through rocks before toppling off of Rainbow Falls, I came to wonder what my world, my literal visual reality as well as my emotional connectedness to Nature would look and feel like if I spoke a different language. What are the worldviews that are encapsulated in a language that is less transactional than English? What would my being look and act like if it was primed by a more holistic and interconnected interpretation of reality? For example, being in Hilo as I was, we can take the Hawai'ian language as an example. Would my entire picture of reality painted continuously through my brush-strokes on the movie-screen of consciousness look and feel totally different? If so, would I inherently act differently in accordance with the world that I interact with and see? Perhaps the language is more romantic, or fluid, or connective. My friend whose family is from Lebanon told me that Arabic is essentially a religious language, with connectivity to the divine in many of the concepts and words. Yet, even in that, translation and language as a whole always seems to come up short of the real unfolding of the moment. The moment is so much vaster than mere ideas relayed into words. Language, after all is the freezing of reality. It is merely a thin veil that separates the unfolding verbiage of process into a still-life noun.

In order for us to embrace subtlety and presence we must begin to detach from our reliance upon explanation. An explanation is not the truth; it is merely a way to conceptualize it. Whatever we call it, label it or talk about it, can't be how it really is, because all we are doing is creating a thought and the thought is not the reality. It is a still-label of the reality amidst the constantly changing wholeness. The reality is what is unfolding every single moment at such a rapid discontinuity that it appears continuous. Thought is trapped in the past and in the future. Thought is a screenshot of perception, smacked with a label and boxed into syllables and sounds. How could this ever be the expanse of all existence and consciousness that is weaving together in the moment? We often forget this while we attempt to relate cross-culturally. If you label God as Allah, and I label God as Buddha, and she labels God as Jesus, who is to say just because of the difference in names, we're not all saying the same thing? To meet behind the understandings of language are where we find some of the roots of our interconnectedness.

We often attribute so much to our thoughts, forgetting that

our thoughts are not reality. Language is just a tool to attempt to wrap our minds around the world—it is not the world. These labels themselves separate us from what is happening, and some languages separate less. Some languages depict nature as more of a living, breathing entity of which we are a part than English does. For example, while I was at the Ute Indian Museum in Montrose, Colorado, one of the videos showed Clifford Duncan, an elder of the Ute Indian Tribe, describing the importance of the depths of language.

He states,

> "The language that we speak today, we use it to communicate. But the other part to that, it contains words that have a spiritual connection to nature or to higher level spirit. Words that we cannot put into like English. That's why its important."

As we delve into the existential truths, we see that outside of our language, which builds the constructs of our reality, there is no separation of rock and squirrel and sky to us as human beings. We are but a parcel of the same mass. Perhaps clinging to language, thoughts and ideas is one of the roots of our superficiality. We are on a collective journey to stop clinging so tightly to our labels of what we think reality is.

THE LOSS OF ATTENTION AND THE GAIN OF CONDITIONING

Another frightening part of these trends into superficiality in my eyes correlates with the eroding of attention span. Attention is one of the keys to entering into the subtleties of Truth. The shorter this becomes, the shallower the states of being become. We also bundle up attention in our minds rather than our Hearts, thoughts rather than feelings. How can we be fully present for someone unfolding their layers if we are distracted by what is going on in our own minds? If we are thinking about what we want to eat later or how many likes our Instagram posts receive, how can we ever be vulnerable and experience an authentic connection? Authentic and vulnerable connection requires presence. Presence lies in the merging of the mind and the Heart. And we, like birds distracted by something shiny to add to their nests, flitter away the days without penetrating any sort of fertile depths at all, leaving the seeds of our inherent spiritual natures dormant.

Furthermore, from the point of our birth, until the point where we are reading this now, we have been deeply conditioned, which continues through the strengthening of our habits. These conditions physically manifest as neural pathways. Our parents were conditioned by their parents, who were conditioned by their parents, and so on. My mother admitted to me recently that her mother, my grandmother, was known as 'the worrier'. Now my mother is a worrier, having been conditioned to worry. What a trip! As Ram Dass puts it in many of his lectures, "we all entered into somebody training."

This issue of deep conditioning is not linear. Rather, it is a multi-dimensional, multi-generational phenomenon. Plus, this only takes into direct familial exposure, not even environmental and technological. In fact, the conditioning goes so deep that it even affects our expression of our DNA. This is what the study of transgenerational epigenetics goes into. We won't delve into that here, but I highly suggest looking into it. It is simultaneously fascinating and disturbing.

Now, that being said, not all conditioning is necessarily bad. In fact, we must get out of our definitions of bad and good. However, I am talking about the conditions, the stories rather, the falsities that we continually hold onto that cause harm. The stories that separate us from witnessing and participating in the ultimate Truth of reality. We can view this as divisive. Divisive from Truth. This ultimate Truth, called by many names, is the pure manifestation and expression of consciousness and is represented by our greatest abilities as human beings, which are normally rooted in compassion. As we recollect what has been lost in these regards, we continue walking a healing pathway of multi-generational, multi-cultural trauma that has stricken the planet and Her people deeply and gravely.

The biggest condition of them all, which is encapsulated through the stories we tell ourselves, is our separateness from each other, the Planet, and essentially our existence as an aspect of the divine/consciousness itself. This separation results in the exploitation of the land, the animals, and the people who stand in the way, because it feels fine to harm something outside of ourselves. This is why we attempt to personify things rather than listen to their specific, unique language. We may think that tree isn't alive like I am alive, therefore it doesn't have a right to live, it is just a tree, and trees are meant for paper and desks. We've been deconditioned from feeling the pain of the Earth. We've been deconditioned from feeling the pain of the rhinoceros going extinct because we have been conditioned into a belief that the planet is ours for the taking. If we could feel these things, or merge the Heart and the mind, there is no way we would continue doing the things that we are doing. Our Hearts would break, over and over again. We would see that as the world is being destroyed, so are we. This is why we find ourselves in the middle of the crumbling wreckage of resource diminishment, abuse, obsolescence and consumption that is ecocidal on levels apparently unseen in the history of the world. Actually, the Hopi discuss that this is actually the Fourth World that has followed a similar cycle of humans being consumed in greed and creating destruction, but we will leave that for a later time. In sum of this paragraph, this illusion of separation is the condition from which all others arise.

To attain peace, we cannot add on anything. In fact, we must strip it away. Enlightenment is not a construction project; it is a demolition process. This is one of the main confusions about spirituality. Many view spirituality as a constant acquisition of experience, culture and the like. However, we and everything that we perceive, and don't for that matter, are already divine. Consciousness is not exclusive. The entire mass of the knowable universe is encapsulated in the smallest atomic particle in our bodies. We are already a part of it all. The true spiritual journey is just removing the veils of stories and conditioning that prevent us from experiencing this existential Truth of our own divinity and interconnectedness. Complexity only adds to the division. We are demolishing the layers that separate us from our true nature.

We are in fact, with the conditions and stories that we tell ourselves that are not real, preventing ourselves from finding peace and living lives that are harmonious with our human community and the planet. As we place a false image of reality in between us and the reality that is expressing itself, our movie reel becomes skewed. Cyclical tapes of patterns and thoughts roll over and over, connected by the reels of our conscious habits. We do this, at first, through language, as discussed above.

When I was in a hot tub somewhere in the woods of Western Massachusetts, I was having a conversation about language. My friend Terry and I came to the conclusion that language is the first prison. However, as we discussed it further, we realized that it can also be a prism.

Every aspect of our lives has the capability to enslave us or to free us. From language, comes our conditioned cultural stories, some from childhood, some epigenetically passed down, some not even our own stories. They could be your friend's story that she told herself and you absorbed it through mirroring. These can be stories such as, "My parents are the reason why I am how

I am" or "If my friends don't message me then they don't care about me" or "I am a burden to my family and friends." Whatever they may be, these images of what we think reality is, play out on the film screen of existence via the patterns that we hold in our belief system as true. Even if they are not. All of these stories prevent us from truly being present because we are trapped in thought which is somewhere in the past or future.

Our story of what is, is the division that exists within us. There is no one to point the finger at here. There is no one who can decondition you but yourself. If your neighbor has worked on themselves, you do not automatically inherit their inner-work. It doesn't matter what anyone else thinks you should do. Remember that you are your own medicine and your own poison. You are your own captor and your own source of liberation. This is the beginning of the journey of deconstruction. It brings the responsibility back to you, not the outside world, not the trends, nothing outside of you.

What are the main barriers to responsibility? Trust and faith. Do you trust that you can heal yourself? Do you trust yourself to be able to adapt, ebbing and flowing with the natural tides? Or is it easier for you to step outside of yourself and allocate that responsibility or blame to the universe, the government, or your parents? We are so quick to give away our power to others who appear to have more credentials than us because we don't trust ourselves.

Once we can move into a space of trusting ourselves, which is essentially the universe and every single other centralized agent we pin our power to anyway, we will be led to sovereign growth. The growth happens via de-growth. The growth happens in relation with Nature. The destruction yields creation, which will yield fruit for everyone. It is cyclical, not linear.

I've viewed this cyclical phenomenon in the context of our current time on the planet quite often. I first experienced this insight while living in Cameroon. I could really understand the Earth's macroscopic circulatory system of time when I began to put it in the sense of conditioning. From the beginning of time, we work our way out of the absolute Self. The Bible calls this the fall; many other traditions describe something similar. We build languages, structures, societies, and cultures, only to see that we are headed for destruction, hedonism and a loss of freedom. We hit the apex, and begin our trajectory back down to a different location. Similarly, the West has reached the so called pinnacles of society and development, only to find itself dissatisfied, and there have been movements back towards communes and living in alignment with Nature. However, many countries in the world who have been aligned with Nature and not tasted development seem to need to go through the rise and the fall as we have due to the spreading of capitalistic and consumptive ideology. When we all fall back down, naturally, it is to a different place. Nonetheless, we work our way back towards ground level, base level, Earthen level. As we begin our de-growth, we weave through dirt and wire fences, false beliefs, stories and conditioned reactions, boarded up shops and ghost towns until we reach a point of stillness and acceptance of it all. The sun is rising, and the carrots are growing right on the plane where we all started. Back to the only thing of value; that which provides life. We are a part of it. Nature. Home.

JOURNAL PROMPTS:

1. What are the personal stories you've been telling yourself are true? Example—I am worthless. I should already be successful (add in definition of successful.)

   Note: When I did this exercise, I came out with about 50 personal (not even societal) stories that are not true at all, but that I have been conditioned to believe.

2. What are the societal stories that you believe in? Example
—The richer you are the more important you are
3. What habits or beliefs have you accumulated that are toxic?
4. What habits or beliefs have you accumulated that are healthy?

Journal Prompt 1:

What are the personal stories you've been telling yourself are true? Can you know for sure that they are true?

Journal Prompt 2:

What are the societal stories or narratives you agree with or believe in? Why? Can you know for sure that they are true?

Journal Prompt 3:

What habits or beliefs have you accumulated that are toxic? How can you change them?

Journal Prompt 4:

What habits or beliefs have you accumulated that are healthy? Are any beliefs healthy?

Our Skewed Value System

"This is what the bourgeois political economists have done: they have treated value as a fact of nature, not a social construction arising out of a particular mode of production."
—David Harvey, A Companion to Marx's Capital

"Such a value system might be responsible for the fact that the burden of unavoidable unhappiness is increased by unhappiness about being unhappy."
—Viktor Frankl

As we go into value, to summarize the first quote above, the political proponents of capitalism have created what we deem as valuable based on the system seeking propagation; not by Nature's inherent value. Nature's inherent value is priceless. Capitalism's model attempts to put a value on Nature and then extract from it using the orders of supply and demand. This model only works because price correlates with time, and time is an agreed-upon illusion that is viewed linearly. This value model is a framework upon which we build metrics to measure our superficial growth upon the 3D plane. We are currently not measuring our growth or value pertaining to the subtle depths of the human experience. We cannot pin a commoditized value to something that is priceless. If we truly recognize this, our blind acceptance of our value system crumbles. Part of the unlearning process is to begin to see that our current values are programmed ideals based on an extractive system's desire to continue its existence.

Capitalism's root is to maximize self-interest. This is a self-fulfilling prophecy of sorts. Although capitalism and the rise of innovation through 'civilization' have helped to resolve many global crises, capitalism also creates crises such as poverty, war, pollution, gentrification, homelessness, hunger, unemployment, and deforestation. It builds itself a model to make money off of the issues that it creates, and then labels it philanthropy. Yet because of technological force and neo-imperialism, it is still the most widely adopted operating system on the planet. This brings us to the polarities that such a system creates, which in turn breeds suffering.

One of the main falsities of capitalism is the illusion of scarcity. Scarcity creates competition, and competition in turn creates separation because of the 'us and them' exclusionary nature of finite resources. It also creates a means to control. This control to monetize scarcity is in opposition to an abundant worldview in which the Earth, although finite in physical resources such as land, metals, water, can well provide for every person on the planet. It also is in opposition to the fact that we are more productive and innovative in collaborative, less risk-averse systems rather than competition. When our imagination becomes atrophied because of competition, we lose our ability to think outside the box in profound ways. When the end goals are not profits or results, but rather, the process, the innovation platform becomes a whole lot more holistic, less fragmented, and purposeful. The cut-throat nature also decreases as people have literal mind-space to roam. Control is diminished alongside the fears of riskiness, which in turn allows creativity and imagination to thrive.

This knee-jerk reaction of consumption fueled by our desire to control is highlighted by Marx when he describes what fetishism is. Fetishism by definition is the excessive or irrational devotion or commitment to a certain thing. Our value system has been set to feed the means of the mode of production, which is dependent upon resource extraction and exploitation. To put it briefly, we have an irrational commitment to consumption and accumulation that is fed by the imposed value system's dogma of competition over collaboration. This dogma stems from the attempted control over a finite amount of resources that we desire to surround ourselves with based on the fear of insecurity.

Competition is rooted in two things, identification and accumulation. The identification is with our individual selves that places others outside of our circle of benefit. When we accumulate material and immaterial things, we feel more secure and safe. We are buffering our own fears of death and unworthiness by surrounding ourselves in external stimuli that temporarily makes us feel safe or fulfilled. As opposed to lessening our dependence on external stimuli for fulfillment, we are habitually trained to rely on superfluous needs to make ourselves feel inflated and worthy. Our prefrontal cortexes are in overdrive, creating stress and issues that we no longer have. Most of us are no longer fearful of being attacked by a wild animal as we roam the woods, yet we stay in a fight or flight mental environment creating things to worry about.

The clock continues to tick based on our current value system on how much longer humanity can survive on this planet with massive inequality and population growth alongside a continued exploitative existence. We must look for the root of why we desire this outcome of our collective lives.

IDENTIFICATION LEADS TO ACCUMULATION

Identification leads to accumulation. Why is this? Accumulation is based on desire. Desire is based on the premise that something has value to 'I' if it is acquired. This acquisition cost is what fuels our current value system. This is then extrapolated and commoditized until we function within the unit economics of a human being. Our souls are being sold, commoditized. The priceless entity of a human life has been slapped with a value label that is transferable to fiat currency. Since value is based on two illusions, the illusion of linear time and the illusion of separateness, respectively, it is an abstract and non-attainable reality that is false by Nature. It is acting currently as merely a mechanism to continuously wring out our untrained desire systems, which is key to the current meta-economic system of capitalism and oligarchical collectivism, or dependency on centralized modes of power. This system continually fabricates needs out of thin air and in doing so disconnects us from our true needs as human beings which lie in simplicity and connection with Nature.

These core basic illusions and abstract ideas of time and separateness render our entire value system horribly skewed, since time inherently is not linear. Viewed another way, time is the interval between a thought and an action. As beings who are part of Nature, we operate on cyclicality. When we say history repeats itself, it is because we are not learning our lessons in this curriculum of humanity. Samsara is being trapped in the cycle of death and rebirth. When you are able to break free of the cycle is when you stop getting caught in your own separateness which is fueled by a fictitious identification model based on societal values and conditions. To escape samsara and to stop repeating the detriments of history, we must begin to unlearn who we think we are.

Therefore, our monetized value system is forever trapped

in the past or the future context. When we are fully present in the moment, there is no thought, therefore, there is no time. Henceforth, when present in our existences, there is no need to accumulate because desire is a thought. We share what we have when we can if this feeds others in need in a beneficial manner. We become fluid and connected with Nature's rhythms; the constant rising and passing away of phenomena. We are comfortable enough with our being and do not need things to make us feel worthy and of value. We share with those who need to be shared with, we maintain and keep what is necessary for our survival and flourishing, and the natural ebb and flow of resources and energy moves accordingly. Greed has no value. In fact, it stagnates value. Greed prevents those placed at odds with the inner-workings of the operating system from obtaining value. However, with our current interest system, we are rewarded for greed; hoarding wealth that accrues transactional value. A bodhisattva never accumulates. A bodhisattva acts in accordance with right-action, has no attachment to the action's results and moves along without expecting reciprocity. As we will discuss later in the chapter about Ayurveda, accumulation is the beginning stage of disease formation.

Okay, let's bring it back to a practical level now. Why does a delicious rice noodle soup in Vietnam cost $2, while the same soup in the U.S. costs $10? Because costs are based on the time value of money. Does this therefore state that people's time in other places has less value—that the fruit of their labor, literally, is less valuable? Therefore, do they as human beings, have less value if their time is worth less?

This premise of the value engine rides on the economic condition in which time is linear, when in fact physics shows its non-linearity in accordance with Nature's cyclicality. Let's take a look at nature's growth and decomposition process. We don't really know where seeds began, which is already a mystery. But let's start from the seed. The seed becomes a tree, which yields fruits, which fall and spread more seeds. Animals may eat the seeds and carry them to new places. New trees grow, old trees die, and the soil acts as a medium for this exchange. Mycelial networks spring up before and after this process, assisting all along in the decomposition and regenerative nature of this cycle. Nature consumes itself continuously as a mechanism of eternity. There is no starting point, there is no ending point. The Ouroboros, the ancient alchemical symbol on the cover of this book which is discussed by Joseph Campbell in detail, represents this mystery of cyclicality and Nature consuming itself by using a snake that eats its own tail. Birth, death, birth, death, rising, falling, rising, falling, it's all within the hoop. The hoop has no beginning and no end, it is not linear, hence impossible to value because it all comes from and leads back to itself. The value of the hoop is in the continuation of balance.

So, to get back to our last example, who's to say that Bill from Yonkers, USA is of more value than Nguyen of Vinh Hy, Vietnam? Economists will say it's because of the amount of money that they can put back into the system, via consumption. This is what GDP is. GDP is flawed because it is based on consumption, which does not take into account externalities. If it did, every country's GDP would be negative on an extrapolated finite graph of resources based on planet Earth. That's why oil will hit its peak. That means even internet data will hit its peak. On our linear model of scarcity, what won't hit its peak?

Some economists, such as those involved in the prominent publication of the World Happiness Report (i.e. John Helliwell) and Laurie Santos of Yale are looking into different metrics for measuring happiness, which coincide with different ways of measuring value. It feels quite obvious that this trend should've been implemented a long time ago, since it is very clear that happiness is not derived from consumption. However, perhaps our logical minds had to go about a round-about experiential learning model to learn the hard way that as long as we continually accumulate external stimuli to create happiness, we will come up short. In other words, we have to learn that happiness is not derived from external state changes. This requires a habit shift based on a new understanding of value.

Bhutan has been operating on the GNH, Gross National Happiness for quite a while now.[3] That said, even the current model of the World Happiness Report is flawed because it is pegged to the external world of reciprocity as the measure of happiness. Realistically, and this has been proven by the richest and the poorest people, your monetary value does not determine your happiness. Neither does your attachment to stimuli out of your control, which is the entirety of the external world. We have a hard time surrendering to the fact that the world is out of our control. Only when our internal states can become stable enough within the constancy of change can true joy unfold. Therefore, the longer we keep ourselves pegged to input from the outside world for our happiness, the longer we will continue to operate on an exploitative paradigm of resources in order to fill our emptiness.

Are we really still convinced that consuming will buy us happiness and freedom? Let's also not limit consumption here to material or physical goods. Consumption also plays a part in belief systems, knowledge, ideologies and the like. Is consumption now just a habit we cannot escape? Why do we consume? As long as we continue to view the external world and the curation of an environment that we believe will make us happy, we are never going to be content because the nature of reality in a dualistic field is that everything is impermanent. In other words, the environment that we are so delicately crafting cannot last. Every time something changes, if our internal system is attached to it, we will be thrown into a state of turmoil. This is at the Heart of

Buddhism. Clinging to anything creates suffering. As Ram Dass comically says, if we do continue to cling we will be "cast back to outer darkness."

Back to our value system that is based on finite resources. Let's propose a question. What is something that is by its essence limitless and cannot hit its peak? Spirit, which is eternal, absolute, and immutable.

Nature doesn't have desires; all it does is serve. The serving is not selfish. It isn't represented by conditionality; it doesn't operate on a linear model. Trees don't get upset or have expectations of how many mangoes you will pull from their branches. If you don't pick them, they will fall and be recycled into something else. If it doesn't rain for a week, the trees don't get pissed and just walk away to find more rain. They weather the reality, just as if it were to rain every day. They adapt with the ebbs and flows of itself. Are we able to adapt to the ebb and flows of ourselves, without clinging to the emotional responses that our habitual value system creates? Whether or not trees experience emotion is a different story, as emotion is just energy (e) in motion, and has nothing to do with the innate tendency of Nature to be selfless in its service to animals and humanity.

If you look into the *vrttis*, which are the mind-modifications in Yogic science, it states that to be detached is to no longer have selfish-desire, or a desire to gain anything from anything else.

When you want to gain something from anything without giving value back in return, it is an exploitative relationship. Immediately, we find ourselves in a conundrum. We were given Nature, we inherited it for free, and now, we privatize it to make profits off it without giving back to it. In fact, we just keep taking and taking. What are large scale oil corporations giving back to nature? What are solar manufacturers giving back to nature? Is there taking and giving in balance?

All of this manipulation in the name of development is to

exploit the land for our own selfish means. Adam Smith, who proposed the free market, also had an idea of fairness within that market. However, in this exploitative reality, we are all forgetting one part—the planet! Our entire market system isn't fair. We get 100% of our goods and resources from the planet, yet only some businesses even give 1% back to the planet. Talk about theft. Talk about an unequal value exchange. The entire framework is upside down. And those companies like Patagonia and those who are members of 1% for the Planet, which is a global movement inspiring businesses and individuals to support environmental solutions through memberships and everyday actions, still only give 1%, and act like they are doing some mitzvah. If we really wanted to operate on a free economy based on fairness and non-separateness, the planet would be the recipient of a constant ebb and flow of care and stewardship that doesn't leave soil stripped, resources dwindling, animals slaughtered, human groups oppressed and the skies polluted.

TRAPPED IN TRANSACTION

On an individual level, whether we look to gain wisdom from a book, or gain sex from an attractive new mate, something gained, inherently means something given, lost, or taken from the other side. This is, if a value-exchange is not agreed upon. This is duality, our current systemic and conditioned state of consciousness. Duality is a cycle, a gentle sway to opposite sides of the poles until we can find a meeting point in the middle. Until we find the middle way through, we will always be skewed and out-of-balance. We as humans were put here to escape the cycle and return back to a place of balance. With our current abstract concept of capital which doesn't truly honor the value-exchanges that are happening between Nature and ourselves, our ultimate motivations—greed, maximizing self-interest, and the pitfalls of value—are trapped in the commoditization of time. We are trapped in a cycle of transaction which locks us into imprisonment. We are trapped in these terms of give and take. Imagine if it was share and receive, would we be able to function more connectedly and without as much greed?

What I've noticed throughout my involvement in the launch of various businesses, even social enterprises, is the constant concern about margins and their value of their time. Questions such as, "will this be feasible for me, show me what you've done before, what are you getting from me, what's your hustle, sounds good but what is the pitch, why are you doing this?" are all too commonplace. I get it, businesses do require overhead and variable costs to keep the doors open, I studied finance in university. However, should that take precedence over the purposeful functioning of an organization building itself for the utility of the people?

While in this transactional trap of launching businesses, I saw myself stuck trying to respond but unsure of how to do so. Transactionality, or operating on the illusory perception of the constant exchange of things of equal value, is a mental pattern, a neural pathway that was blocking holistic progress. It's this constant loop of humanity stuck in siphoning off value without giving back a value greater than or equal to what is received that creates our skewed system. Our existing monetary system is a figment that designates the livelihood of an individual or group, which enables the holder of more money to control those who have less. So, if some executive of a cobalt company is earning millions of dollars while the miner in the DR Congo is getting less than $3/day plus dealing with unsanitary working conditions with a constant forced child labor, there is no value exchange equilibrium. It only appears as such, and consumers have no way to currently track through transparent measures how the company is honoring those along its supply chain. In fact, very few people seem to care. Imagine a place where, how companies can view our data through Terms and Conditions, we could monitor the corporations operating procedures through data about their supply chain to ensure the proper treatment of people, animals and the environment across the board. This level of corporate accountability seems nowhere in sight.

Even when the ideas of business collaboration are meant to supersede this division created by personal gain, greed, and specialization, it seems we are always trapped in this economic game that results in disequilibrium. The disequilibrium stems from an uneven transaction based on unaccounted-for externalities of gain and loss. Therefore, there is never any freedom from the existing system of value which is rooted in attachment towards selfish desire which results in accumulation. I feel this is but a habit from which we need to detox. Perhaps a Master Fast Cleanse system could do the trick.

HABITS AND HABITAT

I was very competitive growing up. If I won the game, someone lost it. I didn't care, because I won. If I did good, I got a chicken club sandwich at Wendy's. That was my reward. If I did bad, I didn't get the sandwich. This reward punishment model is so deeply ingrained in most of us that we couldn't even necessarily understand empathy and the fact that our so-called winning isn't really winning at all. It was hard to even imagine a way of life outside of that level of competition. Competition is a habit. We're put down if we don't win, made to feel worthless. Sports preach it, school preaches it. Our habits, reinforced by societal norms, formed our habitat. Habits of reward and punishment, or craving and aversion became neural pathways that guide our formation. Now, our neural trails through the forests of our brain are so well trodden that it becomes difficult to not slip into them as we forge new trails within our minds towards extrication from this existing value system.

As we can see, the word habit is directly tied in with habitat. Our habitat, or our environment, is a place where we reflect our habits. We can use conditioned response as a synonym for habit. We live in a world of our collective habit projections.

Our mental habitat, or external world, is coated in violence, war, discrimination, confusion, inequality, oppression, superficiality and manipulation. As we have begun to see this habitat with "wtf is happening, this is enough" eyes, there are beginning to be movements towards the opposites of these qualities that are rampant in our internal habitual structure and therefore external habitual structure. Combined individual habits are reflected and co-created in the collective. However, even in our move to the opposites of these systems, we are creating another ripple that will lead us back towards the other end of the spectrum because of the see-saw effect of competition and attachment. The middle ground lies in decreasing the polarization between the two sides of the spectrum by lessening our attachment to our conditioned opinions.

If we are to become more collaborative, we must practice non-attachment, or vairagya in our relationships with ourselves, others and to our habits. We need to become non-attached to the results and non-attached to the means. We can have a responsibility to do something, but as soon as we possess the results with a responsibility for something, it becomes harmful to us. The differentiation of the responsibility 'to' versus the 'for' is an important distinction.

It is summarized esoterically as follows:

"The goose does not intend to have its reflection cast on the water, as the water does not intend to catch the goose's reflection."

The goose and the water are both interacting with the world

in an effortless manner, not trying to cast a reflection nor catch it. Yet, the reflection is there.

Lao Tzu states, "Nature does not hurry, yet everything is accomplished."

One can participate in the world, but until one practices non-attachment, it is very difficult to not succumb to habits of desire which stem from identification with our perceived beings. This results in the habit of accumulation to provide us security which is perfect for the continued functioning of our economic OS. If we do not then get what we want or what we expected as the result of the action, we become angry or sad, throwing us back into the cycle of re-compensation for our goal and the tumultuous waves of attachment.

If we deconstruct the value system, we end up needing to redefine value. How can we put a value on things outside of time? How can we put a value on the vastness of the mystery which unfolds in each moment? How can you put a value on a psilocybin experience that was one of the most profound of your life but only lasted 8 hours? How can you put a value on a child being born? Knowledge that can help a whole village? Wisdom to live a purposeful life? Compassion? A smile?

These things are priceless: no matter how much you pay, you cannot acquire them. Therefore, they supersede our value system, as they're outside of the time value of money. Time becomes blurred in vast experience. When we move outside of time, or the commoditization of our lives, we begin structuring new forms of value. One can pay $4,000 for a trip to Kenya to see the Masai, and not get anything out of it but a few nice pictures and a memory for the memory bank. These memories soon will gather dust and serve as a trophy on an altar to be reminisced about before memory fades away and we die. The beauty of the fleeting moments in our lives is where value rests.

The true value system is based on us. What is our value to

us? You are not a commodity to be strung out homogeneously as currency is. Our value is to transcend ourselves and our little stories of reality, which coincide with the deepening of purpose into self-transcendence. Then, there is nothing to do but free others with that awareness, which is an acting of a consciousness stretched beyond our identity and selfish desire for gain. The value is in the extension of ourselves beyond ourselves and into collective liberation. Whatever we can do in the moment to move towards that direction, we do.

All of this being said, how did we get so hoodwinked into thinking that everything had to be dog eat dog, individualized, and identified? As we accumulate wealth and drive around in a Mercedes, there are people on the streets in ragged clothes picking lettuce scraps out of the garbage. We normalize this juxtaposition out of the illusion of our individuality, privilege and self-righteousness. Perhaps, like the cyclical nature of time that we are merely a part of in our identified selves, we needed this time of forgetting to remember. It is part of the cycle, it is part of the search for balance.

That being said, the main façade and reason why I see our group-oriented,consensus reality operating systems so deeply entrenched in this mis-identification of separateness is the manipulation of language or image to spin an individualized and relative truth out of the absolute Truth.

THE ROOTS OF MISINFORMATION

The Yoga Sūtras of Patanjali, which will be discussed later in this book, state, and I paraphrase, "If it's not in holy scripture as reference, how can we know it's true?" I take holy scripture here to mean transcribed through the experiential wisdom of those who have searched for and found a path of harmonious evolution and assimilation for human beings.

In the sūtras, there are three ways. The first two are relatively straightforward; experience or inference. Examples: First, I experience a chair by sitting on it. Pretty straight forward. Second, I infer that it is a chair because I've heard chairs look like that and are for sitting and that woman is sitting on something that looks like what I saw and functions how I heard. Makes sense.

The third one is what arises now in our current time, which has been called Babylon, which comes from the Aramaic root word *Balal* which means 'to confuse'. This has also been called Kali Yuga. A land of smoke and mirrors. This third way relates to taking on wisdom, knowledge and/or words from a person who is an authority on these words or a lineage. In ancient times, the lineage and authority structure was sacred and the teachings kept in them were undiluted. The teachers were undeniably "cooked" as Ram Dass says, and their teachings were effortlessly absorbed through darshan, tribal councils or various sharing mediums. This provided a steady and trustworthy framework for faith in the wisdom and paths that they taught because you believed in them.

The current perversion of the third way lies in a few different places. First, people in authority are motivated by money, power, or influence, and they speak what will pay them or make them more influential. For example, the American Diabetes Association promotes type 1 carcinogens because their pharmaceutical company sponsors are the producers of the medicines to counteract harmful food inputs.[4]

Second, people want to monetize their knowledge and see a quick way to do that, so they adopt the imagery or identity of that which is authoritatively trendy. For example, yoginis all over Instagram who catch people's attention with cute butt pictures so they gain followers, but in reality actually may have no idea what Yoga is or who Patanjali might be. Their amount of following convinces us that they are an authority, and based on our value system of more is best, we believe in them. This is an example of consensus reality. Third, there is not a platform that allows you to discern its usage via the things that you get to experience and then attribute value to according to your experience. Essentially, a retroactive payment engine for experience is not available. Everything we do is pay up front, which leaves everyone with heightened expectations. When those expectations aren't met, then we think we got hustled. We end up in a world where we lack trust because we think everyone is trying to hustle each other. "What do they want?" we ask ourselves. "Why do they want to put me on? What'll they get from it? Was that really worth $50?" Here comes in comparison.

What if there was nothing to get? Where does the absence of conditioned values lie within an economic system? Could the experiences themselves have a value, not connected to economics, which is the existential gold of true transformation?

The gold, the true wealth, is in the service or sharing itself. The service and help that is not motivated by help itself. True service operates similar to the concept of the gift economy. When we are not attached to a commoditized value system, we act out of gratitude and selflessness. We share and we receive. These intangible assets are priceless, because we are connected to what is being served on such a deep level without any value expectation models that we open up fully, enabling transformation to occur. Nothing is bought nor sold, but there is an equitable receiving of the gifts from each other.

When this happens, we step out of the value we place on our own time, our compensatory identities, and our monetary wealth, which are merely metrics of the current value system based on linear time. When we step out of these conditioned shields that have formed an impenetrable fort around the vulnerable Heart within us, we are able to connect deeply on a human to human level, spirit to spirit level, presence to presence level. We share the breath.

This is the meaning of 'alōha' in the Hawai'ian language. Hā is breath, and alōha is the sharing of that breath and presence in this sacred moment in time and space, something never to be repeated exactly the same way again. This hā, the breath, is also where the term hāole comes from, pronounced 'howlie'. If you've ever been on the islands, a hāole is a tourist, usually a white person. The term literally means 'without breath' and comes from the colonizers shaking hands rather than breathing each other in forehead to forehead, as Hawai'ians traditionally did at that time. By acknowledging the shared breath and the shared presence, we acknowledge our own humanity and the agreements between family. When we don't acknowledge it, we are cast back out into division and ultimately violence and exploitation. We all have a right to breathe—that is the universal right to life. When you consider your breath more important than another's, there is an issue there.

Freedom is priceless. Sharing eye contact with your barista after a sip of your soy mocha latte and hugging your mother are free and priceless. Just as the sharing of breath is existentially what links us all to this precious thing we call life itself, we cannot put a value on a life. Life is all living things. At some point, most of us have had this realization. If not, you must ask yourself why.

EXPLOITATION HAS BECOME NORMALIZED

If you still are having a difficult time grasping a world devoid of this engrained value system, consider your actions within it.

Most of our being and day-to-day actions are feeding the system that we don't want because we want things within it. Many of us try to minimize our participation in the system by limiting our interactions within it, a sort of systemic renunciation. However, we have not been able to avoid it entirely, plus now we are pushing it away. We use transportation, buy iPhones, whatever. We cannot have the desires and wants of the systemic aspects of life without the system itself. So, as long as we remain attached to desires for things within this structure, the system cannot dissolve. The system honors exploitation and usury. Usury seeks to use the power that it already has to gain even more—to take what could be easily shared with others and keep it for oneself. I find it necessary to define exploitation now because some people may be getting the meaning twisted.

Exploitation is the action of making use of and benefiting from resources.

It connotes treating someone or something unfairly to benefit from their work. It also connotes an imbalance of exchange. This is very accurate. In fact, we did this right off the bat with Nature. We inherited this beautiful planet, and were never charged for it. Now, we take it away from each other and label it as 'our land' or as 'private property.' We steal the land and its bounties from the indigenous peoples, who cared for it without greed, and then we do not give back in return to those people or the land itself, we just take, take, take. In fact, we exploit these people, oppress them and attempt to silence them. Just as the indigenous peoples of the Americas were long pushed out into the desolate reservations from fertile and ancestrally-connected lands, the voices of animals and the trees cannot be heard by a cognitively dissonant population. Regeneration and stewardship are at the opposite side of exploitation. Exploitation, extraction and hyper-growth is at the root of our entire toxic operating system. It is built on thievery, which continues to occur every day. But it is not necessary to continue the discussion on the base derivation and definition of the word exploitation. We will focus on the above aspect of making use of resources.

As it is now, the majority of humans operate in this system of exploitation of resources. Resources are labeled capital, from natural resources like land and animals to human capital like spirituality and labor, to energetic capital via psychological warfare. In the current functional model of the world, which is built upon our value system of the time value of money, we structure this system to deem certain things more or less important. This correlates directly with value. What are we comparing it to? More or less important than what? What sort of a life is a life without freedom? What sort of a life is a life without human touch, connection and fun? Without water, food and shelter, there would be nothing to even base our values on as we would perish. The land freely gives these to us in exchange for our participation. These are the things of true value, and they occur within a partnership of equilibrium. We are in disequilibrium because of the amount of fabricated needs that we add on top of our survival needs and needs of community as well as the lack of value exchange back to the planet.

According to Yoga, we are thrown out of equilibrium by the *gunas*, which are propensities for disequilibrium. The *gunas* operate through the process of the senses. Our senses process input and discern from it. The sensory path normally goes as follows: your senses perceive something, a desire arises, and that thing is perceived through some condition to be valuable. We then act on the value, normally craving more of something we view as positive, and wanting less of something that's viewed as negative.

CRAVING AND THE RISE OF HEDONISM

Value is currently rooted in craving or hedonism. Hedonism states that if you can get closer to a state of the desirous model, which is rooted in pleasure, comfort, or something positive, then it is worth whatever the cost. We are taught to avoid pain, avoid suffering, avoid the other side of the spectrum. We want to do things and buy things that make us feel good, so we chase them.

This aspect of the spectrum of duality is aiming in the direction of happiness or, ultimately, freedom, which is often expressed, in our current societal model, as pertaining to money or material objects via "I want to do whatever I want and I need . . ." or "I will be fulfilled or complete if I had . . ."

Many Eastern spiritual traditions have told us repeatedly that this is not feasible, because the external world is impermanent and whatever pleasure is derived from something external will always change, decay, and go away, which in turn creates suffering. This is the Second Noble Truth of Buddhism; the cause of suffering is attachment to things that are impermanent.

The heliocentric model has displayed that if you chase your own tail continuously, or try to 'keep up with the Joneses', there will always be something new or someone doing something more curated and cool, so you can never succeed and you end up chasing, or running after unattainable states of being. You end up running forever. The objects of desire change, but the desire to obtain hasn't. Isn't it ironic we are called the human race?

Our hedonistic model fits in with that of prophets like Aldous Huxley. He writes about the rise of hedonism in Brave New World. In this book, Huxley provides a dystopian future in accordance with George Orwell in 1984, but comes at it a little bit differently. Neil Postman in his book *Amusing Ourselves to Death* states,

"What Orwell feared were those who would ban books. What Huxley feared was that there would be no reason to ban a book, for there would be no one who wanted to read one. Orwell feared those who would deprive us of information. Huxley feared those who would give us so much that we would be reduced to passivity and egoism. Orwell feared that the truth would be concealed from us. Huxley feared the truth would be drowned in a sea of irrelevance. Orwell feared we would become a captive culture. Huxley feared we would become a trivial culture, preoccupied with some equivalent of the feelies, the orgy porgy, and the centrifugal bumblepuppy. As Huxley remarked in Brave New World Revisited, the civil libertarians and rationalists who are ever on the alert to oppose tyranny "failed to take into account man's almost infinite appetite for distractions." In 1984, Orwell added, people are controlled by inflicting pain. In Brave New World, they are controlled by inflicting pleasure. In short, Orwell feared that what we fear will ruin us. Huxley feared that what we desire will ruin us. This book is about the possibility that Huxley, not Orwell, was right."[5]

We can marinate on that.

SMALL SHIFTS IN THE VALUE SYSTEM: BLOCKCHAIN TECHNOLOGY AND THE EXPERIENCE ECONOMY

Today, small shifts in the value system have started to emerge. I will highlight two examples.

First, let's look at the blockchain. In simplified terms,

"the blockchain is a decentralized, distributed ledger that records the provenance of a digital asset . . . This is important because makes the history of any digital asset unalterable and transparent through the use of decentralization and cryptographic hashing."[6]

It is introducing a novel idea in cryptographic keys to the financial system to cut out the middle-man who acts as a custodian, or centralized agent of trust. This middleman, when regarding currency, is the bank who is the holder of your money, and who can do with it what they please behind the scenes and you would have no idea. This cryptographic key is meant to allow transparency for all parties involved, rather than allowing custodians to use people's money for interest rates and other self-maximizing measures. It also makes sure that anonymity can still reign. Many people I know view the introduction of cryptocurrencies and blockchain technology as the incoming way of the financial world.

Blockchain is a nice step forward from our current monetary and transaction system because of this introduction to transparency and non-dependency on monetary custodians. However, monetary vehicles such as Bitcoin, and the use of it to run a new transactional system are still dependent on our current value system based on some sort of currency that we peg it to, whether it be USD or Yuan. You make your money by having more of it, which still incentivizes greed and accumulation. Therefore, the root of the currencies is still inherently tied to polarity in the sense that there is a finite amount of Bitcoin, so a gold rush feeling comes in. Even when you divide it into satoshis, which is the smallest unit of a Bitcoin, there will inevitably be those who are heavily invested in reaping currency-tied wealth as well as those who are not as able to take advantage of the supply and demand.

The rich and poor dynamic does not disappear because it is tied to finite resources. Therefore, all of the dualistic problems that we face now with our current financial system—scarcity and abundance, wealth and poverty, health and illness, will still be there. We have not shaken out the root of the issue.

A friend of mine who lives on the Big Island of Hawai'i and manages a cryptocurrency portfolio told me that he can witness the collective emotions of humanity while watching a stock-screen plummet or rise based on speculation. The emotions he says he witnesses are fear and greed.

I asked him what is at the bedrock of fear and greed? We came to the conclusion that perhaps it is love. However, as fear and greed continue to be the main emotional stimuli behind markets and will continue to be so even with a digital currency systemic shift, could these inherent emotions be reconditioned to no longer be necessary in the human world of technological innovation? Can we operate from the only true Universal condition that lies at the bedrock of all emotions, love? Or do we not trust ourselves enough outside of a system that we are sick and tired of, based on our reliance upon it? Can we use the technology to enable our own reconnection to the land, which provides our sovereignty? Can we be rewarded for sharing rather than accumulating?

Blockchain is trustless and eliminates the need for the intermediary but the cryptocurrencies that it has created are reliant upon the same two emotions as the current stock market.

The goal here is autonomy. But, how can you be sovereign within a meta system that has structured your very definition of sovereignty? I am interested in a system design using blockchain (or not) that can recondition the human to allow these emotions of fear and greed to come to a natural cessation. Where the stand-alone sharing and receiving is the operating principle. Perhaps this is truly what the gift economy can bring. No carrot, no donkey, no stick. Simply the evolution of a global collective consciousness beyond the meta-system in which we are trapped. We may begin to spread a new value engine which rewards people for sharing and punishes them for accumulating to recondition value.

No matter how we continually stem from craving and aversion, the objects will naturally change as Nature changes. But as we remain attached to our selective subjective experience and the hierarchies that function within the human system of conditioned reality, like pain and pleasure, the chain will not be broken. We will never have peace without war, therefore we will forever remain in turmoil. Perhaps this is just the way it is. Maybe we are not equipped to enter into non-dual states as a collective. Maybe our economic OS cannot experience a complete revolution. I do not know. All I do know is that until we become adaptable and equanimous within our own desires and biological sensations, discerning what is truly us and what is just a societal condition, which requires our taking full responsibility for ourselves, we cannot escape the cycle of suffering that governs our lives because we are attached to it.

Second, as of now, subgroups of people are looking to accumulate experiences over material things. This will be discussed in more detail in the next chapter pertaining to the experience economy. The pitfall is that we end up with the same result of accumulation, as people are amassing quantities of experiences rather than qualities and depths of experience. We still are operating on the need to accumulate. To push this factor, many experiences on platforms like AirBnB and Triple are being marketed in a way that makes them feel enlightening based on aesthetic, exclusivity and price point. It could be something like Horse Whispering in a Desert Highland or Unleash the Inner Masculine Burlesque Dancing, with price points and curation to a T. Therefore, those who pursue certain experiences often are looking to gain something out of them, immediately building in ambition and expectation into an experience. This is still extractive. They are trying to make themselves more of something, therefore less of something else. This is like trying to see your organs while you just keep adding on more and more levels of clothes. We do not need complexity added on. We need it stripped away. Oftentimes experiences can strip complexity and identification away, but not if our models are involved in a deep manner trying to build ourselves up and gain something from the experience itself.

We are becoming more and more complex through our experiences, when the ultimate goal is to become more and more simple. We are becoming more and more hardened and callous through our accumulating of knowns, rather than more and more soft and innocent from our entrance into the unknown. Without stillness, how can we truly experience anything? And without experience, how do we derive meaning? As long as experiences privilege quantity over quality, we make the sacred nature of experience profane and render its integration hollow and meaningless.

GUIDEPOSTS: MEANING AND PURPOSE

In accordance with meaninglessness, what is meaning? One of the things I've thought about is how the interpretation of the loss of individuality through the path of simplicity may lend itself to people seeing the world as meaningless. However, when I asked my partner, Marisa, "what is meaning?" she was unable to define it at the time.

While in India, we were riding in the back of a rickshaw right outside of Balmuri Falls in Mysuru, witnessing dragonflies floating in the air above a field of flowers. The sun was hitting the dragonflies, and they looked like tea lights effortlessly rising in the wind. "Is there no meaning in that?" I asked. We often limit our meaning and purpose to the tether of our accepted value system. Ultimately, meaning comes in as connectedness to something greater than ourselves. Meaning is meaningful because of how quickly it can pass away.

I believe that meaning is the unlabeled sensation or feeling that something awakens in you via the direct connection to it. Some call it love, joy, serenity, beauty, or peace. Nature mirrors the vast expanse of consciousness more accurately than humans since it has less conditioned imprints and its existence is based on pure sacrifice. Hence, people seem to be able to find meaning and connection in Nature. When you see a mountain, you are seeing the mountain within yourself. The beauty or feeling that comes over you is the wellspring of meaning that rests in your

True Self. The mountain is but an aspect of it, and we are but an aspect of the mountain.

The word that emerged on this rickshaw ride from Marisa regarding meaning was purpose. I asked, "Is not the purpose or meaning of all things to lead you back to your True Self?" Synchronicity, serendipity, and co-incidences (there are no co-incidences) can help act as guideposts in our lives. Once we begin to see the signs as interconnected, and whether we should lead or follow, life becomes a treasure hunt of the Soul, and interconnectedness only expands. If it brings you closer to that wellspring of joy and love within yourself, it has purpose and meaning.

Many people have been culturally trained to imbue certain things with meaning. These could range from an owl, to a feather, to a shadow on a rock, to a rainbow. Symbols help us to move towards deeper connectedness with ourselves. Purpose and meaning are the same, and their derivatives can be as simple as evoking direction, emotion, or feeling that moves your being towards stillness and into remembrance of the subtler, more nuanced parts of the interconnectivity of life. This leads us to what this current buzzword of 'remembering' really means.

Remembering seems to be using our current illusory and separated state of "I", (Ryan J. Kemp) which exists in duality (opposites), to look at the Truth that we are not in fact separate from this fabric of existence (everything) which in turn moves us from being somebody (ego) to no-body (Self). Put more simply, we move within Nature or duality into Oneness through the undoing of our identifications and labels. Oftentimes the remembering can come into play the more that we forget. If we forget, or fall out of alignment, as soon as we realize our forgetfulness, we are back into the remembering.

Sri Ramana Maharshi states in Day by Day with Bhagavan 5-1-46,

"Where are you now? Where is the goal? What is the distance to be covered? The Self is not somewhere far away to be reached. You are always that. You have only to give up your habit, a long-standing one, of identifying yourself with the non-self. All effort is only for that. By turning the mind outwards, you have been seeing the world, the non-Self. If you turn it inwards you will see the Self."

This requires a literal psychological death of our impression of who we think we are, over and over again. That is how we are reborn into the Spirit.

DO WE REALLY WANT TO CHANGE?

The question remains, are we really ready to change? Change is not some continuous, small shift. Although it may appear to move in increments, change represents transformation or alchemy. We must consciously evolve toward a place where our internal habitat is completely devoid of the duality created by our habits of division. This is represented by the Yogic *guna* of *sattva* or calm-abiding. In other words, unaffected by external conditions to designate your internal state of being.

Hopefully, we all consciously evolve to be less and less aggravated by all of the stimulus coming from the outside that spins us into disequilibrium, burn-out, and confusion. Acting in alignment is not aggravation, in the sense of doing things that are morally correct, but if we attach to the righteousness of our side and polarize the other in an 'us versus them' ideology, we are right back in the same place of disconnection.

The path forward is one which cultivates the internal systems of peace, beyond the duality of war. It ushers in a dropping of the labels of opposites and witnessing them as parts of one whole. As long as we oppose, reject, and neglect by not embracing all of it, including people who may oppose us in political or religious dogmas, which are merely habitualized points of view, we will remain trapped in the swings of these cycles. Freeing ourselves starts with an internal habitat shift through the reprogramming of our habits. We must break the cycle within ourselves. We must toe the line in-between the Yin and the Yang, the Middle Way. As we do this, others are given silent permission to do the same in their own way.

This is why meditation is such a powerful technique, because you are directing all of your attention inward to assess your internal habitat rather than your external one. However, it is often difficult for people to truly look into this internal habitat because they are overwhelmed with memories, to-do-lists, sensations and anything that is being created in accordance with thought; which is separated from the current moment in its basic sense.

Once we cultivate this internal habitat of stability, we will see a direct change in our external habitat. It begins to look like a mere substratum of collective projections playing itself out. This is based on our continued karmic impacts and imprints that are reinforced by the habits of living within a dual system. For example, whenever I find myself around family or old friends, I have been able to cultivate a space where I can see how old patterns of interaction in the relationship are merely on repeat, like a broken VHS player. This space of seeing that they are merely old patterns then allows me to step back from the trodden trail of reactions and consciously evolve towards a new neural pathway.

When we no longer react to the world, but respond instead, we are free to bring compassion and love into all of our actions. As we witness everything as our own Self, and anything we do to this projection is mirrored from the internal world to the external one, responsibility and understanding of our own ability to empower is gained. To truly align with the mantra, "do unto others as you would have them do unto you" is a step in the right direction. If we can really honor this, it would be amazing. It is so simple that it seems difficult.

In conclusion, our current value system is a mere habit. This habit stems from the misaligned desire to accumulate because of our false belief of separateness from existence itself. It is the habit of transaction which stems from selfish desire, which uses the notion of gain/loss, purchase/sell to operate in duality in an unbalanced, exploitative way. Extricating ourselves from this habit, in an internal sense of reaction to desires, ripples out into the very habitat and systemic structure and state of the world. No longer must we sit in a world in which we are often dissatisfied when it doesn't fit our models. We can begin to create the changes within our own structures of value by valuing ourselves through responsible action and reconnection to our disavowed parts. The process may be slow, but the moment of realization can be quick. It all starts from within.

JOURNAL PROMPTS:

1. What are some things that you personally value? How many of these do you think have been conditioned by society for you to value?
    a. Once you've written these down, see how many of them you are able to purchase.
2. What does society tell us to value? This is not only for material possessions. Do you believe in this value-system?
3. If money was not an issue, how would you live?
4. What habits do you have that create your own habitat? What habits do we have as a society that create our own habitats?

Journal Prompt #1:

What are some things that you personally value? How many of these do you think have been conditioned by society for you to value? Once you've written these down, see how many of them you are able to purchase.

Journal Prompt #2:

What does society tell us to value? This is not only for material possessions. Do you believe in this value-system?

Journal Prompt #3:

If money was not an issue, how would you live?

Journal Prompt #4:

What habits do you have that create your own habitat? What habits do we have as a society that create our own habitats?

CHAPTER THREE

What the Experience Economy is Missing

"No man ever steps in the same river twice, for it's not the same river and he's not the same man."
—Heraclitus

"My goal is getting free from all of the things that separate me from everyone around me."
—Raghu Markus

As many of us know and we touched on gently in the last chapter, the experience economy at this point in time is beginning to gather steam. Spearheaded by AirBnB, you can sign up for experiences from locals around the world as you travel: drinking coffee with a local in Copenhagen, making hand-made pasta with an Italian grandmother at the base of Mount Etna while drinking red wine, whatever it may be. These experiences are well and good and they are opening up a way for people to approach the mind-set of travel rather than tourism. Also, they are opening up understanding as many people are becoming aware that one must delve into the one's deeper layers of interconnectedness through experience.

So, what is the difference between travel and tourism? In my direct experience of traveling the world for the last eight years, there is a big difference. We will use Hawai'i as an example for this, since I am currently living on the Big Island and it is familiar to me.

TOURISM VERSUS TRAVEL

Tourism in its basic sense, is a stagnant commodity. It driven by accommodation such as resorts (i.e. Kona Marriott, Four Seasons at Hualalai) which are essentially real-estate monopoly pieces placed around the globe, many of them on indigenous sacred sites. They provide more expensive stays than homes, impersonal accommodation, and cookie-cutter bus and escort services to tourism spots such as waterfalls and beaches. More often than not, unless controlled by a responsible entity, these tourism outlets create more environmental and cultural damage than good through the superficiality of shopping and consumption. Tourism is a massive industry because of partnerships with multinationals, tourism budgets from municipalities, airlines, and governments. They funnel people into specific activities that more often than not are not indicative of the day-to-day life of the place which people are visiting. Culture turns into a commodity, like a luau.

However, at this point in time, perhaps even that appears better than having the culture completely erased, and this is the predicament in which many indigenous peoples find themselves. Their cultures have become entertainment. Many tourists, who oftentimes look like adult toddlers, snap selfies and waddle around taking in the basic aspects of the sites. Tourism normally leads you to have many souvenirs of a place, perhaps some memories or snapshots of specific places or moments in time, but overall, the culture, way of life, and deeper understanding of the location, embedded in the language and topynomy, is seldom touched upon or remembered in a way that will impact the day-to-day life of an individual or family. In other words, tourists rarely experience true spiritual deepening; they skim the superficial layers of a place, often not remembering names of rivers, mountains or much more than a shaved ice they got in Kona.

Travel, on the other hand, is an unfolding process. When you are really traveling, you begin to experience a way of life, a world view, or specific aspects of a culture or the natural environment of a location that deepen your experience of yourself. This normally creates an increased level of awareness of the interconnectivity between human beings culturally and the natural world. As you travel, the world begins to appear interconnected on depths that have not before been experienced and normally, you are positively affected by levels of increased compassion, global awareness, alternative historical perspectives, conservationism, cultural sensitivity, and interest.

By highlighting the different patterns of humans and traditions of culture and reality relayed through language, ultimately, travel will lead you only deeper into your own self. You will begin to unravel much of what you have taken for granted, felt entitled to and believed to be accurate or true, since there are so many ways of living, believing, worshipping, and eating. Therefore, the deeper you go, the more your identity unravels because you witness the copious worldviews that our planet shares; the plethora of ways of being human. Traveling is a surefire way, if approached in the manner of open-mindedness, to break down barriers within your own compensatory identity and understand that experiences are merely a way to move deeper into the mystery of life and inter-being. You begin to see that we are indeed not separate, or non-dual, existentially to anything that exists. Travel breaks down the ego, which is the possessive 'I' feeling that leads us into separateness. However, if approached with a selfish mind state, it also has the capacity to build the ego up.

One eventually sees, if traveling deeply enough, that one is only journeying within oneself. The world and its inhabitants become a gateway and a mirror. This mirror is the continuous play, or Lila, that will unravel through a process over time all of the knots of conditioned values, stories and the like that keep one from truly experiencing the here and now of the moments that are unfolding without attachment to thoughts that separate them from time and space itself. The play of life becomes lighter as we take our own identities less and less seriously by releasing them into the vast expanse of time.

Now, to bring it back to the experience economy, AirBnB's moving people towards less-commoditized experiences that actually offer an introduction to a local's way of life is a move in the right direction—into the change-process-orientation.

However, we now need to break down experience as a whole, and determine why we enjoy racking up experiences. There seems to be a common theme that the more places we have gone, or the more experiences we have in our life, the wiser we are. That is because we believe that accumulating experiences means accumulating wisdom. This is what the experience economy is missing. In Truth, we can never accumulate experiences. They are just happening. And as long as we maintain this accumulation-based mentality around material and non-material entities, we will stay missing the point. We keep trying to grasp at meaning when the core basis of meaning is in its fleeting nature.

Decreasing desire to get something from experiences deepens our experience. Desire in our current world is mostly related to wealth, power and influence, pertaining to money which relates to sexuality which relates to the core human need to feel connection. Freedom, if you look at the word, is free. Many, like Noam Chomsky will argue that freedom is not free, but that is only because we have separated ourselves so much from others in the scheme of the accumulation of wealth, that we create polarities of emotion such as envy, judgment, hatred, anger and ultimately, war.

At least from my experience, the most powerful experiences are those which I have never paid for, the ones that sporadically occur without any organization or transactional structure whatsoever. They occur when I am not trying to extract anything from the experience itself. This is because without any monetary exchange, expectation disappears. The expectation is rooted in comparison, and comparison is the death of joy. Expectation pulls you out of the moment into what you want the moment to be. Some sort of money normally sets these expectation models off kilter because of the time value of money. This means whatever you see your time as worth, we compare to what we are extracting out of the experience, as if we could accumulate it like a commodity. This theoretical concept of worth is illusory in Nature. The value of one thing cannot be compared to the value of another thing. We try to compare where our time could be spent rather than how we are currently spending it. It is embedded in our language; we are spending or investing our time. While we're lost in the expanse of possibilities elsewhere that our minds chase with jealous pleasure, we miss the experience. It follows that monetary expenditure does not align with fulfillment. We have erased the depth of the experience by trying to derive value from it.

Furthermore, since our minds have evolved to chase every possibility, which manifests as a blessing and a curse of the current millennial generation with careers or lifestyles for example, we are never inherently fulfilled because the grass is always greener cliché. The mind has been trained this way, Joni Mitchell sings about it too, "don't it always seem to go..." And as the moments pass us by while we think about what else we could do or how much we should've gotten from such an experience, we could be un-training the mind to un-chase every possibility, to be rooted in the present moment, and to be alright with that. As opposed to FOMO, the fear of missing out, you can have JOMO, the joy of missing out, as Tonya Dalton says.

CONTENTMENT

The halting of the trying to derive value from the experience is contentment. It is the understanding that nothing from the outside can make you feel any different or more joyous than your internal environment right here and now. The experience is merely a gateway into this joy. Contentment is directly correlated with eliminating your own internal sense of identified value within this structure we call time. As that is slowly dissolved, all external things lose their attachment and ability to affect you via expectation because you see it all as a condition of whatever you think you should be doing or should be getting versus what you are actually receiving at that very moment. We can be nowhere but here and now and it's all game that our mind plays to keep us from looking inward. Everything becomes a lot simpler.

On the chalkboard outside the Yoga Shala at Yoga Gita in Mysuru, India, a quote about simplicity struck me.

It stated, "Simplicity is maximizing the ability to just live with [what is] happening."

As we reflect on and bring attention to our predicament as a whole, which is merely a part of the whole, we see its inseparability from everything else that is unfolding. We cannot view you, as your named entity, outside of a relationship with another entity. This is a good place to begin moving towards this direction of contentment. This is the law of interdependence, otherwise known as dependent arising in Buddhism.

The roots of the experiential movement are solid. The entire movement stems from the understanding of the necessity to experience something to truly understand it, whether that be a way of life, a culture, or a skill. As tourism has now moved into Ayahuasca and other plant medicines, there is a more mainstream recognition of the correlation between experience and wisdom. To a certain degree, this is correct. However, the state of presence, vulnerability and stillness within the experience is the key factor that is often overlooked. That being said, there are also levels or depths to an experience, and these levels directly correlate with the levels of stillness and openness within yourself as you enter the experience. There are pitfalls to experiences that get you caught up in a phase of the experience rather than continuing fluidly with the process. We attach to our experiences and believe they are absolute. We build out our experiences to have a goal, yet the more goal-oriented we are the more presence we lose. Beyond the actual experience, there is the next step of process-integration which is often neglected after impactful moments have been lived which often toss people into confusion.

STILLNESS IS THE KEY TO SUBTLE EXPERIENCE

As to why stillness is a key factor within experience, let's use the example of walking slowly versus walking quickly in a museum. The slower you walk, and the slower you are moving around, the subtler the details of your experience: the color of someone's shirt near the Manet, the smell of coffee on the second floor, the pointillist genius and imagination of Georges Seurat next to the man in the pink shirt with the tilted head. If you're moving quickly around and through the museum, the experience will be shallower and many of these nuances will remain unnoticed. In sum, presence and stillness facilitate subtlety and deepen experience.

In addition, the depth of experiences very often is now motivated by the ego, or in this case, a societal-validation seeking mechanism. The subtlety is being sullied by the intention of many an experiencer to have others see them experiencing something so that there is some sort of recognition or validation. Social media is a large proponent of this. Perhaps we want to be wiser so we have some sort of hierarchical placement over others or so we can monetize it or use it to proliferate our worldviews over others. This is using the wisdom of experience against its goal of connectivity by setting it within transactionality. The more these pride-driven intentions arise, the further from the portal or origin of experience we are moving which is neutrality and immutability.

One of the main guardians at the gate of deep experience is control. Control is all but an illusion. We think we are afraid of the unknown, but as Krishnamurti states,

"One is never afraid of the unknown; one is afraid of the known coming to an end."

Like stated above, control is a fear of our known world coming to an end. Control is a desire to hold onto something that is in the past or hold onto an expectation of how it will be in the future. Control is a mechanism to attempt to maintain continuity so our entire identified lives don't crumble before our eyes. Mathematically, many attempt to explain control in probability. What is the probability that human beings would have evolved to this point in time, on a Goldilocks zone planet to enable us to come to consciousness and question the whole existence of our species via the formation of language? Where is our control in those hundreds of millions of years of evolution? Do we control where our breath comes from? We often brush aside these deeper layers of how little we are in control by justifying how much we claim to know. The more you understand that you don't know anything, the less control you need to feign to maintain the illusion of stability. As you relinquish control you step into vulnerability.

Wisdom does come from experience, but we can only truly experience something from a point of presence where we are not caught up in our own control mechanisms, conditionings, mind-chatter, and memory. At that point, if we can silence those parts of our mind, we are not experiencing the moment as separate. We are not grasping at or craving a specific outcome. If we are enveloped in these aspects of our thought forms, then the true stillness of experience, which generates wisdom, will always evade us. We will remain separated from the moment through a thin veil based on our thoughts of the past or future. Tick, tock, tick, tock. There it goes, right out the window. Oh wait, here comes another experience from which to learn!

If we start looking at Nature as a totally impermanent and interconnected set of ever-changing phenomena, where not even our leg is the same as it was before we started reading this sentence, we cannot accumulate anything. Which one of those trillion particles rising and falling away every millisecond is your 'I'? We are renewed every moment.

GO BEYOND PREFERENCES

A piece of true wisdom lies in the acceptance of, not indifference to, the moments that arise without clinging or attaching to any expectation or end result. This includes accumulation of experiences searching for an intended result. When we are looking to associate or disassociate from moments or people based on our preferences and being able to isolate the presence from our thought forms, we are caught in our own trap.

In The Third Patriarch of Zen, it states,

"The Great Way is not difficult for those who have no preferences. When love and hate are both absent everything becomes clear and undisguised. Make the smallest distinction, however, and heaven and earth are set infinitely apart. If you wish to see the truth, then hold no opinion for or against."

Our preferences prevent us from accepting reality for what it is. And the more we cannot accept reality and the gifts that it provides, the less gratitude we feel. For only when we relinquish the control to try and build up walls of safety exactly as we want it, can we begin to taste freedom. The more the knee-jerk reactions of control via preferences emerge, the more we feel unstable. Being unstable is natural. Don't fool yourself. You begin to relinquish control by relinquishing your attachment to your preferences. Now, this doesn't mean blindly accepting anything, especially in an instance of people attempting to siphon your own power or exert control over you; discernment is key. However, it does entail releasing attachment to models of behavior after a certain event, rather than who we are now. Discernment is not attachment.

By releasing our attachment to our preferences and expectations, we relinquish attachment to what we believed our identity to be and what we thought we needed to survive. In this regard, we begin the journey back towards the origin point of all experience which is, as Chögyam Trungpa puts it, the primordial dot, or potentiality. We are all nodes of potentiality waiting to experience our own potential.

True nonviolence is in the decomposition of your own identity. When you tap into the depths of experience to the point where you are no longer experiencing for gain, the true understanding of inter-being will arise.

Now that we have looked into why and how our trained value systems' desire to accumulate extends even into our own ideas of experience, we will use Ayurveda as a mechanism to look into how this accumulation-based mentality results in the physical and mental dis-ease of our planet.

JOURNAL PROMPTS:

1. What have been some of your most powerful experiences? Did you pay for them with money?
2. What are some of your preferences or expectation models that prevent you from truly experiencing freedom?
3. If you have experienced tourism versus travel, which one was more powerful? Why?
4. How often do you sense yourself looking to experience something to gain value from it? Do you view yourself as an accumulation or combination of all of your experiences?

Journal Prompt #1:

What have been some of your most powerful experiences? Did you pay for them with money?

Journal Prompt #2:

What are some of your preferences or expectation models that prevent you from truly experiencing freedom?

Journal Prompt #3:

If you have experienced tourism versus travel, which one was more powerful? Why?

Journal Prompt #4:

How often do you sense yourself looking to experience something to gain value from it? Do you view yourself as an accumulation or combination of all of your experiences?

CHAPTER FOUR

Accumulation = Disease:
An Ayurvedic Diagnosis of Planetary Illness

"Can we bring about in the very essence of our being a total revolution, a psychological mutation, so that we are no longer brutal, violent, comparative, anxious, fearful, greedy, envious and the rest of the manifestations of our nature which have built up the rotten society in which we live our daily lives?"
—Jiddu Krishnamurti, *Freedom from the Known*

"The capitalist world-economy needs the states, needs the interstate system, and needs the periodic appearance of hegemonic powers. But the priority of capitalists is never the maintenance, much less the glorification, of any of these structures. The priority remains always the endless accumulation of capital, and this is best achieved by an ever-shifting set of political and cultural dominances within which capitalist firms maneuver, obtaining their support from the states but seeking to escape their dominance."
—Immanuel Wallerstein, *World-Systems Analysis: An Introduction*

Ayurveda is one of the oldest life sciences known to humans. Transcribed in Sanskrit, the roots of its name lie in the two words: *Aayus*, which means life and *Veda*, which means science or knowledge.

In January of 2020, I was in Kerala, India studying Ayurveda. I was curious about learning the beginnings of an ancient science that is often viewed as contradictory to modern, allopathic medicine because of its holistic nature. In brief, Ayurveda is utilized to maintain health and prevent disease from forming by understanding the elemental makeup of the physicality of a person and the mediums of nutrition delivery. From here, ailments can be diagnosed based on the causation of disease in the physicality of a human organism using the elemental makeup of the person. Herbal medicines can then be applied to alleviate the ailment using the proper mediums that match with the elemental makeup.

Ayurveda is guided by the five elements, called *Panchamahabhoota*, of which all of existence is constituted: earth, water, fire, air, and ether. It is not literally these things, but more of the characteristics or functionality of each. Earth represents solidity, fire represents heat and transformation, and air represents mobility. These elements in different combinations build the human constitution of susceptibility, called a *dosha*, of which there are three: *vata*, *pitta*, and *kapha*. You can never be one of the doshas alone; normally you are mainly two of them. It is very rare to be equal parts of all three doshas, and that is a fine state of health according Ayurvedic practitioners.

Food inputs, like humans, are also made up of the same elements and have certain qualities of the elements which are called rasa. These are flavor profiles expressed in the food, such as astringent, bitter, spicy, sweet, pungent. Accordingly, in a physical sense, if you understand your *dosha* constitution and you ingest the correct food combinations prepared in the correct way, you will be a healthy individual.

Ayurveda states that the cause of all disease is undigested

food particles, which creates build-up in the body called *aama*. *Aama* is the accumulation of these food-stuffs. Medically, this can be viewed as mucus in the intestines, colon or inflammation in the body. *Aama* begins to affect the *dhatus* which are the humors of the body, starting from the lymphatic system all the way through the bones to the reproductive system. Dr. Arnold Ehret's Mucusless Diet Healing System follows a similar ideology around the fact that the inflammatory response based on improper food inputs is the main causation of disease. Many people I know personally have healed chronic ailments by adopting a diet that does not create mucus accumulation in the body.

It is important to look at Ayurvedic science in the terms of biological/physical diagnosis of the root causes of illness; we are what we consume. If we consume things that are not beneficial for our bodies, consume in excess of our needs or out of alignment with our system, we will become ill. Anything superfluous of what we need is poison. Allopathic medicine is focused on the suppression or healing of symptoms. Symptoms are our bodies' way of speaking to us. Our current health-care system suppresses symptoms with pharmaceutical drugs to get rid of any inconveniences. By suppressing this language of the body, we become unaware that we are forming diseases and chronic ailments. This is a simple etiological understanding. This is where Eastern medicine differs from Western medicine; the Eastern medicine pathways from acupuncture and cupping to Ayurveda see the bodily symptoms as a sign on a roadmap towards the root of the issue, which the goal of the treatment is to alleviate rather than suppress.

However, in this section, we will be looking into how this understanding of accumulation we have discovered in a philosophical and practical context can reach far and wide beyond the physical organism of the human being. We will ripple out to the collective mind-space of humanity as well as the macrocosmic understanding of the Earth's physical body and its diseased condition at the moment. As we look at our own organs such as the heart, lungs, and pancreas, we can look at Earth's organs as the ocean, rivers, mountains, forests, animal life, plant life, and prairies. Earth is a living being that is looking to maintain balance and homeostasis. What are we accumulating that is affecting our physical health? What are we accumulating that is affecting our mental health? What are we accumulating as a species that is affecting the Earth's health? How do we get back into balance?

In the last section on the experience economy, I wrote that we are looking to accumulate experience because we are looking to accumulate wisdom. The common theme here is accumulation. Remember from the first chapter, enlightenment is a demolition project, not a construction project. Simplicity is not attained by adding on complexity, it is attained by stripping it all away. Harmony is not attained by accumulation; it is attained by fluidity. Fasting, which is coming to a halt of consumption, is one of the main routes to healing. We can fast physically with food, but we can also fast on many other levels of our being.

The section below will depict my interpretation using Ayurveda as the principle for the current planetary condition derived from the human condition of the desire to accumulate. We will be moving from an organismic view from microscopic human to macroscopic planetary. This will be depicted in the flow of disease formation from an Ayurvedic point of view.

According to the principles of Ayurveda, disease forms in six steps.

Stage One: *Sanchaya* or Accumulation

As mentioned before, in Ayurveda specifically, which addresses this accumulation in the elemental biology of an individual, this is the first stage of disease. Food inputs affect the *dosha*, or biological constitution, which is affected by an *aama* accumulation in a specific site in the body.On an existential and philosophical level, if you look at the accumulation from another perspective, we must look into ourselves and see our desire to accumulate. Normally in life, we accumulate many models of how to live. These can be conditionings and habits, rules and laws pertaining to morals, financial ideas of our value system, influence and power through energetic sway, material possessions that bring us comfort and security, and experiences with the goal of either building the ego or acquiring wisdom. The list goes on and on.

A rule of Nature is any accumulation of anything causes distress or disease in an organism's system. This is because in Nature, in accordance with the *Dhamma*, there is no accumulation of anything. Everything is rising and falling away, being recycled and regenerated. Flowers don't cling to blooming. They bloom and wilt. Trees don't accumulate fruits trying to save them for some other season or their next door neighbor Ralph who likes the fruits more. They grow and they ripen and they fall and they rot. Everything is constantly in a cycle of renewing, rising and falling away. We have extrapolated this out to the planetary ecosystem earlier by seeing that our conditions or habits are reflected directly into our habitat.

As many of us recognize, we accumulate ways of being that are conditioned through societal responses and values, wealth and material possessions, influence or power. Something as simple as picking up a reaction from your parents and allowing it to control your reactions to a situation rather than coming from a place of freshness or newness is an example. Rarely it seems in our society do we cultivate the space to take a step back and see what is happening. We are so busy. We accumulate belief systems about worthiness, success, political ideologies, or other people's judgments that remain stuck over time and form our realities thus.

How can we sort through the ideas we have accumulated, and come out at the present moment? How do we begin to fast from the consumption of our own opinions and ideologies? We tread the same trails over and over based on our accumulation of past experiences like an old trail in the woods riddled in poison oak and thorns. These past experiences prime us to react to our current situation even if they are completely different, rendering us repeating the same outcome. We are looking to move towards repeatlessness. Our worries about possessions, thoughts of the future, all of them do the same. Belief systems are self-enforcing, and very often in a fear-based, death-phobic society that pins worth to monetary value, they honor a negative feedback loop of extraction and exploitation. All of these accumulations are literal weight and density upon our beings. They are the dementors, to reference Harry Potter, of innocence. The vampires of freshness and newness. They all lead to reactions or provocations, which is stage two of disease formation, in our beings that create a lack of ease.

Stage Two: *Prakopa* or Provocation.

At this stage, where accumulation creates provocation or aggravation, signs begin to appear. Once again, from a philosophical standpoint, these aggravations in an individual could be viewed as the avarices of human beings stemming from the fear of separation, insecurity, impermanence and death. We live in a death-a-phobic culture. The fear of death exists because of our first separation anxiety; the illusion that we are separate from existence. Because of this fear, we look to accumulate a wall of safety between ourselves and the inevitable, and push it away. If we can drop into the feeling from the mind to the Heart that we have been doing this living thing for eons, much of the weight and pressure we feel day to day would be lifted. If we understand that death is yet another transition, we would admire it as a boundary to be embraced. It simply requires a shift of our vantage point.

As the fear springs forth of death it is transmuted pertaining to the loss or absence of the accumulation, therefore, a perceived absence of security and safety. As we don't feel sturdy within ourselves, we pad our vulnerability with external stimuli. In strictly the human case, a comparative sickness arises regarding those who are accumulating more, therefore creating the presumption that they have more security, comfort, and ease. When we see others accumulating more, because we have been taught in societal conditioning that accumulation of things is good, a sign of wealth, we start identifying ourselves as inadequate or unworthy. Advertising feeds into this story of inadequacy quite powerfully. From here sparks the chase; the human race, the collective provocation based on our value system.

The aggravations of the mind such as desire, aversion, greed, and envy stem from this root which is connected to accumulation. The desire to accumulate stems from the possessive nature of the singular 'I.' We form cravings or aversions depending on the stimulus and how we have been trained to view it through our accumulated conditionings, and from this our provocation is created.

Once it is provoked, as we interact in the external-world, our energies and provoked accumulations begin to spread to those we interact with, just like a virus. No COVID masks can protect you from ideological viruses! Toxic belief systems such as racism and chauvinism, patriotic ideologies, anything that excludes another in a sense of hierarchical collectivism, are sicknesses that are the provocations of accumulated conditions and beliefs. These belief systems can be spread through person-to-person contact, television programs, and social media. Our accumulation of the habit of escalation rather than de-escalation assists in the driving of these provocations to stage three, the spread.

Stage Three: *Prasara*, or Spread (Dissemination)

Biologically, Ayurveda states, if this accumulation has been provoked in one site, typically a specific area of the body such as the lymph nodes, it will spread throughout the body looking for new sites to accumulate and provoke the system. In our case, let's use the individual as a specific site of the planetary body. This individual is infected with an imbalance of a societal operating system such as exploitative capitalism and global imperialism based on resource accumulation which manifests in greed.

As this provocation occurs in each one of us, we will naturally represent it, sometimes unconsciously, in the OS. Since we operate inside of the system itself that is meta to our operating existence, it provides the stimulus for which we blame our reactions upon. All of our diseases form within its structure. Another beautiful quote by Krishnamurti echoes this statement:

"It is no measure of health to be well adjusted to a profoundly sick society."

As our society is so sick, sometimes it is difficult to see the dissemination of the sickness. Many of us accept abuse as normal. Many of us accept the violence of envy, ruthless competition, and aggression of business as normal. Many of us love horror movies, play violent video games, and eat the flesh of animals, and consider it normal. Someone cuts us off in traffic and we flip them off, we consider it normal. No, that is sickness. Blind reactivity is sickness. Why react? You are spreading disease and violence.

It is important to really look at ourselves and not shy away from these truths. We are all violent people on some level in some way, shape, or form. Most will always divert responsibility for their own reactions onto the outside world. That's called deflection. However, if you can take responsibility for your own accumulation and provocation, the spread that we are describing that comes from accumulation can come to a standstill and you can prevent the advancement of these mental diseases and halt the disease formation process. Responsibility diffuses reactivity and halts dissemination. It begins with decomposing denial. By stopping and recognizing what is happening within you, you can halt and reverse the process here and lessen your accumulation and provocation. It is quite simple in concept, really. This is a good stage in which to recognize it, and this is often where most people wake up.

Sometimes, and this is why psychedelics and traveling are such powerful tools, it takes one to leave their current environment of comfort, or dimension of safety, for a drastic shift to rattle the bolts around in their being for them to see what's happening on an individual and larger scale.

Stage Four: *Sthana Samshraya* or Localization

In Ayurveda, this stage is when the disrupted *dosha* now localizes in a tissue outside of its main seat and begins to disrupt the function of that tissue (*dhatu*) or organ. Localization, by definition is the fact of being or becoming located or fixed in a particular place.

In our philosophical analysis, the spread or dissemination has attacked fully an entire systemic part of the organism which renders it vulnerable for the manifestation; which is stage five of the disease formation process.

We can use specific ideological geographies as the elemental values of our system as a visible form of our habits in our habitat coming to detrimental localization. These include the continuation of exploitative practices in the Amazon forest, burning fossil fuels for continued energy consumption, over-farming and destroying the soil. We can continue to use specific geography of humanity as the elemental values of our system as a visible form of our habits in our habitat coming to detrimental localization with shootings like the one in Orlando in 2016, indigenous land destruction, treaty dishonor and imprisonment like Standing Rock, corporate greed that steals your data under the guise of Terms and Conditions, dictatorships that starve the people because of corruption, systemic racism and oppression. The list goes on as our mental accumulations provoke, spread, and localize across humanity and the planetary body.

Stage Five: *Vyakti* or Manifestation.

In this stage the disease manifests in its full-blown, clearly identifiable form. In Ayurveda, this is recognized as the functioning of the tissues being disrupted by the complex of *aama* mixed with the imbalanced *dosha*. In one example in Ayurveda, if it is of the *Kapha dosha* and *aama* localizing in the head and neck, then scratchy throat and heaviness which was a localization in the head is now experienced as the full-blown syndrome of congestion in the form of a common cold, sore throat, sinusitis, or an allergy attack.

Now, we as humans have been hard at work accumulating, provoking, disseminating and localizing, so these manifestations are differentiated and varied across the entire planetary organismic system. They are stemming from each one of us internally by our complicit participation in the structural integrity of this systemic operation. We can view these manifestations from our root cause of accumulation via pure destruction of entire peoples, geographies through tar sands and mining, ecosystems' biodiversity being shattered, endless war, and violence. Essentially, the destruction of our shared natural world is being labeled as development, construction and progress. It has all stemmed from accumulation. Environmental reactions like changed seasons that result in abnormal rainfall or drought, agricultural season change, coral reef death, et al are often commonplace.

Did you know that between 15 and 17 percent of the Amazon rainforest has been lost, and if the amount of cleared forest land reaches 25 percent, there won't be enough trees cycling moisture through the rainforest[7]? That will cause the rainforest to dry out and degrade into a savanna. Beekeepers across the United States lost 40.7% of their honeybee colonies from April 2018 to April 2019. Without bees, there is no food[8]. Greenland and Antarctica have lost 318 gigatons of ice per year since 2003, according to new ICESat-2 research. One gigaton of ice is enough to fill 400,000 Olympic-sized swimming pools. These are all vyakti, or manifestations of the macrocosmic planetary organism now falling victim to these habits and being extremely vulnerable to the next stage, which is the final stage of disease.

Stage Six: *Bheda* or Chronicity (also called Disruption), which normally results in death

At this sixth stage, the disease becomes so embedded in the tissues that the body's natural repair mechanisms are not able to reverse it. Then the disruption of functioning becomes a long-term or permanent disorder, normally leading to decay and death. For example, the Kapha disorder could become chronic or perennial sinusitis or rhinitis.

On a macroscopic level of the planetary organism of Earth, we can view this as a complete upheaval of the planet's homeostatic functions, which is already unfolding in widespread fires in unheard of places such as permafrost zones in Siberia and Alaska, seawater temperature rise which creates massive sea-life catastrophes, glaciers melting faster than ice in your Gin and Tonic, air quality PPM being the equivalent of smoking a pack of cigarettes, and pandemic upticks. If the accumulation does not stop, it is not a question of whether Earth will survive or not. It is a question of whether human beings will survive or not. Look at some of the wealth-leaders in our society, they are already planning their escapes with the current space-race unfolding with their companies, Blue Origin and SpaceX.

The focal point in this discussion is simple. In order for us to prevent this manifestation from deepening its chronicity, which normally kills the organism, like cancer in a human being, we simply have to work backwards within the external world of consumption as well as the internal worlds of conditioning to cut down on our current and future accumulation.

Here are three pragmatic examples.

First, energy. If we are weighing the pros and cons, renewable energy versus coal or nuclear is a vast directional improvement of the energy industry for the environment. But it is not the long-term answer. This is because renewable energy is not renewable. Where do the silicon cells and plexiglass for the panels, the metals, normally aluminum, for the frame, the wiring, and the inverter come from? Where does the energy to power these manufacturing processes of renewable energy come from? Nothing is actually renewable unless it mirrors Nature completely. Biomimicry is absent in energy generation at the moment. Therefore, renewable energy does not solve anything and actually continually aids us in consuming more and more energy under the guise of sustainability and helping the planet. It is a Band-Aid in the First Aid kit, necessary as a transition in wound healing, but not the final solution.

What we need to address is our accumulation of devices and the desirous need for energy based on our hedonistic lifestyles. Four A/Cs in your unit? That's not very responsible. The answer is to cut down on consumption which renders the need for so much energy generation futile. Project Drawdown is a great resource for these sorts of inquiries of how to implement solutions in your day-to-day life.

A second example is eating seasonally and cutting down on meat consumption instead of always having the demand for such foods that are being flown, driven and shipped all around the world. This includes us complicity wreaking havoc on our agricultural lands and environment as large-scale meat operations do. Almonds in the desert of California that drain the aquifer, and we wonder why California is in a drought? Bananas and papaya in New York City in January? The logistic demand places a huge stressor on the environment in many respects, as well as our health. Eating out-of-season and most of the time, not ripe foods which release all sort of chemicals into our system as well as the absorptions of trauma-systems from the animals that are killed en masse to fuel our insatiable greed and desire of our taste buds over the lives of sentient and innocent beings. We will talk about this later in the chapter on the cause of the restless mind states of rajas and *tamas*.

Three, waste. Plastic, paper, glass, et al. Buy a nice Keep Cup or coffee mug if you want hot beverages on the go. Shop at stores with bulk foods. Use the same canvas bags to shop, beeswax wraps for food instead of foil or Ziploc bags. Make your own hummus. Compost your food waste. How much are we willing to sacrifice convenience for true sustainability? Or do we just like the word sustainability because it makes us feel good?

There is absolutely no need for this statistic found on Dumpsters.com blog: "the average American consumer produces just under five pounds of trash each day, while a family creates about 18 pounds. Multiplying those numbers by 365 days for the year, it all adds up to 1,642 pounds per person and 6,570 pounds per family." [9] That's insane, yet viewed as normal operating procedure. Cuckoo, cuckoo.

After all, the basic of accumulation which is the causation of disease stems from our over-identification with our identities. Technology feeds directly into this over-identification and in doing so, only proliferates the likelihood of irrelevance and misinformation which pushes the trend further.

Please see the chart below, which describes some of the accumulations and the resulting personal, global catastrophes as well as remedies.

Accumulation (Mental and Physical) Diagnosis Chart:

Accumulation of...	Personal Result	Personal Remedy	Some Global Results
Righteousness	Anger, judgment, inflated sense of self	Selfless service and non-attachment (to being correct/right)	Violence, war, political unrest, inequality, environmental devastation.
'Knowing' what will happen next, feeling secure	Fear, anxiety, restlessness	Non-attachment, self-inquiry, vulnerability	Fear of the 'unknown' is one of the roots of all the current global issues because we attempt to control nature.
Material possessions	Wealth, greed, gluttony, addiction, inauthenticity, resentment, fear of shame, lack of contentment, extrinsic self-worth,	Non-attachment in the sense of material and mental possessions, selfless service	Poverty, terrorism, political unrest, massive environmental catastrophes for resources, indigenous genocide
Sexual cravings	Lust/objectification	Non-attachment, self-inquiry, selfless service	Rape, pornography, gender inequality, child sex trafficking
Self-identification with individuality, vanity	Pride, egoistic, selfish, external validation needed	Vulnerability, self-inquiry, selfless service, non-attachment	Division and separateness, hierarchy, selfie-craze, social media craze

Accumulation of…	Personal Result	Personal Remedy	Some Global Results
Self-inadequacy, lack of trust in yourself	Doubt, lack of faith, fear, anxiety, insincerity, confusion, self-pity	Self-inquiry, vulnerability	Immigration issues, terrorism, violence, political unrest, lack of trust in others.
Comparisons	Envy, emotional baggage, desire for control, confusion, self-pity, hypocrisy	Vulnerability, selfless service, non-attachment	Division and separateness, depression
Thoughts about the past or future	Sadness, anxiety, business (opposite of stillness), lack of mindfulness	Selfless service, non-attachment, self-inquiry	Insecurity and fear of the "unknown", control mechanisms
Information (external)	Pride, ego, pompous-nature, know-it-all-ism, judgment, prejudice, entitlement, arrogance	Non-attachment, self-inquiry, vulnerability	Fear is one of the roots of all the current global, issues fear of the "unknown"
Poor nutrition	Laziness, inaction, distraction, indecisiveness, poor lifestyle choices	Vulnerability, self-inquiry, selfless service	Complicit violence, inaction on issues within community, globally
Things you want to keep hidden	Dishonesty, hypocrisy. selfless service	Vulnerability, non-attachment,	Division and separation, hardened heart, depression

JOURNAL PROMPTS:

1. What are some things that you personally accumulate in material form? In mental form?
2. In what ways are you contributing to the destruction of our world? How can you ameliorate these?
3. Where does disease lie within your mind? Is it the result of belief systems, ideologies, or identification with self?
4. If you could think of a few ways in which you could cut down on the accumulation of consumer goods or belief systems in your day to day life, what would they be? How would you put them into practice?

Journal Prompt #1:

What are some things that you personally accumulate in material form? In mental form?

Journal Prompt #2:

In what ways are you contributing to the destruction of our world? (this can include plastic and trash waste, energy usage, gasoline, eating meat, etc.) How can you ameliorate these?

Journal Prompt #3:

Where does disease lie within your mind? Is it the result of belief systems, ideologies, or identification with self?

Journal Prompt #4:

If you could think of a few ways in which you could cut down on the accumulation of consumer goods or belief systems in your day to day life, what would they be? How would you put them into practice?

CHAPTER FIVE

Technology and the Disease of Identification

"There is an immense suffering that comes from self-importance."
—Pema Chödron

"We're here to awaken from the illusion of separateness"
—Ram Dass

I'll start this chapter out with a shout-out to East Forest. His East Forest x Ram Dass album is amazing. There is one song on it called 'Electric Sea' that mirrored my feelings about technology for a long time now; which is the muddling of a larger human being identity with the microscopic 'I' that becomes the highlight of the platforms that we use. The selfie-craze that started who knows how long ago was one of the first parts of this misidentification that has now rooted itself deep into the culture of technology itself. Everywhere you go, everything is becoming more customizable through invasive advertising technologies and cookies, which leads to higher and higher expectations that must be delivered per the customer's satisfaction. Our expectation models are somehow linked to the elimination of privacy that has been thrust upon us since 9/11 and the Patriot Act, all in the name of safety. This invasive technology has also become normalized.

The issue continues that the satisfaction, or happiness of the customer is pegged to what unfolds per its expectation models per this technological knowing. These models are becoming more and more pressed for perfection. We are weeding out, or pushing away imperfection which is naturally occurring as we concurrently weed out creativity and authenticity. The result? We all become closer to homogeneity based on cultural models while thinking we are different. Craving special-ness yet trapped in sameness. The more we continue along the lines of 'our own' models, which are fueled currently by our conditioned value system, the more we will feel entitled. This emotion or feeling of superiority or hierarchy over others which is inherent in our identification of ourselves and our opinions as right, is a violent and toxic emotion because it leads to deeper and deeper division between people, other species and Nature.

Righteousness is toxic because ultimately it does not matter who is right and wrong. Everyone is on their own journey and has trials and tribulations to go through. In functionality, it does matter; 2+2 is not 9. Nevertheless, it is not functional in the realization of connectedness with people. If living in a peaceful world is what you want, then you must become peaceful yourself. And to do this, you must accept others for where they are at, not force them into realizations that you think that they need and let them live out their journeys how they think is appropriate. Sharing information is fine, but most of the time, unless it is asked upon us to share, we should hold our tongues.

Regarding righteousness, Ram Dass says,

> "Righteousness ultimately starves you to death. If you want to be free more than you want to be right, you have to let go of righteousness, of being right."

When we become righteous, which can be viewed as valuing our opinion more than others, we push somebody away immediately, which creates a divide and a separation. It makes us view them as something that we are not, or that our journey is more valid than their journey. This is the cut that deepens the wound of separation. If everything is perfect as it is in this mysterious unfolding, then people are exactly where they are at for reasons that we may not fathom.

When I personally experience righteousness, it feels like I am shining the trophy of my own egoic statue while simultaneously allowing others small imperfections and smudges to come to the forefront. It's all another identification that keeps us trapped in a dualistic understanding of separation and functioning of the world.

In Herman Hesse's *Steppenwolf*, there is a great portion where he describes the main protagonist, Harry Haller, judging and critiquing a picture of one of his idols, Goethe, in a professor's living room. Harry basically verbally destroys the picture using the principle of his intellectualization, i.e. that he knows best. This intellectualization of opinions, very common in our society, is an airy concept that prevents him from seeing that every single other being has an equal right to feel a certain way or view something a certain way different than ourselves. Righteousness is yet another attachment to the 'I' that we so greatly protect at all costs with our shields of the intellect. I have plenty of personal experience within this and still often find myself with the same neuroses of self-righteousness which coats itself in a different garb, becoming subtler and subtler. This righteousness leads to us over-identifying with the unique parts of ourselves at the cost of the greater whole rather than embracing the uniqueness of others fully. There is plenty of room for people to practice and worship and live in their own models, so why force an identified model onto everyone? Homogeneity is non-existent in nature.

With our identifications we build out this model of separateness rather than breaking them down into acceptance.

That being said, technology is brilliant for allowing everyone to share their stories, their pictures, and whatever they want about themselves with certain people. The many positives of social media and the group-mind that has formed around social and environmental justice movements is a positive. However, the fact that we then attach our own identification solely to the small 'I' as it is often called, leads us deeper and deeper into our personalities. Personalities do not love; they just want something. We are not a noun; we are a verb. Anything that we constantly limit ourselves with, from the ego to the person we think we are, is selling ourselves short of the infinite gift of compassion which is rooted in acceptance.

ORIGINALITY IS AN ILLUSION

Perhaps this desire of personality lies in the fact that we believe ourselves to be original, innovative, and more special than others. What a drag! Let's make something clear, there are no original thoughts. Not even the thoughts of this book are original. Our thoughts are generated second-hand through an education system that is based on a culture, a language and exposure to the interpretation of intelligence. We translate or channel messages into a language that must have been delivered or originated from somewhere. An application of knowledge can be original in its function and application, but no thought in itself is original. In Ayurveda, they say that the knowledge of the science was recollected from the ether by Lord Dhanvantari; it had always been there. He just brought it to the surface. This alone can free us from always trying to be special, which is such a bummer!

How much pressure do we bear, as we walk around all day trying to separate ourselves from others based on the illusion of novelty? As we drop that, societal pressure goes away because all of our expectations of ourselves disappear. We stop trying to fit in and stand out simultaneously. We have nothing more to defend and protect, we're just a part of it all. We are embracing our imperfections, which are unique in themselves.

Another aspect of division that technology has enabled us to enact with this perceived originality or special-ness of our own being is to lose the responsibility for the harshness of our own words and critiques to others. This is based on our own righteousness, stemming from our perceived separation. There is no courage in sitting behind a keyboard or a phone and typing something to someone else to try and prove your own point. Publicly shaming others and 'cancel culture' come in here. Mistakes are beautiful, they allow other people to learn. Even calling it a mistake is labeling it something that has a negative connotation. You cannot learn without these steps. Plus, many times, people are just looking at the same elephant from different angles. Once again, it doesn't matter if you are wrong or right. If the message being delivered through you is pure, it is flexible and adaptable enough to take into consideration the reality that you do not know anything. In another person's eyes, their opinion is just as valid as yours. Whether you are right or not from a belief system standpoint, ultimately doesn't matter. You can let go to the clinging of opinion.

PATIENCE IS COURAGE

To really get down into courage we must become vulnerable with ourselves. This means we really have to get down into patience. Forgiveness finds itself a home in patience. Forgiveness is for giving. This self-identification with and indulgence of our own self-importance has rendered us completely reactionary to anyone who doesn't agree with our perspective. We place ourselves on our own pedestal, as if we feel that we are unheard, unseen, or challenged when we think that we have no right to be. Reaction is not sovereign. Responsive action is sovereign. Reactions are conditioned by the stories we tell ourselves. Responsive actions are not.

As Pema Chödron states in one of her lectures called *Don't Bite the Hook*, patience is the action against a knee-jerk reaction to harden the Heart and lock-down tightly into a them/us, friend/foe relationship with another. When she references these things, she is assisting us in understanding a beautiful, ancient book spoken by Śāntideva on the Bodhisattva path, called the *Paramitas*, or perfections, in Pali, the ancient language of Gautama Buddha.

The Six Paramitas (as according to Mahayana or Tibetan Buddhism) are listed below[10]:

1. Generosity (*Dāna*)
2. Morality (*Sīla*)
3. Patience (*Ksānti*)
4. Vigor (*Vīrya*)
5. Concentration (*Dhyāna*)
6. Wisdom (*Prajñā*)

Here, we are focusing on the third *paramita* of patience. Patience can be used as a shield from our own patterns because if we are centered enough to sit with the discomfort that is brought through anger arising in the body and mind, we will have nothing left to fear or deflect from because we are not fearing the emotions themselves. We begin to be able to view the emotions as passing phenomena that may be triggered from the environment, but do not need to be acted upon. Patience is a prerequisite to peace.

Pema Chödron states in one of her lectures,

"Peacemaking is as contagious as violence, but we have been programmed to escalate rather than to de-escalate."

It occurred to me recently that emotions are a phenomena of the mind and are therefore trapped in duality as well. They are somewhat entities upon themselves. To free our emotions from this trap of identification we must just sit within the feeling that arises from our mind's interpretation and story about what an emotion feels like to us via sensation. In this objectivity, in sitting with the emotion, if you can, you are able to witness the emotional phenomenon as a fleeting entity. It only exists as such, and without a label other than the subjective sensations that arise within the body, it comes and goes. For me, when anger comes in, it feels like I become a dense block and my head becomes thick like glue. Sadness feels like this a well of water that is overflowing uncontrollably and spills out of my eyes. The emotion itself is interdependent of you. It is a collective, objective phenomenon and each may experience that passing emotion in a different way.

CONFLICT IS AN INVITATION TO INTIMACY

We tend to shy away from emotionally jarring experiences. However, conflict is an invitation to intimacy. It opens you up by exposing the core wound which your ego protects. Those who trigger you are your greatest teachers; they show you what is left to be cleared out, uprooted.

As Ram Dass says, "the teacher can show you exactly where you aren't."

Anger can be a portal into love, for vulnerability is a portal into true connection. Our emotions are our own teachers, like symptoms of the body. They are medicine for the illness of our minds which we complicity abide by every day. By accepting the illness of the society that we function within as normal, we can never find the cure. Our patience as a patient is to see through this illness as an antidote to our complacency; to live in a world that conditions and reinstates these emotions in the first place.

The first step of our conscious resistance starts with the resistance against ourselves to be vulnerable.

The subtlety of the mind is accessed by the subtlety of the body. As you begin to track your emotions and bodily feelings, you begin to walk the pathway back to your being. Truth has no lineage. Symptoms arise at edges, as disavowed parts of the whole. Our own concept of freedom gets in the way of freedom. Our concept of our own identification, with how we identify, locks us into limitation.

The most succinct pathway I have seen to begin the movement from limitation and deconditioning to liberation and freedom is the process of Ashtanga Yoga. We will discuss what Yoga is in the next chapter.

JOURNAL PROMPTS:

1. When do you find yourself avoiding conflict? Is it a tool for you to keep yourself safe?
2. How does the current environment of social media make you feel? Does it create more suffering or peace within you?
3. Why do you think patience is so hard to cultivate? In what ways could you cultivate patience in your day-to-day life?
4. Where do you find the borders or boundaries of your own resistance to your vulnerability? Where do you find you are the most vulnerable and open to share your deeper truths?

Journal Prompt #1:

When do you find yourself avoiding conflict? Is it a tool for you to keep yourself safe?

Journal Prompt #2:

How does the current environment of social media make you feel? Does it create more suffering or peace within you?

Journal Prompt #3:

Why do you think patience is so hard to cultivate? In what ways could you cultivate patience in your day-to-day life?

Journal Prompt #4:

Where do you find the borders or boundaries of your own resistance to your vulnerability? Where do you find you are the most vulnerable and open to share your deeper truths?

CHAPTER SIX

So, What is Yoga, Really?

'Yogás citta vritti nirodhah.'

"The restraint of the modifications of the mind-stuff is Yoga.
—Patanjali Yoga Sutras, Samādhi Pāda 2

*"Although a man has not studied a single system of philos-
ophy, although he does not believe in any God, and never
has believed, although he has not prayed even once in his
whole life, if the simple power of good actions has brought
him to that state where he is ready to give up his life and
all else for others, he has arrived at the same point to which
the religious man will come through his prayers and the philosopher through his knowledge; and so you may find that
the philosopher, the worker, and the devotee, all meet at one
point, that one point being self-abnegation."*
—Swami Vivekananda, Karma Yoga

As many of you are aware, Yoga is very popular now—it has
become a worldwide phenomenon. When the word Yoga is
brought up in conversation, most people immediately think
about some physical practices of stretching or stress reduction.

However, this is only one small aspect of the Yogic Science. As of now, there have been many styles of Yoga, from Vinyasa Flow, to Bikram, to black-light Yoga, beer Yoga, and even goat Yoga. Originally, there were no styles of Yoga, just four paths; *Bhakti* (devotion), *Karma* (selfless service), *Gyana* (wisdom) and *Rāja* (Ashtanga). They all converged, ultimately leading to the same place. In this chapter, we will be reviewing aspects of all that intertwine with Rāja Yoga.

We can start by sharing a few examples of what traditional Yoga is not. Yoga is not an Equinox class, it is not Lululemon pants, it is not styles of stretching, it is not physical fitness or exercise that you do once a day. Yoga is an entire life-way that interacts with the external and internal worlds.

We've seen what Yoga is not, so what is it? The word Yoga comes from the Sanskrit root *yug* (or *yuz/yuj*), meaning to yoke or join together. It represents both the unification process and pathway, as well as the state of union itself. If we accept this translation, then Yoga is only necessary at all because our current state is separation.

If we did not have a sense of separation, or if we did not engage in the process of separation through action, we would have no need to actively engage in this experiential science. But, as the global trends suggest, we do have a yearning for Yoga. Up to 20.4 million people in the U.S.A. alone now practice what is labeled as Yoga[11]. However, is what they are practicing really Yoga? Or is what they taste, which is enough to keep them coming back, but a mere drop of the diluted liquid of a sacred river leading to the oceanic mass of interconnectedness? The presence of this mass yearning indicates that more and more people are recognizing separateness and how it limits our ability to authentically participate in the fullness of life.

Historically, it is said that Yoga was introduced to the West by an Indian sage called Swami Vivekananda, who was a deep devotee of Sri. Ramakrishna. Vivekananda demonstrated Yoga postures at a World Fair in Chicago in the 1890s. This generated much interest and laid the grounds for the welcoming of many other Yogis and Swamis from India in the years that followed such as Paramahamsa Yogananda and Sri Krishnamacharya.

When you introduce a mere drop of ink to a glass of water, the ink becomes diluted. Similarly, the purity of teachings as of now is not maintained by those who have experientially attained what is occurring in this experiential science. This happened down the line from perhaps the 1950s onward. Tightly-maintained lineages had sustained the accuracy of the practice. However, a global telephone game began, which enfeebled this sacred science, making it what it is today, an ambiguous buzzword with copious packaged styles for capitalization.

As this watering down began to occur, many people started to see that Yoga could become a business. People were having pains from sitting at desks all day. People were feeling disenfranchised by their lack of connection to others. The removal from Nature had already long begun. The race to claim territory in the spiritual-business-race began. Teachers who may not have been at the level of spreading the Truth, but perhaps had more of an enterprising mind, took hold of the bare bones of this information, came up with a cool twist and hitchhiked onto the philosophy to begin to spread it. Or, beings who were not fully 'cooked' began to teach and yet the avarices of humanity were too strong, and the guru power trips started. The result of this perfunctory spreading is rampant misinformation and lineage erosion due to the unaligned intention of spreading something to create it into a profitable industry for selfish reasons. It also began to lose the intricacies and principles of the Yogic science rooted in the *sutras* for the sake of market customization and demand.

This trade-off has rendered places like Rishikesh, India, which I visited in 2017, as a Yoga-teacher-manufacturing facility.

People go from all over the world to be granted pieces of paper that certify them to teach Yoga. However, even if the school is certified, these newly minted teachers may not even necessarily know what the true goal of Yoga is by the end of their training. This is not to say that there are no good teachers in Rishikesh or those who have created new styles. Nevertheless, the process of what Yoga is going through now, as many things in this world have gone through due to the commoditization of value through the homogeneous structure of money, seems to have taken a turn toward quantity over quality. The intention has been lost. Yoga in the modern eye has lost its depth, and has succumbed to the market demand for shallowness and superficiality. As such, stillness and subtlety, two of the keys of any spiritual practice, are being ignored. These subtle depths are where you find the transformative factors of Spirit which Yoga seeks to unionize.

As we mentioned above, Yoga is the Sanskrit word which, when attempted to be translated into English, means approximately 'union' or to 'yoke together.' Okay, so many people may know this. But, what does this union really represent?

THE UNION OF PURUSA AND PRAKRITI

This core basic principle beyond the word 'union' is not commonly discussed in classes by most teachers who are spreading teachings as well as hosting workshops and retreats around the world. In fact, if people knew that what they were doing with this experiential science of Yoga was to facilitate their own psychological death, their own dissolution of identity, I doubt as many people would be trying to look cute in Lululemon pants to go step on the mat and practice. Nor would it be hosted at your local Equinox before you head off to work.

Union in the multidimensional interpretation of the Sanskrit word means the union of the *Purusa* and *Prakrti*. I'll break these words down below for easier comprehension.

Purusa can be translated as 'Self' or as 'Consciousness'. Purusa exists in an un-manifest form, or the pure potentiality of energy. This potential state, or the vacuum of enormous energy, is the non-dual state, or, no dividing polarity of existence. It is the stillness of eternity from which springs our diversely patterned reality. In quantum unification theory, this metric relates to black hole physics and entropy.

This *Purusa* in Yoga is the substratum of consciousness as a whole, the interconnected force which is unwavering, completely encompassing and unitive in its material and immaterial wholeness. You can view a substratum as something like a film screen upon which everything is playing out. This includes the subtle layers such as intelligence and wisdom itself, the mind and all of our thoughts, out to the grosser, material layers such as the physical body, your coffee cup and your boss's Prius. These material layers only appear to be continuous and solid.

As the ultimate and unwavering state of consciousness, the *Purusa* is the state of being which is discussed when human or non-human beings attain a state of liberation or enlightenment; they are no-longer tethered to their limited concept of themselves, their time-space locus or the 'I.' The 'I' is a part of *Prakrti*. The Soul or the Self (with a capital 'S') is what is represented by *Purusa*, and this consciousness is existentially the same across all phenomena unfolding in the Universe. It is the immutable and unchanging Truth; non-duality.

Prakrti can be interpreted as 'Nature', or duality. Nature exists in manifest forms, which are expressive forms of energy in specific design patterns; sacred geometry in the form of the Phi ratio are examples of this. These patterns designate function and formation. *Prakrti*, being dual, means that everything within nature is made up of polarities such as good and evil, hot and cold, light and dark, rich and poor, peace and war. This includes every spectrum in between these two polarities as well.

In the Tao this is called the Yin and Yang and is represented by two halves which are connected by a thin line. I have begun to view the thin line as the middle way, the way through the duality. This line merges the dual natures to become the pattern itself. As this pattern is expressed endlessly outside of time and space, you no longer are trussed to birth and death. Therefore, you are moving beyond samsara, or the cycle of birth and death. On that note, if any of you have not seen the beautifully directed film titled 'Samsara' by Ron Fricke and produced by Mark Magidson, I highly recommend that you watch it. It is a non-narrative film that acts as a guided journey that explores the human experience.

IMPERMANENCE: THE LINK BETWEEN BUDDHISM AND YOGA

Anything in *Prakrti* or Nature abides by the wavering factor, also known as impermanence. It is continually changing every microsecond of every moment of every day on the atomic level. This principle is called anicca in Palī, the original language of Gautama the Buddha, or anitya in Sanskrit. *Aniccā*, is a compound word consisting of "a" meaning non-, and "*nicca*" meaning "constant, continuous, permanent." While '*nicca*' is the concept of continuity and permanence, *aniccā* refers to its exact opposite; the absence of permanence and continuity. This illusion of continuity ripples up to the more gross levels which we are able to observe directly as changing cycles such as the seasons, life and death, newness and innocence to deterioration and obsolescence.

Our bodies, breath, minds, wisdom and intelligence are all a part of *Prakrti*. The Yoga, or the union, of these two fields is when the human being has sufficiently navigated him or her-self to the point of an experiential level of understanding in which they are witnessing that *Prakrti* is an illusion, and existentially there is no mine, no 'I.' Therefore, there is no longer division or separation between the immutable Self and the ever-changing self. What we are discussing here is not a conceptual understanding or an intellectualization of Oneness. That conceptuality is relatively easy. This is the experience of it, which renews itself moment to moment in apparent continuity, like the in and out breath.

Whenever we cling to the attachment of continuity, we suffer. This is the link between Buddhism and Yoga. Both guide the practitioner into the natural cessation or relinquishment of attachment to the mind-stuff, the *vrittis*. S.N. Goenke, the lineage carrier of Vipassana who brought it to the Western world through his teacher Sayagyi U Ba Khin, describes the four attachments that the mind clings to. Goenkeji states,

"There are four types of attachment that one keeps developing in life. The first is attachment to one's desires, to the habit of craving. Whenever craving arises in the mind, it is accompanied by a physical sensation. Although at a deep level a storm of agitation has begun, at a superficial level one likes the sensation and wishes it to continue. This can be compared with scratching a sore: doing so will only aggravate it, and yet one enjoys the sensation of scratching. In the same way, as soon as a desire is fulfilled, the sensation that accompanied the desire is also gone, and so one generates a fresh desire in order that the sensation may continue. One becomes addicted to craving and multiplies one's misery.

Another attachment is the clinging to "I," "mine", without knowing what this 'I' really is. One cannot bear any criticism of one's "I" or any harm to it. And the attachment spreads to include whatever belongs to "I," whatever is "mine." This attachment would not bring misery if whatever is "mine" could continue eternally, and the "I" also could remain to enjoy it eternally, but the law of nature is that sooner or later one or the other must pass away. Attachment to what is impermanent is bound to bring misery.

Similarly, one develops attachment to one's views and beliefs, and cannot bear any criticism of them, or even accept that others may have differing views. One does not understand that everyone wears coloured glasses, a different colour for each person. By removing the glasses, one can see reality as it is, untinted, but instead one remains attached to the colour of one's glasses, to one's own preconceptions and beliefs.

Yet another attachment is the clinging to one's rites, rituals, and religious practices. One fails to understand that these are all merely outward shows, that they do not contain the essence of truth. If someone is shown the way to experience truth directly within himself but continues to cling to empty external forms, this attachment produces a tug-of-war in such a person, resulting in misery."[12]

He then goes into Gautama the Buddha's process of understanding that the 'I' is a result of the initial separation between un-manifest and manifest which is held into accord by the four causes of the arising of matter, basic principles of the mind-matter continuum. It is created, according to the *sankhārā*, or strong reactions that the mind clings to with regard to the world perceived by the senses.

Goenkeji explains it as follows:

"The entire external universe exists for a person only when he or she experiences it, that is, when a sensory object comes into contact with one of the sense doors. As soon as there is a contact, there will be a vibration, a sensation. The perception gives a valuation to the sensation as good or bad, based on one's past experiences and conditionings, past saṅkhārā. In accordance with this coloured valuation the sensation becomes pleasant or unpleasant, and according to the type of sensation, one starts reacting with liking or disliking, craving or aversion. Sensation is the forgotten missing link between the external object and the reaction. The entire process occurs so rapidly that one is unaware of it: by the time a reaction reaches the conscious level, it has been repeated and intensified trillions of times, and has become so strong that it can easily overpower the mind."[13]

The four parts of mind are classified by their functionality and result from contact of a stimulus via our five sense conscious-nesses plus the mind. This is taste, touch, sight, hearing, smell and, in comes thought. The amalgamation of these five sense doors, or sensory parts, form the thought of 'I' when it latches onto physical matter. The matter is the physical body. The route of the mind from stimuli to reaction are classified as:

1. Cognition, or consciousness, which can be thought of as the ability of an expression of functionality to witness;
2. Recognition, which is the formation of a thought pattern based on the stimulus that was cognized;
3. Feeling, which stems from the recognition of something in the system;
4. Reaction, which is normally formed in the pattern of desire which is rooted in craving, a positive desirous function of an object/stimulus, or aversion, a negative desirous function to be free of the object/stimulus.

As these parts of mind or parts of consciousness manifest, they create the formation of the 'I' or the 'me'. From here comes possession, the feeling of my or mine. Our strongest feeling of this is most directly connected with the physical body. We often confuse ourselves with the body. The body itself is more of a vehicle that has been loaned by nature for consciousness to manifest itself through. But we attach so deeply with it as our limitation. If our body becomes injured or old, we become miserable. Is what is looking out of your eyes getting old, or is it just your vehicle? If your Volkswagen Beetle gets old or gets a ding from a rock flying off the road, do you confuse the vehicle with yourself? Yoga assists to merge the lines between the body and Nature, so the vantage point becomes inseparable from the viewer. This returns us back to the subtleties of interconnected discontinuity through experience.

POSSESSIVE VALUES

Our entire value system as we have seen is situated into a possessive 'I' context; an individualized context. Because of this collective illusion of me and mine, we develop desires to fuel and fulfill that 'I.'

These 'I' desires manifest in two forms, craving and aversion. Basically, these are the desires to associate positively with something that has been perceived as good by the senses or a desire to disassociate negatively with something that has been perceived by the senses as bad, respectively. These two definitions are already completely subjective and culturally based. In many ancient linguistic traditions like Sanskrit, the separation of these two things does not exist.

When these individualized reactions to the senses form, the plethora of desires and aversions fall continuously; we never recognize that the internal world is already whole without the external world. In fact, there is not even a divider other than in our perceptions of the language which provide a basis for the division of these two worlds. Just like there is no unconscious and conscious mind, there is only mind. The more we label things in this separate context, the more we are separating and segmenting ourselves. We block out our connection with source consciousness by intellectualizing our connection with source consciousness.

That being said, the reactionary nature to the sensory world does not need to be eliminated. It is not like your senses will disappear, they will always be there. Then again, becoming more non-reactionary or equanimous to stimuli is important because it reverses a conditioning pattern of the mind to constantly pin its possessive desires and fuel for craving and aversion to the external world. This practice is commonly called sense extrication, or the fifth limb of Ashtanga Yoga known as *pratyahara*. This sense extrication is also explained in Buddhism.

S.N. Goenke states,

"As one continues observing oneself, it becomes clear why kalāpa arise: they are produced by the input that one gives to the life flow, the flow of matter and mind. The flow of matter requires material input, of which there are two types: the food one eats and the atmosphere in which one lives. The flow of mind requires mental input, which again is of two types: either a present or a past saṅkhārā. If one gives an input of anger at the present moment, immediately mind influences matter, and kalāpa will start to arise with a predominance of fire element, causing one to feel a sensation of heat. If the input is fear, the kalāpa generated at that time will have a predominance of air element, and one feels a sensation of trembling; and so on. The second type of mental input is a past saṅkhārā. Every saṅkhārā is a seed which gives a fruit, a result after some time. Whatever sensation one experienced when planting the seed, the same sensation will arise when the fruit of that saṅkhāra comes to the surface of the mind.

Of these four causes, one should not try to determine which is responsible for the arising of a particular sensation. One should merely accept whatever sensation occurs. The only effort should be to observe without generating a new saṅkhāra. If one does not give the input of a new reaction to the mind, automatically an old reaction will give its fruit, manifesting as sensation. One observes, and it passes away. Again one does not react; therefore, another old saṅkhāra must give its fruit. In this way, by remaining aware and equanimous, one allows the old saṅkhāra to arise and pass away, one after another: one comes out of misery."[14]

The objects of our desire will always change, because *Prakrti*, or Nature, is always changing. Until we look at the root of the issue which is a lack of control of our conditioned desirous sense, we cannot be free of the continually evolving material worlds that fuel our consumption of more curated, more hip, or more buzzwordy objects. We will always look to supplement our imagined un-whole self with the changing external world if we do not recognize our innate wholeness. We manifest the craving and aversions to move through them by accepting them. We are all just practicing relationships with ourselves.

Essentially, all the information thus far in this chapter is leading to the fact that the experiential science of Yoga was recollected to lead us into an integrative understanding of the non-duality or non-separateness of existence by providing a pathway to master the modifications of the mind, *vritti*, which involves deconstructing the 'I' sense. Can we accept that our entire current state of the world which is rife and rampant with disconnection and separation is perfect for us to evolve back towards unity? Only in the duality of the disconnection can we find the unity.

On the Yogic journey, you will be totally transformed from a seemingly limited physical, mental, and emotional person into an illumined, thoroughly harmonized being—from attachment to likes and dislikes, pain and pleasure, success and failure to peace, joy and selfless dedication.

One of my favorite models that helped me to understand what the point of Yogic practice is, is represented below. It is called the Pancha Kosha, or Five Sheaths. It was one of the tools of learning used at Yoga Gita in Mysuru, India with Sri Vijay Gopala. Some information is listed below.

PANCHA KOSHA—THE FIVE SHEATHS

In this model, you see five concentric circles. The further out in the circle you are, the more gross or material the realm of consciousness, the closer to the small circle in the middle, the subtler or fine and invisible.

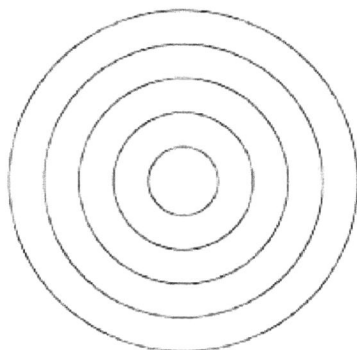

Anamaya Kosha (Body) – This is the outer ring of the circle. It is in the physical and material dimension, the body. This realm is totally exposed and subject to natural decay and the changes of *Prakriti*, aging is a prime example. Asana practice is connected here by moving the body in specific patterns for many different meanings, in accordance with a harmonious continuity of the breath. That is the next subtler sheath.

Pranamaya Kosha (Breath) – The breath is the second ring of the circle, prana. The prana is life force. This *Pranic* sheath is subtler and vaster than the physical sheath. Breath is the link between the physical body and the mind. Breath can vary in subtlety, but the subtler the breath, the deeper linkage to the mind and the Self. When fully absorbed into the pranic sheath, you no longer need breath.

This is where part of the confusion about modern day breathwork remains; it is attached to the aim. The goal of *pranayama* is not to rely on the breath but to move beyond the breath. The breath is only necessary if you are exerting effort in the body. As you reduce effort in the body and mind, or reduce do-ership, you reduce the necessity of metabolism, which is the sum of all chemical reactions that occur in living organisms that enable the physical body to function. Therefore, breath regulation or *pranayama* is a route to subtler planes of pranic, or non-physical energy systems.

However, since the breath body is subtler than the physical body, many breathwork techniques can easily harm the body. The energetic channels of the *ida*, *pingala* and *sushumna* are thinner than even a human hair, so techniques such as holotropic breathwork, where you essentially over-oxygenate yourself by hyperventilating to rebirth can actually be harmful to the subtle energetic layers of the breath body and even the physical body. This is why tetany, a symptom of tetanus where your body locks up, is a common result of over-oxygenating the body. We, in our culture which is obsessed with feeling something, become averse to the cessation of anything and crave some sort of stimulus or validation of effort. We have become so numb from societal living that when we receive any sensation through a natural process such as breath, we cling to it like we have achieved a certain state. This is still attached to the doing and not to the being. Pranayama is the reduction of the breath, not the overexertion of it. Processes like **anuloma viloma, kapala bhati and ujjayi** are subtle forms of breathing that enable us continued spaces of non-breath between the breaths themselves. For more information on these techniques, you can refer to the back of the book in the Glossary.

Manomaya Kosha (Mind) – the mind is called the *citta* in Yoga. *Citta* is the sum total of three factors. The flow of traditional thought goes from a–c and is referenced in the *The Yoga Sūtras of Patanjali.*

  a. Manas – desiring part of the mind;
  b. Buddhi – intellect or discernment;
  c. Ahamkara – ego or 'I'

Every thinking person will go through these stages. Within the *citta*, there are the *vrittis*, which are mind modifications. The deeper you penetrate the superficial layers of the mind, the more you find material that is not penetrated via common day-to-day activities. The *vrittis* are as follows:

  1. Pramāna – correct or right knowledge
  2. Viparyaya – misconception, or incorrect knowledge
  3. Vikalpa – verbal delusion or imagination
  4. Nidra – sleep
  5. Smrti – memory

Vijnanamaya Kosha (Wisdom) – this layer is the ability of discernment always from an objective or neutral angle. It has surpassed the mind in existential subtlety and has no perceived owner.

Anandamaya Kosha (Self, or bliss) – this is the eternal state of *Purusa*, which is the connective force of bliss or love that connects all things.

From this understanding, the traditional science of Rāja Yoga (Ashtanga) is structured via eight limbs, providing a practical pathway to move with the body through the breath, through the mind, through wisdom, and into the Self.

STHIRAM SUKHAM AND EFFORTLESSNESS

The key that is often overlooked or misinterpreted in Yoga that was shown to me regarding asana practice is effortlessness. It is highlighted in the Patanjali Yoga Sutras via the thread of *sthiram sukham*. *Sthiram* means stability and *sukham* means comfort. Our teacher, Sri Vijay Gopala, shared with us that the postures are practiced to harmonize the physical expression of the individual with the existential expression; from effortful to effortless. The movement into effortlessness cannot arrive by continued effort, but must cease naturally by the relinquishment of the effort itself.

This means that the *asana* postures are not practiced to express a particularity of form. As long as there is particularity, there is finiteness in the expression. As you move deeper and deeper into the subtlety of allowing your effort to cease, you move towards the pure expression of the union of *Prakriti* and *Purusa* on the physical level. The ultimate landmark here is when the borders of the body begin to merge or dissolve and the body loses its identity. Universal vision is a technique used in *asana* practice that assists with the movement beyond form. This moves you out of a do-er role, which naturally moves you into effortlessness. How else could one hold an *asana* position for hours on end? Definitely not by trying to do it. We can view this in the phrase of getting out of our own way.

Making the Yoga practice a 'doing' is one of the most basic

mind traps. Other mind traps like goal-oriented practice, judging your progress, loss of contentment, putting effort into the practice, all have to be realized as pitfalls to effortlessness. Yoga assists in moving us away from doing and into being, from reaction into stability.

THE EIGHT LIMBS OF ASHTANGA YOGA

The word *Astanga* or *Ashtanga* means eight limbs. *Ash* is eight, *tanga* is limbs. Similarly, to Buddhism having the eight-fold path, there are eight integral and holistic limbs of Rāja Yoga that must be practiced and advanced upon in succession in order for the other limbs to be activated to their highest potentiality. When you are on this path, you are said to be on a path of *sādhana*, or practice. According to the sūtras, the limbs are as follows:

1. Yama – abstinences. These are mostly guidance given how to be with what is while interacting with society. It is a balance between your truest life expression and societal life expression;
2. Niyama – observances of how to treat yourself during your life practice
3. Āsana – posture practice
4. Pranayama – breath control/regulation. This is used to harmonize yourself with life-energy, *prana*
5. Pratyāhāra – sense extrication, sense withdrawal. This can also be viewed as a shift in particularity or singularity of observation. You are no longer being tethered to the reactionary state of sense consciousness, you witness the happening of phenomena without attaching to them
6. Dhāranā – concentration. Also said to be in a non-dual state, establishing a state beyond any egoic 'I identification.

7. Dhyāna – meditation, or continuity of a non-dual state. Alignment with 'what is'.

8. Samādhi – contemplation, absorption, superconscious. Stillness of the body in total comfort, no breath needed, mind freed from 'I'ness.

In planetary terms, I'm unsure that everyone can really practice Yoga to this utmost flow. However, in my eyes, we can all start at the basic first step of the Ashtanga Yogic pathway, the *yamas*, in order to reflect within ourselves and understand how these qualities can be key in the current paradigm shift and transitionary state.

These aspects of the *yamas* are nothing new. When respected and honored with discipline, they will enable us to respond to the world in a more compassionate, non-attached and loving way. These three characteristics help us to slowly lose the attachment to our 'I-ness,' which creates insecurity, possession, accumulation, and disease of all sorts. There will be some comments after the basic translation consisting of my additions to our modern context and vernacular. These *yamas* are in accordance with The Yoga Sūtras of Patanjali.

Yamas—otherwise known as the *mahāvratam* (great vows) are below. These are not something to be skipped over and looked at in a trivial sense.

B.K.S Iyengar states,

"Practice of asanas (physical postures) without the backing of yama and niyama is mere acrobatics."

Ahimsā – non-violence.
This is representative of no pain or harm caused via words, thoughts or actions. This does not relate only to killing, as the word himsā means to cause pain, and *ahimsā* means to not cause

pain. All enmity ceases in one whose presence is in non-harm or non-violence. Even without obtaining 100% perfection in *ahimsā*, we can practice it. Just like Mahatma Gandhi exhibited in India, any practice of non-violence will elevate us to a higher, more peaceful and connected state of being. A few examples of practicing *ahimsā* can relate to not eating meat, not harming others with your words or reactions, not attaching to the experiences of envy or harmful emotions that create division, and letting go of grudges or stories.

Satya – truthfulness, not lying.
This correlates with honesty or transparency which, in my mind, is directly tied to vulnerability. Nowadays, many people are using the phrase 'radical honesty'. Honesty is anything but radical. In fact, to say that honesty is radical is quite scary to think about! That means we are walking around in a world full of liars, hiding our true selves from one another like scared animals. That's no environment for openness, trust, collaboration, compassion, empathy, or love. That's no environment for togetherness. No wonder we are all separate if we sacrifice our honesty for societal constructs of respectability. We are framing ourselves out of our own truth.

Honesty is a basic principle of communication and action, and should be simple. Yet, our overly-sensitive egos get in the way because we are afraid of being vulnerable. Like a hermit crab moving shells, the perceived supple and soft interior that has been wounded intentionally or unintentionally throughout our lives is cautious about exposing itself. This caution creates the lack of connection that is rampant in the world today as well as reactionary states of being that polarize us in politics, religion and social justice.

Exaggeration is also a form of lying, as it stretches the truth. This could be from personal experiences such as, "that cliff jump was like 40 feet high", when it was actually 20 feet, to business exaggeration or false-marketing. One that I catch most often is people speaking and sharing information when they really don't know what is true or not, but they want to appear like they know rather than appearing inadequate and having the humility to say 'I don't know.' If you are always honest, vulnerable, authentic and true, there will come a time when all you say will come true, because nothing but truth is emanating from you. As stated in the Sri Swami Satchitananda translation of the Patanjali Yoga Sūtras,

> "With this establishment in honesty, fearlessness comes. One need not be afraid of anybody and can always lead an open life. When there are no lies, the entire life becomes an open book. But this comes only with an absolutely honest mind. When the mind becomes clear and serene, the true Self reflects without disfigurement, and we realize the Truth in its own original nature."[15]

With that freedom we are released from the burdensome energetic density that we carry within by not expressing our own inner truths. We give ourselves permission for our own release. We only suppress our authenticity because of the conditions of seriousness and respectability that society engrains in us. We when we become free of some of this weight, we are free to be light and accepting, with compassion for other people who judge us. We have compassion that they are on their own journeys and we are unable to completely understand what they have been through that has brought them to the place they are at now. We become able to fully embrace our own honesty, which in turn allows others to embrace their own honesty and truth. A permission is granted from the experiencer to those who are on the brink of experiencing. Although we cannot force another's awakening, providing a safe space for other's unfolding through our own self-acceptance is a gift in itself. It is as if by unlocking the place of Love within ourselves, we grant them the key to unlock their own Hearts as well.

Here, vulnerability is of the utmost importance, as it leads to real authenticity and true safety. Denying our imperfections makes us hardened. Embracing our imperfections creates a softening. Our imperfections are in fact our uniqueness. Rather than structuring our lives around the attempted achievement of perfection, we can relax a little bit and allow the imperfections to simmer into a delicious soup of human-ness. Being able to share the truths that sit inside of you waiting to be expressed in relationships with others, perhaps with anonymity at the beginning, but eventually without, is beautiful. It creates authentic human connection, which always results in the opening of the Heart. Real Heart openings are transmittable.

Asteya – non-stealing.

Non-stealing seems pretty straight forward. The current definition of stealing is to take another person's property without permission or legal right and without intending to return it. However, because property is an illusion that has a forcefully-agreed-upon structure enforced by law, we believe it to be true. This definition also limits the theft to human beings, rather than including Nature. We can never truly own anything; we borrow it. We even borrow these bodies. We are impermanent creatures, therefore ownership is by Nature temporary and false. We do not even own our own breath, *so how can we call ourselves owners? As the saying goes, "we don't inh*erit the land from our ancestors, we borrow it from our children." Land must be treated with care and respect so as to protect it.

This principle of the futility of land-ownership is rooted in indigenous cultures as well, such as the Hawai'ians. There was no concept of land ownership, in fact, it was more like the land and humans we're in communion with one another rather than any hierarchical framework of owning. Kauikeaouli, or King Kamehameha III in his 1841 Constitution of the Kingdom of Hawai'i, reaffirmed that the land was traditionally held by the chiefs and the people in common, and that no man, including the king, could own any part of it. Six years later, convinced by foreign advisors that land ownership would benefit his people, he undertook to distribute land in what became known as the Great Māhele. But, Hawai'ians did not conceptually comprehend land ownership, believing that the land is immortal and could not truly be the property of mere mortals, and began to allow others to buy it. Today, the law of Kamehameha III that still survives grants public access along the shore for harvesting food from the sea. Otherwise, perhaps the greedy hotel chains would have gobbled up all of this land too in dishonored treaties and language confusion.[16]

You can see the primary differing worldviews represented here; arrogance created from a limited understanding of Nature versus humility and a commune and relationship with it. We've turned the world into a good to be bought and sold. It is not. It was gifted to us, and we are taking from it without giving back. It's even in the Ten Commandments, thou shalt not steal. This non-stealing also relates directly to gratitude. If we accept things constantly without gratitude or continually exploit and take from others or the planet without reverence, this, as mentioned above, is a form of theft. We steal because of greed. And we have greed because of the illusion of 'I' which creates desires to possess to increase our self-security.

We all mostly want to do a little and reap a lot, and this is exacerbated by the 'overnight' billionaires in the start-up culture which is fueled by millions of dollars of venture capital money looking for the unicorns. These capital injections are often so they can get a quick-pocketed return after 3-5 years. That's why sometimes it is referred to as vulture capital. To quote *Fight Club*, these "innovative solutions to modern living" that are being created are mostly bereft of meaning and are full of fluff. In fact, this is creating a brain-drain of the talented minds that could be solving world issues and tackling the root causes of many of the problems on the planet. Their energy becomes diverted into making money to fulfill societal models of ambition and desires to accumulate. Top graduates from universities around the country are creating apps that help people navigate grocery stores or that deliver new puppy toys monthly to one's doorstep or consulting on oil and petrochemical derivatives. We are looking for a steal, a quick ticket up and out, and we end up stealing our talent away from ourselves, and away from things that truly matter. This leaves us lost and confused searching for purpose. Not to mention the fact that a CEO in certain businesses may earn up to 80 times the amount of other employees, which in itself is a theft through inequality. Thievery is, in a way, forgetting how to live with the collective as ourselves. By forgetting to care for all Earthly-stakeholders, whether it be in the specific business or not, we increase suffering and reduce compassion, rather than its opposite which is beneficial for all life. Everything is intricately tied together.

The ideation now in most all universities and institutions is tied into the greed-conditioned system that is meta to us within which we operate. Even these institutions are looking to funnel graduates into reputable companies so their job placement numbers go up and perhaps they get a bigger endowment. This has always reminded me of 'the claw' from *Toy Story* where all of the three-eyed-aliens look the same, act the same, and talk the same, sitting in the same machine waiting to be picked by the claw. Pertaining to this movie reference, I view the claw as the continually changing exploitive economic system which sets rules, regulations, and conditions upon how you must speak, act and look to fit in with the culture of development and 'civilization'. This culture looks to proliferate more and more sales of things that matter less and less because of their movement into commoditization and obsolescence. As the true value of the planet diminishes, many who appear mindless to it's deterioration who lack the critical thinking skills to make a transcendent decision fuel this demand, all for the sake of a dollar. Jim Morrison sang in the song 'Five to One', "trade in your hours for a handful of dimes." Isn't it a pity how we are the thieves of our own time all for some agreed upon value system that lacks gratitude and reverence?

Brahmacarya – continence, or moderation of any sense drive. This one is often a tough one to swallow. I know even I do not honor the *brahmacarya* or celibacy vow completely. It may be tough for most of us to wrap our minds around, as sexual drive is so built into our human-being. However, celibacy is not the ultimate point here. What brahmacarya is focusing on is a way to maintain vital energy within the body, which is said to be generated through the root chakra, the seat of kundalini or life-force. Part of this yama is to decouple sexual desire from love, to enable love to be present without the craving of sexual desire. If love is based only on physical contact, then the mind will never be satisfied with one person. Love as an all encompassing force does not cling to expectations or desires of sexual intimacy.

We find ourselves today, in a relatively oppressed sexual society, conditioned by the juxtaposed puritanical mindsets of sin proliferated by the Church and contexts of pornography and advertisement. These polarized reactions have built in deeply rooted triggers of sexual craving, desire and repression into every action. From a woman licking an ice cream cone on the street to you buying a new shirt or dress at the store, most everything branches into a sexual root. The funny thing is, if you have ever been to a nude beach, most sexual charge dissipates, for me at least, when you see the naked human body. The level of separation between what clothing shapes versus what is actually under there falls away and there is nothing left for the imagination to create.

Clothing and the hidden reality that lingerie and other garments create helps to exacerbate the sexuality of the human being. Everyone's got the same equipment, what's to crave? Something like pornography is literally draining the life-force energy from millions of people across the country, not to mention conditioning them into a deep misunderstanding and craving for often abusive sexual intercourse and harm. This trend of sexuality leads to objectification. Objectification, according to Wikipedia, is the act of treating a person, or sometimes an animal, as an object or a thing. It is part of dehumanization, the act of disavowing the humanity of others. This dehumanization process is programmed into our value system as well through the use of currency to deem worth. In fact, one of the blind-spots of objectification and dehumanization is that by dehumanizing or utilizing others as objects, we are truly dehumanizing ourselves. When we objectify others and in turn ourselves, we drain our life-force energy, literally through masturbation before this reproductive energy can be transmuted into vital life energy. This is rendering many people unable to build physical or mental immunity to illnesses, cravings or desires in all parts of their lives. In Yoga, it is said that sexual energy that is preserved is transformed into a subtle energy called *ojas*, which when stored creates *tejas*. *Tejas* is an aura or energy of calmness yet sharpness, glowing yet welcoming.

Aparigrahā – non-greed, non-grasping.
This is essentially operating on the paradigm of non-hoarding.

Hoarding is defined as the process of accumulating something, normally for future use, but also accumulating items with little to no use and experiencing distress at the thought of discarding them. We also feel distress at the accumulated parts of our own identities, and when we begin to see that they are no longer serving us there is a part of us that grasps onto them. Yoga defines greed and hoarding as a form of stealing; blocking the reception of gifts. Our society currently rewards massive levels of accumulation on many levels, from wealth accumulation to knowledge accumulation, all of which build on the layers of identification that we coat our divinity in. As we become non-attached to who we think we are, we allow what we really are to be revealed.

For operating on the gift economy, this is one of the necessities to understand. We are currently operating on the take economy. The gift economy will not function if people are giving gifts with the expectation of receiving something in return or as repayment. Accepting gifts can often bind us and make us lose our neutrality towards a person or a situation. True giving is giving without attachment to reciprocity, or their reception of our gift. To become unbound by giving or receiving is the equanimous state to be in that enables the uninhibited flow of resources from those that have more to those that do not have enough to meet their basic needs. It is natural. If one tree has an excess of water from the last rainstorm and needs less to survive than another tree, it will communicate and send water through the underground mycelial root system to allocate its extra water to help the other tree have its growth needs met. The Hidden Life of Trees by Peter Wohlleben is a cool book to begin to get a glimpse into this world.

Many, including Charles Eistenstein as of recent, have written about a potential feasible economic example of this state called negative interest rates. Certain blockchain solutions like MannaBase are being created to attempt to tackle the issues surrounding Universal Basic Income (UBI). Essentially, these systems of functionality reward the spread of money through continuing the flow rather than stocking it up in a savings account. Here, you could be rewarded for the actual dispensation of the resource rather than the accumulation. This is a key shift in value that must be functional within our economic OS to counterbalance the current detrimental effects caused by massive polarizations and continual hyper-growth.

YOGA AND THE QUANTUM FRAMEWORK OF PEACE

While practicing traditional Ashtanga Yoga at Yoga Gita in Mysuru, India, it became clear to me that many concepts, like seeds, were lying on the soil of my brain but hadn't had the proper force to sink into the soil and germinate. The simplicity of the teachings at Yoga Gita assisted in this evolution. The integration phase felt very rapid and is still evolving. However, from a philosophical and existential standpoint, one thing now is becoming more and more clear to me which seemed clear to Ram Dass and Krishnamurti, Alan Watts, and many of the teachers and beings who were out there being deeply with these inherent Truths. It stems from the nature of space and time; the *Purusa* and the *Prakrti*.

From these fields, there is one Absolute Unchanging Self (*Purusa*) from which one of the impermanent and ever-changing Nature (*Prakriti*) has emerged. We are all, for the most part, trapped in Nature as we must utilize the duality to go behind it. As a part of Purusa, we manifest the craving and aversions within *Prakriti* (duality) which we must move through to return to the absolute. It comes full circle. Nature, as continually changing or impermanent, is viewed from our standpoints as individualized awareness, in space and time. This is called our time-space locus. I'm Ryan, you're Himani, he is Jacob, the dog is Alfred, the couch is the couch.

Things have forms or patterns of energy; we must eat, breathe. I have a body, and they call me this name and so on and so forth. This consumption of everything upon itself to survive is the mystery represented by the esoteric symbol of the Ouroboros, which is the snake that eats its own tail that was mentioned earlier and is on the cover of this book. It's completeness, often discussed by Carl Jung may symbolize the fact that we need to consume our own egos or identifications to achieve oneness.

It still ties into current discoveries in physics. Empty space is literally 99.9%+ of our being. However, the emptiness is not empty. As said in the Heart Sutra of Buddhism, "form is emptiness and emptiness is form."

In quantum theory everything is arising instantaneously and simultaneously and the atomic material is the same as all material and can be swapped in and out of all of the matter at any moment. Take a peek into Heisenberg's Uncertainty Principle for added learning into this.

This one BBC article states,

" . . . atoms are in more than one place at the same time until a conscious observer looks at them. Think about this for a moment—if no-one's looking at the atoms that, say, make up your hand, they're effectively spread out across the entire Universe. Then when someone, maybe even you, looks at your hand, the atoms instantly coalesce into the hand-like shape you're familiar with."[17]

In essence, we are all the same matter. This matter is mostly empty space, but the empty space is in fact not empty at all. Recent discoveries led by physicist Nassim Harramein lead us towards the recognition that empty space is actually a dense vacuum, with the tiniest particle holding more density than the entire universe. On a quantum level, each particle within us encapsulates and consists of the entire universe. How can we be separate? We are already living in a non-dual state but we are unable to recognize it! The documentary entitled 'Black Whole' discusses many of these topics and you can find it on YouTube or Vimeo. Every part of us is interchangeable at any moment with the rest of the universe. The only route to complete peace is if we are truly no longer under the illusion that we are separate from one another. This may start as a conceptual framework, but the true depth lies in the subtlety of experience of this Truth. What's beautiful is that this Truth, relayed by Gautama Buddha, the ancient rishis of India and indigenous peoples across the world is being proven now by modern physics! An integrated framework of action is where the peace rests. The perceived differences of 'I' and 'you', the division of you and I, collectively us and them, dissipates because we begin to see similarities within each-other rather than the differences. The perceived differences validate us to create division, which in turn creates violence. Violence plays itself out in a constant game of exploitation; give and take, protection, greed, anger, and lust—all "sins" aptly labeled by the Church. All violence come from this perceived division between beings, which inherently is the division that we feel from our whole selves. The root of all of this violence are the desires which manifest from the mind in many forms. However, the basis of desire, which is craving and aversion which results often in righteous violence is really rooted in our desire to reduce suffering and to be loved. The root of it all is connectedness, we are seeking to be connected and welcomed home to ourselves. If we can meet at this ground of embracing our similarities and differences, we enter into the field of togetherness.

Rumi says,

"Out beyond ideas of wrongdoing and right-doing, there is a field. I'll meet you there.

When the soul lies down in that grass,
the world is too full to talk about.
Ideas, language, even the phrase "each other"
doesn't make any sense.
The breeze at dawn has secrets to tell you.
Don't go back to sleep.
You must ask for what you really want.
Don't go back to sleep.
People are going back and forth across the doorsill
where the two worlds touch.
The door is round and open.
Don't go back to sleep."[18]

When we meet in this field, field as in grassy knoll or field as in dimensional, frequential field, we can begin to shift the tides into embracing it all. In our current world, this perceived division continually results in the race for resources and economic control where freedom and justice is shoved by the wayside.

Numbers on a screen or a slip of paper have long begun to designate the value of a life. Our life becomes a number, a commodity, a statistic, data. We become so detached from one another. When we read statistics from the U.N., for example, that 70% of Yemenis or about twenty million people are food insecure (are facing or are on the brink of famine), we don't bat an eyelid. Human life is being turned into a graph, an Excel sheet, a numbers game. Since this existing system continually fuels itself on the oppositeness and separateness created, there is no end to the tetherball swings of existence. As the saying goes, hippies create police as much as police create hippies. Henceforth, we will be trapped in duality, suffering, and essentially turmoil as long as we cannot acknowledge from an experiential level the depth of these truths of interconnectedness and inter-being.

ESCAPISM IS THE ENEMY OF CHANGE

One of many powerful tools in allowing this turmoil to cease is recognizing and understanding that we have been conditioned to escape the present moment from childhood. We've been conditioned to push certain emotions aside and sweep them under the rug. When we recognize our escape patterns, we realize there is nowhere to escape to. The pile under the rug just keeps getting bigger and bigger. We can neither grasp at anything nor can we push it away. No matter where we go, here we are. There is no where to stand but within yourself. Escape is an illusion; it is only suppression, deception or diversion. Like a game of Whack-a-Mole, the symptom being suppressed will pop up somewhere else. No matter how much we seek, do through thought, acquire, revolt or change with a purpose or direction, all of this is an escape mechanism coated in new garb. We are escaping from ourselves. The opposite of escapism is responsibility for yourself, which will naturally create responsibility towards others and open others to take responsibility for themselves as well.

This escape, or diversion, starts as a basis in monotheistic thought, the separation of us from the divine. As the Church began to amass fortunes through sponsored colonial conquest, the teachings of Jesus became disconnected from their inherent Truths. This pulled Heaven from the Earthly realm up to somewhere in the sky, and turned us all into sinners who must repent immediately for our sins to some Caucasian father figure. Jesus was a brown-skinned, Middle Eastern Jew; he was not white. He became white when the Church wanted to manipulate the image in order to spread Christianity. In the United States, our escapism is mostly rooted in puritanical thought from either our English, Spanish, Portuguese, Dutch, or religiously colonized predecessors. These Biblical beliefs are changed from their original state to say that God is outside of us and that he/she/they are the controllers of our fate.

Yoga, Buddhism, and other Eastern maps debunk this theory by stating that all God, and the process of consciousness expression, is navigating the subtleties of our own being back to the purest form of it which is immutable and totally interconnected. This purest form, meaning with no conditioned imprints, is consciousness at its more simplistic. It is eternal, it is infinity. It is a mirror for our own selves and what we carry. If we are no longer carrying any attachments to any accumulated conditions or desires, we no longer feed the identity which keeps us separate. We have entered the Heart. We cannot escape from our current imprints; the only way out is in. We've incarnated into this form to learn specific things to evolve on our individual and collective journeys. These neural pathways that we construct build our respective subjective individual and collective realities. There is no exclusion, we are the co-conspirators in our collective systems. Conversely, in the commonplace narrative of Christian context, our separation from the divine automatically strips us of our power by placing us as the original sinners. We then are facing an uphill battle, needing to repent to our Godly father figure to get into Heaven and avoid Hell. This is reward and punishment. Instead of already being divine, we must confess all our imperfections away to move back into a state of goodness, which by natural deductive reasoning means we start out as inherently bad or evil. Since we're trying to catch up from birth, how will we enact compassion-based shifts to our own direct environments and the surrounding ones? Right off the bat we lose our responsibility by becoming victims. We become bad, rather than our actions being bad. Our souls are not blemished, only our actions are.

We use phrases like "I trust in the Universe" or "I trust in God" as common escapism phrases. Why? Can you realize that you are the Universe? You are God, and God is the unwavering interconnected fabric of consciousness. The trust question orients towards another question; do you trust yourself? Do you trust yourself to adapt and Love your imperfections and your process in relation to others enough and make the right decisions? Do you trust yourself to act with enough pure volition to guide your body and soul vehicle to this imagined far-off promised land, the place that you trust the universe to guide you to? That land is here and now. Heaven is all around us, from the fjords of Norway to the Redwood forests of California. We are our own angel and devil on our shoulder. By diverting our trust onto something other than our integral process within it, we build the capability to move into a complacent and passive role and allow tyrannical forces to absorb our responsibility from us. Although fluidity is important in the wu wei, complacency and comfort from progressing on the path can be detrimental to the true responsibility and work on oneself that must take place to de-bundle the veils of illusion that we have accumulated en masse over time.

To highlight this point, I quote Jiddu Krishnamurti stating,

"You can face a fact only in the present and if you never allow it to be present because you are always escaping from it, you can never face it and because we have cultivated a whole network of escapes we are caught in a habit of escape."

THE TELEOLOGICAL TRAP AND RESPONSIBILITY

Alan Watts also discusses this teleological trap. Teleology is the explanation of phenomena in terms of the purpose they serve rather than of the cause by which they arise.

Our teleological trap is when the mind acknowledges that whenever there is effort in anything you create to escape the process, it cannot be the source to which you are looking to return. This is because that thing you are creating, that imagined freedom-state, cannot be created by the effort of the mind-based system because it is a thought. Thoughts are merely a bi-product within the fabric of consciousness, which it is not meta to. If you can think it, you can know for sure that it is not that. Fire can burn the forest but fire cannot burn itself.

When we acknowledge these teleological traps of thought and attempt to transcend ourselves, our minds can spontaneously self-combust. We realize that all of the effort must lead to effortlessness. This process brings us back to true responsibility for everything that comes up in our being. The reactions to the external world are the alive seeds and successive roots of conditions and traumas that only we can heal.

It is time for us to take our power and responsibility back. This is why a commonplace obstacle that many of us face is the feigning of interest when we want to begin learning or integrating a way of life. It's why new year's resolutions play out so quickly. Do you actually want to do it or do you just like to live within a pipe dream? We feign interest because we are escaping our own responsibility to ourselves.

We don't like responsibility, and we find it difficult to take full responsibility for our own actions without pointing the finger at some outside force. We don't like to look at the fact that we cannot hold ourselves to good habits, like de-escalating anger toward someone who cuts us off in traffic, or building a seemingly continuous improvement or routine. That lack of responsibility, sometimes called discipline, they are called disciples for a reason, is one of the reasons that we are in the current world system. We also lack responsible communities, or *satsang* because of our lifestyles of individuation. Our lack of communal life-way buries us deeper away from validation. We are being weakened morally and disconnected from natural processes by the system itself. To think about a simple but deep level of disconnection, we don't even have to understand where our own food comes from anymore! We just walk into an air-conditioned building, structured in rows like a simulated garden, and purchase colorful, wax-like produce from the aisle before we go home and eat it in front of some screen, forgetting that we're chewing or that the food we are eating is really just transmuted light.

The more readily we relinquish or divert our responsibility or power away from our center, the sooner someone else will take it and centralize it. Hence third-party intermediaries to validate our own responsibility toward one another, like banks and credit card processors. The takers of this power are normally despotic, looking to extend their worldview over yours, siphoning off your responsibility and power like a vampire. No, I'm not talking the Romanian prince Vlad Tepes who's the model for Dracula. I'm talking about a world-view that psychologically sucks the vital essence out of you. It only has power because we give it power. We are accomplices in our own draining. Our actions, despite any system, are based on the willingness to divert responsibility. However, we can always take it back. Feeling powerlessness leads to the inaction that we all live with to make the major transformations that are required to live harmoniously with others, the Earth and our own Hearts. The forgetting is remembering.

As we release our own power, we dig a hundred holes in various places trying to find it. When we do this, we never get to the depth of the aquifer and tap into our clear essence below. We must stop fooling ourselves by thinking that others are more equipped to be the holders of our own purpose and responsibility. We are our own rocks, our own guideposts. Hold yourself accountable to yourself. This is a beginning.

Once this ego-bundle, which we can say is ideas, memories

and conditions, truly realizes the futility of all trying and acquiring, it gives up trying to stand alone because of it is blocking itself from entering into a state so much more interdependent, limitless, pure, and wise than its own locus of control. The separation is always transactional, and not natural in accordance with an eternal, unwavering creative power. Therefore, inherently, space is created between our identification of ourselves and the fabric of existence. This is the Biblical fall from grace.

A REVOLUTION OF THE PSYCHE

This real revolution of the psyche comes in when you have actually, not conceptually, experienced the non-separateness of existence. When you've felt the witness behind the veil of your identity, you become freer to live into the lives we've been given that are all blessings.

In my life experience this occurred very prominently on two nights back-to-back while in Mysuru, India. It became very clear reflecting on these experiences that as much as I thought I was controlling myself and my own thoughts, I wasn't. I was under the guise of a deep-seated condition of the illusion of control. There was quite a level of higher intelligence behind the continued operation of even my physical body when my breath naturally ceased. At that point, it became clear that 'I' was not my body. I wasn't holding my breath; it just came to end. The body essentially switched to utilizing *prana*, because the breath had stopped and the body did not need to metabolize. My mind was completely still, with no thought. And yet, there was still something else there watching my body meditating and watching the still mind. Something was there just watching the motionlessness in a vast, black space that could've been anywhere and nowhere. This happened again the next night where my body went into autopilot and was 'doing' alternating nostril breathing, but I was not participating in the action. It was just happening.

Once again, there was this observer just watching me sit and do *pranayama* floating in an expanse of darkness like a silent movie.

After this second experience, I started crying. It was the first time I experientially knew that everything that is talked about this power, God, Shiva, Buddha, Allah, whatever you want to call it, was real. It was real in the sense of an experience where I transcended myself and yet, there was still a witness to observe it all. When this happened, I realized that major parts of myself, my body and mind, were no longer in my control, there was something still there; literally watching the body and mind unfold. This awareness was still, it was witnessing the happening of my body, lack of breath, and mind.

Henceforth, all of this talk of One-ness and what that means beyond some buzzwordy phrase that we can say, is that literally our Self, substratum or medium of consciousness, is connected as the fabric of existence itself. Our atomic structure is the same as the tree, the ocean, the constellation, your landlady who yells at you when you come down the stairs, all of it. It remains intact beyond the mind and body functionality in identity. We're just different forms and patterns of matter restructuring ourselves every moment in accordance with our world-views. This means existentially and practically, that everything we do, we do to ourselves. We are intricately linked to the system around us. Moreover, as long as we are embodying this sense of division and separateness, the violence of individuality, nationality, righteousness, race, political correctness and patriotism, we are proliferating the same system we don't want to exist by the way that we create its reactions. We all want peace, but we constantly are fighting. We are fighting for Love. How can we have peace if we feed into the warring mentality inside of ourselves? How can we connect our fragmented society if we still disavow all of the disparate parts of ourselves?

On an external level, if you don't like animals being killed, you no longer eat them, because you see that eating animals creates suffering. On an internal level, if you don't like war in the world and want peace, you have to see yourself as connected to all things and become internally peaceful. If you do this, I mean, really do this, in the process you will do less and less emotional, physical or energetic harm to other beings. This starts by doing less and less emotional, physical and energetic harm to yourself. Your own internal violence will naturally cease once you stop warring with your self-worth and begin to embrace yourself for who you are, imperfections, neuroses and all. Often times, what needs our Love most will come out in various emotions.

Very often, this compassionate action and viewing can be surface-level and executed as a front to coax ourselves into believing we are maintaining a level of integrity to our system. This is similar to how recycling is a nice psychological write-off to keep consuming plastic. The best thing to do is to stop consuming plastic. Are you getting angry, envious, righteous, greedy, wanton, defensive against others? These are subtler forms of violence, and the duality still exists inherently within you. It's alright to feel these things, it is a process, none of us are perfect. Patience is key, but keen awareness is required. The more we push anything away the more it comes back to bite us. Persistence in the patience, or having patience with your own lack of patience, is another important step.

As we progress through the simple, pragmatic activities that the Ashtanga Yogic pathway provides, we become more connected to disavowed parts of ourselves. We leave self-denial and self-deception to become vulnerable and honest. We embrace the fact we would rather feel it all then feel nothing. We rock our own imperfections to sleep like a mother rocks her baby. We cradle ourselves and have compassion toward ourselves because we see that these perceived imperfections are just conditions of our personality, and that our personality is not what we really are. We don't attach so much to external things because we recognize that they do not contribute to our wholeness, in fact, they lessen it. We become more aware of when we are creating violence through our thoughts, our actions, our words. We abandon greed at the gateway to enter into a temple of connectivity, abundance and fluidity that cannot be achieved by hoarding. Slowly but surely, our own conditioned identities begin to shift out of individuality and into transcendent ones; community, species, planet, and cosmos. Just as an orca whale's sense of self is dispersed amongst it pod, we can begin to dissolve our self-value into the communities of which we are a part, spreading egalitarian value and benefit to all people depending on their needs.

One of the beginning steps that we can do to facilitate this path into subtlety and sensitivity is the introduction of a sattvic diet. We greatly underestimate how much our diet, or shall we call it a live-it can impact our spiritual path. The next chapter will explain the Yogic and Ayurvedic interpretation of mind-types, and how we can create a still mind with certain food inputs versus creating an aggressive or lazy mind with others.

JOURNAL PROMPTS:

1. How often do you find yourself attached to material objects? Mental ideologies or belief systems? Is it difficult for you to relinquish, or become non-attached to these? Why do you think that is?
2. How often are you able to be honest and vulnerable in the work-place? With friends? With family? What happens to you when you are unable to share your Truth and be received in a non-argumentative manner?
3. What does the term 'effortless' bring up in you? Do you often find your self striving to achieve certain things? How often do you just have space to be?

4. Who are you without the things that you do? What are you without your ambition? Is your ambition the same as passion?

ACTIVITIES:

1. Give away five of your most prized belongings. Witness the level of attachment attached to this stuff. Where does the attachment come from?
2. Go up to a stranger and ask if you can share something vulnerable with them. Observe how that feels. Witness if they want to share something back.
3. If someone blames you for something, try to not react and take responsibility instead. See what happens.
4. Focus on things that bring you contentment in your day-to-day life. Write these down. See if they are the same day after day or if they change. Do your best to align with that joy.

Journal Prompt #1:

How often do you find yourself attached to material objects? Mental ideologies or belief systems? Is it difficult for you to relinquish, or become non-attached to these? Why do you think that is?

How often are you able to be honest and vulnerable in the work-place?

Journal Prompt #2:

How often are you able to be honest and vulnerable in the workplace? With friends? With family? What happens to you when you are unable to share your Truth and be received in a non-argumentative manner?

Journal Prompt #3:

What does the term 'effortless' bring up in you? Do you often find your self striving to achieve certain things? How often do you just have space to be?

Journal Prompt #4:

Who are you without the things that you do? What are you
without your ambition? Is your ambition the same as passion?

CHAPTER SEVEN

Food and the Roots
of an Unsettled Mind

"Food is a dynamic force that interacts with the human on the physical level, the mental-emotional level, and also the energetic and spiritual level. The study of nutrition is the study of the interaction with and assimilation of the dynamic forces of food by the dynamic forces of our total being."
—Gabriel Cousens, M.D., *Spiritual Nutrition and The Rainbow Diet*

"Let food be thy medicine and medicine be thy food."
—Hippocrates

Most of us were taught in passing the phrase, "you are what you eat." Let's substitute eat for consume to spread the multi-dimensional language gap. As of now, we'll keep it limited to food and beverage. Despite this phrase, the entire consumptive food and beverage system in the United States specifically is in an overall horrendous condition. That is, for the consumer. The world's most consumed foods: GMO and sprayed fruits and vegetables, alcohol, coffee, and meat are some of the most detrimental things to ingest from a Yogic and Ayurvedic point of view. Not only do they harm the body, but they are also contributors to two types of mind that hinder peaceful and higher states of conscious evolution. These types of mind are the rajasic mind, which is an unstable, aggressive, and overly ambitious mind and the tamasic mind, which tends to fall into laziness, complacency, and inertia.

We'll start with some basics here. Some people know what is happening with the division between GMO and organic. For those who do not, I will expound here.

According to the Non-GMO project website,

"A GMO, or genetically modified organism, is a plant, animal, microorganism or other organism whose genetic makeup has been modified in a laboratory using genetic engineering or transgenic technology. This creates combinations of plant, animal, bacterial, and virus genes that do not occur in nature or through traditional crossbreeding methods. Genetic modification affects many of the products we consume on a daily basis..."

On the website, it continues to state facts such as,

"More than 80% of all genetically modified crops grown worldwide have been engineered for herbicide tolerance. As a result, the use of toxic herbicides, such as Roundup®, has increased fifteenfold since GMOs were first introduced. In March 2015, the World Health Organization determined that the herbicide glyphosate (the key ingredient in Roundup®) is probably carcinogenic to humans. Genetically modified crops also are responsible for the emergence of "superweeds" and "superbugs," which can only be killed with ever more toxic poisons such as 2,4-D (a major ingredient in Agent Orange). Most GMOs are a direct extension of chemical agriculture and are developed and sold by the world's largest chemical companies. The long-term impacts of these GMOs are unknown."[19]

To deepen this scary fact, I will bring in some facts about Agent Orange. Please remember, this is tied into what we are literally consuming through our mouth to be assimilated into our bodies.

According to History.com,

"Agent Orange was a powerful herbicide used by U.S. military forces during the Vietnam War to eliminate forest cover and crops for North Vietnamese and Viet Cong troops. The U.S. program, codenamed Operation Ranch Hand, sprayed more than 20 million gallons of various herbicides over Vietnam, Cambodia and Laos from 1961 to 1971. Agent Orange, which contained the deadly chemical dioxin, was the most commonly used herbicide. It was later proven to cause serious health issues—including cancer, birth defects, rashes, and severe psychological and neurological problems—among the Vietnamese people as well as among returning U.S. servicemen and their families." It continues to state about Agent Orange itself, "In addition to Agent Orange's active ingredients, which caused plants to "defoliate" or lose their leaves, Agent Orange contained significant amounts of 2,3,7,8-tetrachlorodibenzo-p-dioxin, often called TCDD, a type of dioxin.

Dioxin was not intentionally added to Agent Orange; rather, dioxin is a byproduct that's produced during the manufacturing of herbicides. It was found in varying concentrations in all the different herbicides used in Vietnam.

Dioxins are also created from trash incineration; burning gas, oil, and coal; cigarette smoking and in different manufacturing processes such as bleaching. The TCDD found in Agent Orange is the most dangerous of all dioxins.

Studies done on laboratory animals have proven that dioxin is highly toxic even in minute doses. It is universally known to be a carcinogen (a cancer-causing agent)."[20]

Now, for organic. According to The Department for Agriculture and Rural Affairs (DEFRA) in the UK, they state that:

"Organic food is the product of a farming system which avoids the use of man-made fertilisers, pesticides; growth regulators and livestock feed additives. Irradiation and the use of genetically modified organisms (GMOs) or products produced from or by GMOs are generally prohibited by organic legislation.

Organic agriculture is a systems approach to production that is working towards environmentally, socially and economically sustainable production. Instead, the agricultural systems rely on crop rotation, animal and plant manures, some hand weeding and biological pest control". [21]

In summary, when you consume GMO foods, if they are not organically farmed, which is often outlawed in organic legislation, you are consuming chemical and pesticide-ridden, modified plant and animal products that have no long-term study per human health. Ingredients in these pesticides that you are putting into your body were used by the U.S. military as part of its chemical warfare program, Operation Ranch Hand, during the Vietnam War, which I learned from my recent trip to Vietnam, is called the American War in-country. According to the Monsanto Papers, Monsanto being the company who manufactures glyphosate, they have known for decades the carcinogenic quality of that which they've been spraying yet sales continue to skyrocket.

For clarification, not all organic foods are non-GMO, because organic is normally considered a farming method. For optimal health and the least amount of chemical inputs onto your foods, eating organic and non-GMO will be the best option. The best for you are wild foods and organic heirloom plants which are open-pollinated and maintain a heritage of the plant lineage.

Now that we've discussed these two terms and you understand them, we will focus on the specific categories of foods that we are consuming and their effects on the mind through the body. According to Yoga and Ayurveda, foods are classified into three classes based on the reactions they contribute to; sattvic, rajasic and tamasic. The food input, despite the specific dosha you are, affects the gunas (qualities) of life. In brief these qualities of mind are listed below:

The Sattvic Mind – classified by stillness, clear thinking and presence. This is the state of mine to be cultivated by most yogis.

1. **Qualities of the food:** This denotes a class of foods that are fresh, juicy, light and nourishing.
2. **Qualities of the mind derived from the food:** Sattvic foods promote a clear mind, happiness and peacefulness, fluidity of energy and sensitivity. Sensitivity here means more adept senses; subtlety of sensory awareness. People with this state of mind also tend towards compassion and emotional control. Emotional control means being less flustered by external forces and less reactive. Most have positive natural sleep quality and are normally loving. The original sattvic diet was devised for the development of higher consciousness in Yogic philosophy. These qualities are reflected by their minimal effect on mucus production in the body and the easy digestibility and absorption of the foods. Following this process will lead to a healthier body

that becomes familiar with absorbing the subtler energies of natural foods. As food directly impacts all levels of health, the cleaner you can eat, the more fertile the mind is for advancement and development on a spiritual level.

3. **Foods:** A sattvic diet means not only vegetarian food but food rich in prana. Prana here can be roughly translated to vital life force energy. In the raw food community, this is often referred to as bio-photons. This consists of non-GMO, organic fruits and vegetables, nuts, whole grains and legumes, lightly seasoned foods with not too much salt or chili pepper. It requires avoiding canned and processed foods, and foods prepared with chemical fertilizers or sprays. The less you cook certain foods like fruits, the better.

4. **Soil type and harvest time:** Ayurveda also takes deeply into consideration the quality of the soil that is used to grow the organic fruits and vegetables, harvested at the correct time of year and as close as possible to their ripened state. These foods also help develop ojas which is the immunity and adaptogenic response of the body to stressors or oxidants in the environment.

5. **Way of eating:** This refers to the condition and speed while you eat. For example, you should never eat while angry or sad. The processing of the mind when distracted with emotion will affect the digestion in a negative way. In addition, properly salivating your food, chewing slowly and eating without talking are sattvic qualities.

The Tamasic Mind – classified by inertia; laziness, and complacency. This leads to lack of motivation and energy to serve others or yourself; an attitude of give-me-the-easy-way-out.

1. **Qualities of the food:** This denotes a class of foods that are not fresh, such as canned or frozen foods, as well as

over-ripened, dry, old, foul, or unpalatable foods. This is because they are often over-processed and difficult to digest. The further the derivation or slowing of the vibrational nature of the food itself, the further the consumer will be from a natural state of calm. In these instances, canned, frozen or over-processed foods alter the biological makeup of foods so much that they are deadened, leading to accumulated matter in the body, aama. Aama can be inflammatory responses such as mucus and intestinal plaque which create malabsorption of nutrients into the body as well as a variety of other ailments. As stated above, in the chapter on Ayurveda, aama accumulation is the cause of all disease. In accordance with mucusless diet healing system, aama could be referred to as any inflammatory response of the body that hinders proper absorption and assimilation into the various systems of the body. Phlegm or a stuffy nose is an example of mucus production caused by food.

2. **Qualities of the mind derived from the food:** Tamasic foods promote pessimism, ignorance, laziness, criminal tendencies and doubt. Humans who are dominated by this energy tend toward depression, laziness, excessive eating or drinking, and excessive desire for sex. They also tend to be greedy, possessive, attached to materialistic things, irritable and uncaring towards others. Often motivation is lacking and they need excessive sleep due to the nature of the food processing in the body.

3. **Foods:** Meats such as cold-cuts or preserved meats like prosciutto as well as beef, veal, pig meat (pork, bacon, sausages, ham). Farmed fish is also considered tamasic. Alcohol and any other fermented foods, including vinegar, bread, pastries and cakes. Any stale, overripe or under ripe, tasteless and rotten foods are also considered tamasic. Tobacco as well as any kind of drug and any foods that have

been processed, including those that are preserved in any way, canned or frozen. In addition to these, refined sugars and sodas.

4. **Way of eating:** Overeating or eating when not hungry creates tamas. In modern science this is validated by a study conducted by David Gal at the University of Illinois-Chicago. He states when people eat when they're not hungry, they experience sharper sugar spikes than if they were to eat when they were hungry.[22]

The Rajasic Mind – classified by aggression; ambition and ego-centricity.

1. **Qualities of the food:** This denotes a class of foods that are normally bitter, sour, salty, pungent, hot or dry. This also includes fruit or vegetables that are still ripening but are picked from the tree, bushes, or ground too soon, essentially under-ripe. This is especially common with our demand for fruits and vegetables at all times of the year, businesses are forced to pick under-ripe produce to make supply meet demand.

2. **Qualities of the mind derived from the food:** Rajasic foods promote sensuality, greed, jealousy, anger, delusion, over-ambition, aggressiveness, egoism, competitiveness, desire to control, fear of failure, pride, low qualities of sleep and irreligious feelings. Irreligious feelings correlate with the separateness and division.

3. **Foods:** Coffee is one of the top foods that creates a rajasic mind. Specific animal products, such as chicken, eggs, salmon, sole, trout, lamb, turkey, and tuna are also rajasic foods. According to Yogic philosophy, it is said that you take on the karma of the animal that you eat. When you eat meat, especially the meat that is factory farmed, pumped with hormones and put through torture on its

way to be 'harvested', you are ingesting all of the stress hormones as well that were released when the animal was killed. According to the Journal of Animal Science and researchers at the University of Milan's Faculty of Veterinary Medicine, they have confirmed recently that fear experienced during animal slaughter significantly elevates meat's levels of stress hormones such as adrenaline, cortisol, and other steroids.[23] The hormones released at death are present in the flesh when you eat it. At a cellular level, your body is receiving a message that you too are under the stress of imminent death, which kicks your adrenals into overdrive and causes many other bodily issues.

4. **Way of eating:** Another rajasic quality is eating very quickly, or talking while eating, which hinders the process of digestion. The lack of focus on the nourishment provided by the food creates the issue. Eating while looking at any type of screen is a hindrance to proper assimilation as well.

That's the breakdown of the Ayurvedic gunas resulting in sattvic, tamasic and rajasic characteristics that are created by the foods and drinks that we consume. Every food we consume affects your physical, mental, emotional and spiritual energies. We'll take a crack at a few of these highlighted items that are part of the diets of most developed countries to attempt to see perhaps why these qualities of mind are running rampant on the planet.

PESTICIDES (CONNECTED TO GMO AND NON-ORGANIC FOODS)

Most developed countries' supply chain infrastructure prides itself on the ability to fuel the demand for out-of-season fruits and vegetables, six types of salsas and four types of alternative milks at any given time. Our current conditioned consumer response is to expect to have exactly what we want, when we want it; now. Because of urbanization, we have moved so far from living locally in community, seasonally and even in-country, that many of our foods are literally shipped in from around the planet. Preservatives are used in these instances, many of which, from artificial colorings to sweeteners such as high fructose corn syrup (HFCS) and sodium nitrate, benzoate, and sulfite, have been known to cause many biological issues in the body.[24]

In addition to these preservatives put into food to extend its shelf life because of our disconnection with natural living, we are demanding more exotic, out-of-season foods. Many of these must be packaged, which contributes to a whole other issue of waste. In the packaging itself, many compounds such as bisphenol A (BPA) or phthalates enter food and have negative health effects. If things are being shipped in from around the world, flash frozen and picked before they are ripe, how can they be fresh? How can we expect our bodies and minds to be fresh or healthy by consuming them? These foods are saleable because they are waxy. In reality, they've survived a pelting of chemicals by alterations in their DNA, and are quite under-ripened and over-picked. All of these contribute to qualities of mind such as rajas and tamas; restless, irritable and lazy.

This is where GMOs come into play and assist in the global demand. Crop yields are known to increase because of their genetic resistance to the pest killers (pesticides), which allows poisons such as Round-Up (glyphosate), atrazine, metolachlor-S, dichloropropene and 2,4-D into the food. These yields can create the supply to keep up with the massive global demand for a diversified supply of out-of-season fruits and veggies in varied markets across the world. They look nice, without any pollination marks, which are actually signs of health on plants because bugs know which ones are the best, and can last on shelves; as is suitable for modern, urbanized living.

In fact, GMOs are so key in this demand that U.S. agricultural pesticide expenditures by farming corporations totaled over $9 billion in 2012, accounting for 66% of the pesticide market, and numbers have grown quite significantly since then.[25] Atrazine is also the pesticide most commonly found in American drinking water.

Yes, all of these chemicals protect the plants from pests, but what are they doing to our bodies? In Aotearoa, also known as New Zealand, when I was kayaking in Abel Tasman National Park, I learned that Roundup®, whose main ingredient is glyphosate, was put into the trunks of the invasive species of pine trees to kill them to enable native plant restoration to take place. These trees are dropping dead from a small amount of glyphosate in their trunks, while we are consuming fruits, vegetables as well as even our tap water with these chemicals sprayed or leached into them. The water you use to attempt to wash it off does not suffice for cleaning them off, as it is embedded in their DNA.

The path of least resistance here for all of us will require a re-allocation of effort and convenience. Instead of wanting to eat a pineapple in Boston in January, look to eat locally and seasonally, or, begin to store and preserve your own foods in accordance with preparation methods for winters if you live in locations that have drastic seasonal shifts. In order to move towards a sattvic mind in accordance with these principles of fruit and vegetable consumption, we must eat on-time, ripened seasonal fruits and vegetables from local organic farmers or CSAs with the least amount of processing and packaging as possible. This will also cut down drastically on your effect on the environment from a logistical standpoint, help you tap into your location on a deeper level, and change how the seasons affect your body. Tapping back into the cycles of Nature tunes us back into our body intuition and knowledge that has been woven into our DNA for thousands of years.

ALCOHOL

I have yet to come across one human who thinks that drinking alcohol in excess is good for us. Yet that is exactly what we do. Alcohol is built into the framework of our day-to-day life more so than just about any substance on the planet. It is one of the most poisonous substances known to humans, yet it is legal and prevalent everywhere in the world. It permeates from happy hours, celebrations, relaxation and friendly gatherings. Even outside of a small trend of Dry January which originated in the U.K about seven years ago to give ourselves 'a rest', it is so deeply ingrained in us that when many people think about getting off a hard day's work, they just want a nice cold beer, a glass of wine or some hard liquor to take the edge off.

We've associated alcohol with freedom, leisure, and fun. Happy hours are built into start-up culture to encourage mingling, which pegs alcohol with social connection and builds a crutch of social connection without it. We work for the weekends, just like that old Loverboy song. We punch in at 9 or earlier, punch out at 5 or later, and most bars and clubs are packed right after work or on people's days off, rendering hungover brunch goers thirsty to curb that dog-tail with a curated Bloody, some sunglasses and Advil. It's built into advertisements and fashion; alcohol companies spend close to $2 billion a year advertising in the United States alone.[26]

Advertising imagery taps into our deepest insecurity, that of being unworthy for love, and therefore alone, and scatters our brain with images of alcohol leading to social connection, camaraderie and romance. We begin to picture ourselves in varied scenarios that we are bombarded with day and night. If these aren't met, we become dissatisfied, and then we resort back to alcohol to make us feel better. It's hard to resist when it is everywhere around us and everybody is doing it. This is the hard part about the social-matrix and its apparent continuity. It becomes harder to extricate ourselves from a collective projective system because we feed into it as well to feel a part of something. If you've ever walked down the street in NYC, you will understand this social-matrix of superficial beauty and consumption quite well.

Imagine that alcohol in advertisements was replaced with kava, a South Pacific root that has similar effects to alcohol at its onset, relaxed nature, slight sedation, bodily tingling, the works. The world would be a much different place. Kava doesn't lead toward blackouts and total inebriation which most people have experienced, including myself. Kava doesn't lead you to become an insatiable sex fiend at 3am and end up raping someone. Alcohol sometimes does.

Beyond the conditioned response to look at alcohol as a key factor in our social fabric, the sensation that alcohol renders us must be the kicker, right? This sensation is tricky, as it causes our body to create endorphins which makes us feel relaxed and euphoric. Simultaneously, it is also classified as a depressant. It creates physical hunger, I would add in hunger of the mind as well, and normally increases libido because ethanol stimulates the hypothalamus in your brain.[27] As we are craving the sensation, and most of us are not in control of our cravings at all, especially when the neural pathways have been primed by societal conditioning, we are treading a slippery slope. Now, to get into the Ayurveda, from the tamasic sense, alcohol fits right in as a depressant. It dulls our energy and effaces subtlety. Although it may appear that you have a sudden lift in energy and you think you are being subtle, it acts as an inhibitor of conscious action and subtle bodily awareness. Enter the blur.

In my interpretation of Vipassana meditation, this is because alcohol dulls the awareness of our own bodily sensations plus, in regards to the nature of our mind, or citta, we become disturbed by increasing thought-ripples that harm stillness. As our attention becomes disturbed, normally focusing more on ego-centric actions and tendencies like spending lots of money, sex drive and looking cool, our bodily sensations simultaneously decrease sharply. This results in carelessness with our own emotions and thoughts. This transmits to others. Arguments are very common with alcohol because everyone becomes so self-righteous and dug into their opinions. Rape and sexual misconduct are exponentially higher in 'developed' A.K.A. post-colonialist countries, and alcohol is certainly a part. In addition, compassion and love for other people normally drops off the spectrum in accordance with our own self-centeredness. Overall, although it appears to create a connectedness, it certainly deepens the schism in correlation with the amount of alcohol flowing

The best-case scenario to continually calm the mind and deflate the grandiose image that the little 'I' gets when bolstered by alcohol is to limit alcohol consumption as much as possible. Perhaps start off by letting your drinking frequency decrease to once or twice a week, and slowly move it back to once or twice a month. This may be hard to do if you are bombarded by bars on every corner. If you continue down this pathway, discipline will only help. You don't need to quit cold turkey, but experiment with yourself. Degrees of transition which factor in leniency are important for some. Maybe even try to replace it with kava; you never know what'll happen! I guarantee you will feel clearer and discover new ways to express yourself on a social level the more you take alcohol out of the equation. Who knows—maybe your entire life will shift? One thing is for sure: you'll definitely spend less money.

COFFEE

America runs on Dunkin. Well, America runs on caffeine. Lots of it. Every day, about 90 percent of Americans consume caffeine in some form. More than half of the adults in the country consume 300 milligrams a day, making it America's most popular drug[28]. Hopefully we do all know at this point that coffee is a drug. Coffee is also very acidic. It has a pH between 4.95-5.10 and is extremely aggravating to the mind. Coffee has been linked to hypokalemia, which is when blood's potassium levels are too low.[29] Potassium is an important electrolyte for nerve and muscle cell functioning, especially for muscle cells in the heart. Your kidneys control your body's potassium levels, allowing for excess potassium to leave the body through urine or sweat. The kidneys are controlled by the adrenals, to which caffeine is extremely detrimental.

Caffeine is a stimulant, which can be bad news for someone with anxiety. Add in the energy of the city to the concoction and voila. Most people have anxiety in our culture because a level of inadequacy, uneasiness and mal-performance consequences are built into the operating framework. Coffee's jittery effects on your body are similar to those of a frightening event as it stimulates your fight or flight response. Studies show that this can make anxiety worse and can even trigger an anxiety attack. Put on a biological level, as shown through the process of hypokalemia, coffee attacks many aspects of your endocrine system and kicks your adrenal glands, which release adrenaline, into overdrive. You can even end up with adrenal fatigue if your coffee habit persists.[30]

There is very little research into the adrenals and their function on the whole body in allopathic medicine. However, the adrenals, according to Dr. Robert Morse, a pioneer in the field of natural health,

> "...sit on top of each one of the kidneys, and govern much of the body's health through the production of hormones, steroids and neurotransmitters. In many senses they really are the batteries of the body as the neurotransmitters they

produce act as the electricity that powers every action in the body that you don't think about doing. This includes your digestion, breathing, lymphatic movements, and the general function of all your glands and organs."[31]

In summary, the adrenals are a large contributor towards autonomic nervous system functionality. Therefore, coffee negatively affects your nervous system's functionality. Many scientific studies may have tried to tell us that this is not true, but coffee is a pretty big industry. It makes me wonder, who is funding the studies and the intended results? To continue on the effects, when your body is in fight or flight response, it is difficult to make rational decisions. Most often the responses will be rooted in an emotional and survival reaction to your direct environment. This reaction is mainly controlled by the prefrontal cortex. The prefrontal cortex regulates the expression of fear based on previously learned information. It has been proposed that the prefrontal cortex facilitates fear memory through integration of sensory and emotional signals and through coordination of memory storage in an amygdala-based network[32].

Essentially, this part of the brain is rooted in adaptive responses to threats which were critical for survival; such as learning to avoid cues that predict danger and approach cues that predict safety. These are still in-built today, but were more prevalent when we lived in the wilderness. That said, these cues depend on a highly conserved neural circuitry. Anxiety disorders manifest when threat assessment becomes maladaptive, leading to exaggerated physiological and behavioral reactions to perceived or anticipated threat or inappropriate fear of non-threatening situations. Because roughly 18% of the U.S. population may suffer from an anxiety disorder[33], understanding the neurobiology of fear and anxiety is an important mission. Coffee ramps these neurobiological signals up which increases the potentiality of experiencing these emotional responses based on anxiety. When you are anxious, you cannot be at peace. You are always trying to be somewhere else than where you currently are. Your ambitions are through the roof which turns everyone into a part of the competition. Your brain is like static, white noise on the screen from Requiem for a Dream.

When our brains are within these reactions of anxiety because of the pressure we initiate on our bodily functions, our minds cannot be still. The feeling that I used to get when I drank too much caffeine was that of thick buzzing that facilitated distraction, and relentless mind chattering. Most people consume caffeine because if they are able to transmute this chatter, which sometimes caffeine helps with, it can translate directly into an amount of extreme focus and productivity in accordance with the work environment. However, with all of the stimuli that bombard our beings, it normally comes at the detriment of multi-tasking via the abrupt interruptions of social media desires, phone pings or different external factors.

In brief, as we continually overuse this stimulant, it is negatively affecting our brain and biological mechanisms by triggering fear and anxiety through fight or flight responses in the pre-frontal cortex and adrenals as well as energetic static that prevents deep states of presence and stillness. We are moving further away from the state of mind of peace, connectivity and compassion when we consume this beverage. We are moving deeper into the states of mind pertaining to ego-centricity and endless ambition. These motivations, which our current societal model values, are labeled as efficiency and productivity. However, they are only efficient and productive in one realm. They are harmful to others.

Caffeine is the perfect stimulant for the economy as it fuels maximum output and focuses on the linear model of time on which most businesses are based. The aftereffects of coffee, such as lack of stillness of mind and the continued feeling of needing to do something rather than to be, prevent us from witnessing reality as it is. We would be able to witness the difference between states when we were not highly-caffeinated versus when we are.

Experiment with herbal teas, cacao, and other less caffeinated beverages for your artificial energy kick. Or, implement a ten-minute window in the morning to meditate or do some exercise. Sitting still and breathing regulation may also assist with increasing the amount of energy you have access to without a substance.

MEAT

Meat. It's what's for dinner! You remember that American advertising slogan and campaign aimed to promote the benefits of incorporating beef into a healthy diet? All of these advertising campaigns sponsored by big meat and dairy have completely brainwashed us into thinking that we need to dose up on protein. This includes the myth that protein needs to come from animal products. Another word for animal products is carcass. Flesh. Meat, red meat in particular, despite the advertising slogans, is not healthy. In fact, one serving of red meat in particular per week has been linked to an increase in type 2 diabetes.[34]

As I've experimented with language, I've found that most people are offended if their hamburger is called cow flesh or cow carcass, even though that is what it is. They prefer the sugar-coated emotional disconnect that language provides. Between our language of disconnect such as beef/cow, pork, bacon/pig, poultry/chicken, veal/baby cow, eggs/unfertilized baby chicks, buffalo wings/chicken arms. Language gives us one of the cop-outs by conditioning our brains that whatever we are eating is conceptually separate from the entire process of death and killing.

When you are fully engaged with the process of killing the

animal, you recognize that despite the terms like 'humane' and 'sustainable' and whatever is newly trending, it doesn't matter. You feel the animal's pain and breath slip out of their being to be consumed by you. When you actually go into the process of killing, like hunters do, you end up consuming a lot less meat. We are such a death-a-phobic culture that we find it extremely difficult and appalling to acknowledge the fact that we are funding the killing of other sentient beings for our food. Many of us are privileged enough to not need to eat meat at this point to survive, or get our daily necessities of vitamins and minerals, yet we still choose to do it. Why is that? Convenience? Habit?

To connect these dots, when you eat meat, you are complicit in the murder of animals. Whether or not you kill it with your own hands, or you pay for the convenience of some large-scale producer like Perdue to pay someone to kill it for you, the blood is on your hands. The blood is on your hands for your own taste buds' sake. If you've never seen the movie Earthlings, I suggest you watch it, if you even can. It is quite graphic, as killing normally is.

We are no longer living in a hunter-gatherer society where we must consume meat to survive. In fact, through the destruction of the natural environment, it is rare to even find animals to hunt in areas where they used to graze. If we do, they are in small numbers and new, invasive species take their place and can cause habitat destruction. We've been playing far too much with the delicately intertwined strings of nature's ecosystems. Therefore, this complicit killing comes down to the simple fact that you are valuing your taste buds via a piece of meat, normally used as a carrier of a certain sauce or flavor that is rubbed on or that it is cooked in, over the life of another sentient being. Cut and dry, no pun intended. Never mind the externalities connected with factory farming and meat consumption. According to The American Journal of Clinical Nutrition, the production of one calorie of animal protein requires more than ten times the fossil fuel input as a calorie of plant protein.[35]

According to World Animal Protection:

"The United States has five times as many livestock animals as humans, and it takes a lot of land to grow feed for the meat that ends up on our plates. The production of corn and soy takes up more than a third of America's agricultural land, despite humans consuming less than 10 percent of it. Livestock consumes the vast majority of these crops.

According to an article published in The Guardian, researchers at Oxford University found that without meat and dairy consumption we could use around 75 percent less land for agriculture. That's comparable to the size of the United States, China, Australia, and the whole European Union combined. So, in addition to destroying Earth's water and air, raising animals for meat on a massive scale uses countless acres of land, destroying vital ecosystems, harming wildlife and biodiversity."[36]

CULTURE AND MEAT

Many claim that meat helped in the evolution of the human brain. I am not trying to say that meat never played a key role in human evolution. However, at this point in time with the population that we have on the planet hovering close to 7.8 billion people, which demands more and more meat as cultural or status symbols, there is no positive way to look at it. Yes, perhaps back in the day during the Cambrian age of human evolution we were eating meat and the brain-trophic element in meat of B3 or nicotinamide assisted in the growth of the brain[37]. Nevertheless, I believe that we no longer need to consume it as our brains are as fully formed as possible in a structural sense. Plus, back then, the meat wasn't pumped full of hormones, chemicals and GMO corn feed. These were wild animals eating wild foods, exercising, and breathing in fresh air not polluted by smog. Yes, certain groups of people have to rely on meat to survive. For example, Tibetans in the mountains eating yak meat and milk and the Yupik people in Northern Alaska hunting bowhead whale and making muktuk. This was also well before there was a worldwide logistical system that renders two types of alternative milk to a store in Tashkent, Uzbekistan. As stated above, we no longer need to consume meat simply based on the conveniences that most of us have to acquire our nutrition.

There are many alternative sources less harmful to the environment and to your physical, emotional and spiritual systems than meat. Yes, some cultural traditions are deeply rooted in the consumption of meat. Some cultural systems are also rooted in deep polygamy, sacrificial offerings, and wife-kidnapping. Who's to say that culture should not also evolve some of its practices to serve a larger humanitarian need? If a culture wishes to survive in this constantly changing world and the needs of its people are not being met, should we attach to every single culture nuance out of pride and watch our world perish? Or should we rather renounce a few aspects to enable the proliferation of the more important parts of culture? Cultural attachment is a keen issue and something that is a very interesting conversational topic. I would share that small changes, such as the alteration of small cultural nuances should perhaps be flexible in their ability to be adapted to a more globalized, humanitarian context. Maybe that's just my privilege speaking. However, in my eyes, it is not right to prevent the evolution of kinder ideals by attaching to a cultural identity.

For example, about one year ago, Saudi Arabia granted women the right to drive. According to the New York Times article published on June 24, 2019, "it was a historic move that cracked open a window to new freedoms for women who have long lived under repressive laws. The measure was enacted by the country's de facto leader, Crown Prince Mohammed bin Salman, who also eased other restrictions on women, leading some to hail him as a feminist reformer."[38]

This brings us to the point that although women can now drive, conditions of traditional gender roles may be harder to break. This is a start toward a cultural evolution to be more inclusive of principles and thoughts that have been blocked by their traditional systems of ideology. This is not to mention our cultural system, if you can even call it that, rather than an economic OS. Our economic OS has created the largest speciecide, ecocide, and genocides in all of recorded history, yet we continue to honor it. Talk about a pandemic!

Should certain antiquated system-characteristics of groups be honored because they are rooted in culture? Should culture remain unchanged in a world that is constantly changing? Many cultures shelter themselves from change by embracing a collective identity. Many times, they do this whether or not they are still serving the greater good of the group themselves. When this happens, we cannot package the culture up in a box and put it on the shelf for preservation. Cultures, like people, must be adaptable to the changing world. If not, they will perish just like all things do with increased pressure from the trivialization and exploitation that the modern world places upon them. It is very important to maintain the knowledge and wisdom of a culture, which most often is rooted in language and spiritual practices in connection with Nature. However, certain practices such as women not driving in Saudi Arabia or genital mutilation in Iraq among the Kurds in Erbil for example feel un-needed anymore.[39] There is no reason for the sake of pride in identification to proliferate practices that are bound to create suffering. Attachment and resistance to change only create more suffering.

One exception in culture that seems to be catching on slightly as a trend is going back to Nature and hunting your own food. This I view as a good thing. There is a large difference between hunting your own food and purchasing it from the grocery store shelf. If you are intertwined deeply with the hunt, as stated earlier, taking of the animal's life, preparation, preservation and consumption of the animal creates a much more holistic view of the entire process. Most hunters I have met have a deep connection with animals and nature, plus, they consume a whole lot less animal flesh than the person who is disconnected from the whole process. However, at this point in time, perhaps it is not fully sustainable for approximately 7.8 billion people on planet Earth to hunt; as most of the wildernesses in the world have been continually destroyed for agriculture, logging or mining. The privilege and access to food is a whole other topic that is intertwined deeply with our polarized and exploitative economic operating system.

THE KARMA OF MEAT

According to Yoga, when you consume another sentient, or conscious, being's flesh, you are consuming everything they have consumed. This includes all of the GMO corn and soy, as well as every emotion they have stored within their musculature and energetic being. Yoga goes even further to state that you also consume that being's karma. The more your physical body becomes sensitive, the more this can result in many adverse reactions. I have personally experienced this when I have eaten any meat in the past six years. I will provide an example from my own experience.

I chose to no longer eat any animal products in 2015 and I followed that strictly for many years. I have been privileged enough to follow a fully plant-based diet now for about five years. However, at that time, it occurred to me that holding onto this label of vegan for example was as divisive as my decision to not eat the animals themselves in terms of attachment and identification. Therefore, to break this attachment to a label, I attempted to introduce a small amount of red meat one night to test how my body would respond to it. This correlated to the mental non-attachment to the label. After I ate this piece of red meat while in Prague with my friend Jiří, I went home that night and had some of the worst nightmares of my entire life. The dreams were blood soaked and torturous, painful and graphic. When I woke up, I was in physical pain and was extremely anxious. From that point on, if I have accidentally had a miso soup with bonito or shrimp paste in it, or unknowingly eat cauliflower that was roasted in chicken stock, the energy in my body immediately takes a turn towards aggression and I sense myself becoming more reactive, irritable, and not overall not fun to be around.

This experience of mine added in a realization that there were a whole lot of unknown inputs from the animals that people were not taking into account, many of which are going to affect their mental states as well as their physical bodies. For example, if you were to eat a cheeseburger and that cow was pumped full of GMO corn grown in Iowa, stuck in an area with ten thousand more cows where fecal matter is rampant and the ground is filthy with harmful bacteria, you will be consuming that filth and the emotions that the cow felt while in those conditions. Then, the cow is thrown onto an assembly line, probably already feeling extremely stressed or scared which releases adrenaline into the muscular system, where it smells death, is then hung upside down, gunned in the forehead and then its throat is slit. How do you think the flesh that is being consumed after being processed in a massive factory is going to affect you? The stress is transmitted from the animal to you, kicking your adrenal glands into overdrive, which negatively impacts your immune system, nervous system, and mental state. This step-by-step logic follows suit for every single piece of meat that is consumed. Furthermore, if you believe in karma you believe in reincarnation. The decision-maker in the decision to consume meat (you) is creating karma by harming another being, and you are also consuming that animal's karma into your physical and emotional system. Sounds like a lose-lose to me. I'd rather eat some pumpkin curry.

The easiest way to move about this shift out of meat consumption is to continually limit the amount of meat you consume. Most people start by eliminating red meat, but find themselves still eating chicken and fish. The quicker the better to relinquish the majority of the meat you consume, unless for drastic health reasons that allopathic medicine says you cannot remedy by another token it is viewed as necessary. For your sake, for our planet, and for all of the animals that you are complicit in killing with your decision to consume them, it is best to allow the habit of meat consumption to come to a halt.

In conclusion, what we have discussed above is just the select food and beverages that the majority of us consume in excess. This consumption we've been discussing is not even to mention the majority of household and cosmetic products that we are consuming such as shampoos, soaps, make-ups, dish detergent, and laundry detergent which are laden with toxic carcinogens and fragrances that we are plugging into the largest organ of the body, the skin, without even a second glance. Plus, what about informational consumption? What about the consumption of EMFs? What are we consuming from a media standpoint? Most of our news organizations are completely partisan and spin news to induce emotions of insecurity and fear that will result in increased spending from consumers to stimulate the economy, devalue the environment and create a dog-eat-dog competitive nature between us.

Beyond even these levels of consumption, we extend into a friendship standpoint, a familial standpoint. Do we surround ourselves with toxic individuals and viewpoints that lead us deeper into division, fear and hate, or do we surround ourselves with those who encourage togetherness, compassion and acceptance? Do your friends sing the song 'No New Friends' by DJ Khaled and Drake, or do they embrace those who are different from themselves who could enrich their worldview?

I will never forget that while I was sitting at Kopan Monastery's 2017 November course in Kathmandu, Nepal, one of the nuns stated something so true and profound that it struck me quite directly. She said, "most of the people we call our friends are actually complicit in our self-destruction. The habits and the partying, the discussion and the interests, instead of lifting each-other up and helping us focus on what matters as what true friends should do, our friend groups pull us down into more and more division."

I wish for all of us to continually deepen the process of understanding how what we consume, from food to cosmetic products to information, affects us on all levels. If we can begin to awaken to these realities and take control of our input in these manners, we will set ourselves up for the journey from self-actualization to self-transcendence.

JOURNAL PROMPTS:

1. What are your most commonly eaten foods? Is this out of your own health or out of a cultural model of dietary structure?
2. When you eat non-organic versus organic, are you able to sense a difference in your body, in your mind? When

you eat meat versus don't eat meat are you able to sense a difference? Coffee versus no coffee? Alcohol versus no alcohol?

3. Is the issue with your food consumption one of laziness or difficulty in obtaining proper sustenance? If not, why may you continue bad habits within the food consumption realm?

4. What do you still consume, from any standpoint, from media to household products, that may be contributing to mal-health?

Journal Prompt #1:

What are your most commonly eaten foods? Is this out of your own health or out of a cultural model of dietary structure?

Journal Prompt #2:

When you eat non-organic versus organic, are you able to sense a difference in your body, in your mind? When you eat meat versus don't eat meat are you able to sense a difference? Coffee versus no coffee? Alcohol versus no alcohol?

Journal Prompt #3:

Is the issue with your food consumption one of laziness or difficulty in obtaining proper sustenance? If not, why may you continue bad habits within the food consumption realm?

Journal Prompt #4:

What do you still consume, from any standpoint, from media to household products, that may be contributing to mal-health?

CHAPTER EIGHT

Maslow's Pyramid and the Movement Towards Self-Transcendence

"I can observe myself only in relationship, because life is relationship. It is no use sitting in a corner meditating about myself. I cannot exist by myself. I exist only in relationship to people, things and ideas, and in studying my relationship to people things and ideas as well as to inner things, I begin to understand myself."
—Jiddu Krishnamurti

"Let people realize clearly that every time they threaten someone or humiliate or unnecessarily hurt or dominate or reject another human being, they become forces for the creation of psychopathology, even if these be small forces. Let them recognize that every person who is kind, helpful, decent, psychologically democratic, affectionate, and warm, is a psychotherapeutic force, even though a small one."
—Abraham H. Maslow

To come back to our value, when we think of value, what do we think of?

Normally, people view something of value or valuable as increasing or adding to their individualized sense of self. Therefore, it is worth a trade of their time, or money in our economic model, to acquire it. This value can relate to belonging, perceived worth, the desire to be loved or create positive feelings for someone, or anything attributed to an individual personage's structure. We put value on things if they can benefit us directly.

Our current measurements of value that we strive for do not normally take into consideration the value of providing value for others within our personal addition of value, unless they are in a tight-knit community or nuclear family. They also rarely take into account things such as the externalities of creating this aforementioned value. For when they do so, they lead to market failure because a product or service's price equilibrium does not accurately reflect the true costs and benefits of that product or service in the scheme of our collective world. It also does not account for the value taken.

In other words, in the inverse scenario of value, as opposed to maximizing self-interest, we could maximize total interest while maintaining that our individualized needs are met. The more we give and respect the externalities, the more value is generated on a holistic level. This honors diversity, and includes measures beyond humans, into species and environment. In other words, we take into consideration the value of ecosystem preservation and regeneration. For without this ecosystem balance in which we are just one delicate part, we cease to exist.

This makes more sense to me on a holistic level because essentially our individual value means nothing without our collective value. As each individual person and species is delicately intertwined with the rest, if we hoard and accumulate value for our own selfish means without pro-generating the value for others, including protecting ecosystems, inevitably someone will strive to take our value from us and it will cease to exist. This value can be in monetary wealth, resource wealth, ideological wealth, or anything viewed as the inequality quotient between those not being shared value with. This taps directly into Maslow's hierarchy of needs.

For those of you who do not know, Abraham H. Maslow was arguably one of the most important psychologists of modern times. In a recent survey, Maslow was found to be the 14th-most-frequently cited psychologist in introductory psychology textbooks. On the basis of various indicators, some researchers proclaimed Maslow as the 10th most eminent psychologist of the 20th century.[40] The hierarchy of human needs outlined by Maslow (1943, 1954) is one of his most enduring contributions to psychology.

Maslow breaks down the hierarchy of needs into the deficiency needs versus growth needs. The framework of the bottom four structural pieces of the pyramid is known as the deficiency needs. See the pyramid below.[41]

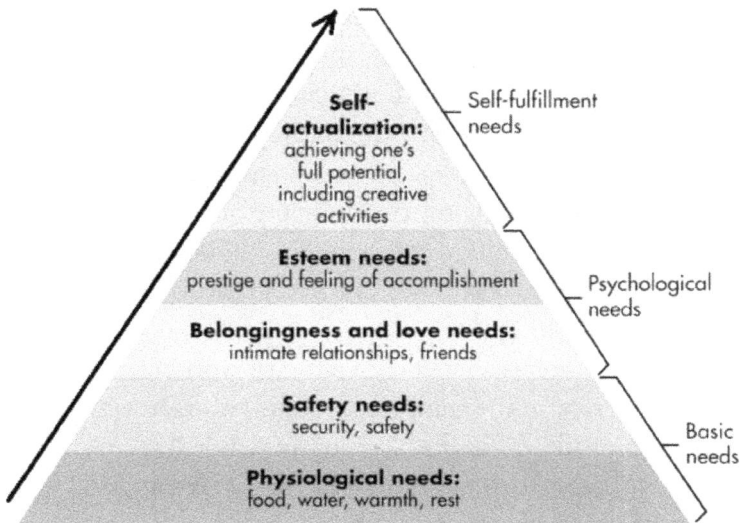

Self-actualization: achieving one's full potential, including creative activities — Self-fulfillment needs

Esteem needs: prestige and feeling of accomplishment

Belongingness and love needs: intimate relationships, friends — Psychological needs

Safety needs: security, safety

Physiological needs: food, water, warmth, rest — Basic needs

If you are to look at the current state of the world, some of the so-called 'developed' countries and a very small percentage of other countries are able to meet the deficiency needs, which in the above pyramid are labeled basic and psychological. This is why these countries call themselves developed. These developed countries in the world develop by using resources from the under-developed, forcing many into unfathomable realms of poverty. The World Bank's 2015 census states, "According to the most recent estimates, in 2015, 10 percent of the world's population or 734 million people lived on less than $1.90 a day."[42]

Without these basic needs being met, nothing else can be met. This is where you can visually see how privilege begins to filter in. Our privilege creates its opposite because of how intricately tied we all are.

In no way, shape, or form can $1.90 per day fulfill the physiological needs on a level for people to begin to work their way up this proclaimed pyramid of deficiency needs towards progress and self-actualization. Most of these people in this so-called bracket of poverty, if you have traveled around to speak, live and learn with them, are most likely wanting to work if they are not already, yet need to expend huge amounts of effort with little to no value exchange for it. The jobs they are vying for are most likely the beginning of the supply chain of logistics which is resource based, especially relating to many of the higher market items such as technology products, road building, agriculture, or keeping the wheels of society like taxis or rickshaws and restaurants churning.

Yet these laborers are left high and dry, working to scrape by on mere survival as the management of these organizations take exorbitant profits off of the backs of this labor. The only reason people with unearthly fiat wealth like Jeff Bezos and Bill Gates exist is because someone somewhere is living in the polar opposite world. This is the baseline of the economics of oppression. Normally those with darker skin in any of these select countries with high poverty rates are the poorest in that specific country.

Now, I'm sure many of us have never even tried to live on $1.90 a day. And if we have, we are lucky enough to conduct it as an experiment. That's what I was able to do while living in Bali-Nyonga, Cameroon. As a privileged person, I could conduct the experiment without fear that I would be unable to come out of it due to lack of monetary resources. So, in 2012 I tried it, to see if I could live on $2 a day. The scary part about the experiment was that, where I was living, and in most of these places where the wage is around $1.90 a day, there is very limited to no clean water. Therefore, half of my money for the day, or $1, was used for about one liter of potable water. If not, then I am encountering a whole other slew of issues that come from dirty water which I would have to compensate for with medicines that hopefully were not expired or bootlegged.

Since I chose to dedicate half of my funds for the day to clean water, I had $1 to eat for the remainder of the day. This doesn't take into account the externality of plastic waste impact. With that $1 for food I was left with, I would buy some bananas from the market or have some beans and a puffy doughnut called beignet, in the evening for sustenance. If I felt like not drinking water one day, or someone gave me some or I humbled myself to ask someone else to give extra, I could eat a different meal such as ndolé or njama njama and fufu. The beautiful thing about Cameroon was there was plenty of community who were willing to share food, so normally, no one goes hungry there. However, that being said, Cameroon is known as the bread-basket of Central Africa, and desert-countries such as Chad without fertile of soil are not so lucky.

Needless to say, by the end of the month, I had dropped a serious amount of weight and felt extremely malnourished, and I wasn't even working full hours in the fields as the farmers were. My brain was struggling to move into a capacity of deeper thinking because I was focused more on when I was going to eat or how I could save money to eat more. Farmers, the very producers of the food that we must consume to survive, are the majority of those who live on this sort of sustenance basis. What sort of upside-down system are we in that the people who keep us alive with food are rewarded the least?

With the rapid changing of the climate and the alteration of the seasons as well as the weather patterns such as monsoons being stronger, and dry seasons being hotter and longer, these farming populations are in great peril. They have very little to lean on for support. Traditional charities move from the top down, and unless there are grassroots solutions to the problems in these communities, the likelihood of these people suffering on a survival-basis-level is almost guaranteed. All of this happens while politicians in those same countries send their children on real-estate shopping sprees in Paris, drive around in Mercedes and have lavish houses in the nicest parts of town. The juxtaposition of wealth and poverty in Africa is riotous, and it follows suit in much of the post-colonialist world based on the leeching of the colonialist mindset of accumulation and the mechanization and exploitation of development.

To return to Maslow's hierarchy, if you do not have food, or most of your time is spent trying to make sure you and your family are well fed, then you have less time to move toward deeper considerations such as self-actualizing. Maslow is quoted saying:

> "It is quite true that man lives by bread alone — when there is no bread. But what happens to man's desires when there is plenty of bread and when his belly is chronically filled?
>
> At once other (and "higher") needs emerge and these, rather than physiological hungers, dominate the organism. And when these in turn are satisfied, again new (and

still "higher") needs emerge and so on. This is what we mean by saying that the basic human needs are organized into a hierarchy of relative prepotency."[43]

Looking at the original model of Maslow's hierarchy of needs as we navigate through the realms of sustenance and basic needs being met, social stimulation and the like, we find ourselves at a point of self-actualization. Sure, we can accept this. But the fact that most people take the self to mean 'me' or 'I' is contrary to the Truth of the matter. As we've discussed, according to Buddhism or Yogic philosophy, the 'I' is an identified illusion, and the only Self is that of existential inter-being. We would not exist without others. Therefore, we can use a new application of Self-actualization (with a capital S). We can stay that all beings must have their needs met. In sum, the Self, or Brahman, is the substratum or summation of existence itself, and we can look at this in a practical way as all sentient species, which, in the physical realm, means all life forms, have their needs met.

Many people in the self-actualizing realm that I know personally are not assisting the Self, or, other sentient beings whatsoever. They are not using their privilege for the common good. Karmically, I feel that privilege exists so that you can utilize it to transcend yourself and begin the service of the collective. Many I know who have privilege are working for large corporations or startups that they don't care too much about or whose mission isn't deep enough for them, yet they're able to curate their cheese trays with more niche bries, manchegos and Bordeaux, have dinner parties with select Spotify playlists and are listening to biohacking podcasts. For the record, I enjoy all of these things as well. However, when many look into this world of self-actualization, it seems they interpret it as trying to optimize their own self-interest. I don't call this self-actualizing at all. This is purely selfishness.

HEDONISM BLOCKS HUMANITARIAN PROGRESS

Very often, people essentially relinquish their desire to help others because they have reached a level of comfortability. Comfortability is the enemy of humanitarian progress, and comes from one of the root causes of self-destruction which we've discussed earlier, hedonism. Hedonism is the ethical theory that pleasure, in the sense of the satisfaction of desires, is the highest good and proper aim of human life. This is one of the major tell-tale signs in Aldous Huxley's book *Brave New World* that the populace would lose their freedom. It is also why humans tend to not care so much about one another as long as their pleasure-seeking mechanism is optimized. If they are receiving pleasure, like rats on a wheel getting fed cocaine, they will continue to pursue selfish desires, abandoning things that do not give them pleasure. In fact, we try to push away suffering. Where do we think we are pushing it to? If we experience pleasure, someone somewhere must also be simultaneously experiencing suffering. This includes the spectrum of the suffering of animals for the pleasure of their taste buds to the suffering of others to produce their goods and services. For example, people continue to buy iPhones even though people at Apple's parts manufacturer's Foxconn's enormous Longhua plant tried to kill themselves. The corporate response of Foxconn spurred further unease, as the CEO, Terry Gou, had large nets installed outside many of the buildings to catch falling bodies.[44]

This attempted avoidance of suffering in the name of pleasure-seeking in itself is extremely harmful. Suffering is always there. Our aversion, one of the roots of desire, can never be fulfilled based on the natural cycles of decay and death in Nature. The natural objective phenomena of energy that quantum physics validates in Buddhism, described as rising and falling away, is the way of all things. As we begin to negate specific sides of the spectrum, our inclusivity of pleasure and comfort only forms it's opposite somewhere else on the planet. As it does, it will toss our curated environment into flux by the desperation of someone else somewhere else to have their needs met rather than optimizing a compassionate response to all beings. We can try to avoid suffering all we want, but by doing this we create its opposite and continue along the routes of selfishness.

DEPENDENT ARISING

This selfishness to optimize our own self-interest and self-pleasure is yet another reason why we are orphaned from depth and meaning. The traditional worldviews of indigenous people long before this OS of the maximization of self-interest was centered on communal, species, and ecological benefit. This early pyramid of Maslow disregards all of the background stuff that was needed for one individual to achieve that self-actualized state. In Buddhism, this is called dependent arising. In accordance with our existing value system, if someone is achieving self-actualization, that means that someone else must not be because they are the production of that labor to enable others to do so. It doesn't acknowledge the externalities of the system; the access to foods which are on the backs of others who are not being paid adequately to meet the first framework of the pyramid, the impoverished conditions of those who have helped in the ability for one to climb this structure, et al. Your own natural wealth is not independent of anybody else. This realization ultimately leads you out of your own story and into the happening and enablement of all that is unfolding around you.

My two original qualms with the original pyramid of Maslow that I had been taught in high school psychology class are twofold. Firstly, the largest myopia and misinterpretation in this traditional pyramid is the decoupling of the interdependency of the collective and the individual in the pyramid, which was touched on above. For without the collective input in relationship to the individual's journey, there would be no individual ability to self-actualize.

Second, from what I've witnessed, the majority of people who believe they arrive at self-actualization do not progress to assisting others. In other words, they squander the blessing that they have been granted with their karmic level of opportunity and privilege to assist others in navigating the pyramid.

Thankfully, after I wrote this section, I decided to do more research on Maslow because I was amazed that this seemed to not have occurred to him. After falling down the rabbit hole of the interwebs, I discovered that Maslow's later work, which is often hidden from plain-sight and psychology classes, included a realm beyond self-actualization. This realm is called self-transcendence, and, in my opinion, this is his saving grace. Plus, it helped me out because it validated even further the intuition that I am receiving around the interconnectedness across many realms of belief and modality and the importance of selfless service.

SELF-TRANSCENDENCE AND MASLOW'S LATER WORK

Maslow defined self-transcendence as when one "seeks to further a cause beyond the self and to experience a communion beyond the boundaries of the self through peak experience."

He goes on to say,

> "As he, that is, the person in the peak experiences gets to be more purely and singly himself he is more able to fuse with the world, with what was formerly not-self, for example, the lovers come closer to forming a unit rather than two people, the I-Thou monism becomes more possible, the creator becomes one with his work being created, the mother feels one with her child. That is, the greatest attainment of identity, autonomy, or selfhood is

itself simultaneously a transcending of itself, a going beyond and above selfhood. The person can then become
relatively egoless.[45]

. . . In conclusion I wish to underscore one main paradox I have dealt with above . . . which we must face even
if we don't understand it. The goal of identity (self-actualization . . .) seems to be simultaneously an end-goal
in itself, and also a transitional goal, a rite of passage, a
step along the path to the transcendence of identity. This
is like saying its function is to erase itself. Put the other
way around, if our goal is the Eastern one of ego-transcen-
dence and obliteration, of leaving behind self-conscious-
ness and self-observation, . . . then it looks as if the best
path to this goal for most people is via achieving identity,
a strong real self, and via basic-need-gratification."[46]

To recapitulate what I shared above, you can self-actualize on
an individual level, however, when you do, your self, or 'I,' will
disintegrate to the point of your merging into the Self and moving into selflessness. This brings us back to the quote we read by
Chögyam Trungpa in the first chapter, "enlightenment is the
ego's ultimate disappointment."

After all, how else would you have gotten to the point of
opportunity to self-actualize without the help of others? From
your parents, friends, relationships in work, animals, the Earth,
et al, everything we do is intricately tied to others. In other
words, for you to self-actualize, some sentient beings on the
planet must have provided you in some way with the opportunity. This is where one of the predicaments with development
lies. It seems that those who are privileged have a potentiality to work their way through the material realms quicker than
those who are economically oppressed, because they can witness first hand how money and materialism do not provide

ultimate happiness. By seeing these things, the pathway begins again towards simplicity and the lesson of lessening. However, until most people have tasted what they have seen in movies or advertisements across the world, it is a distant thought, so those who find themselves 'under-developed', or simple-living, often are craving the material realms. They then get caught in them nonetheless in order to return back to simplicity. It seems part of the process is being unable to leapfrog the necessity of the experiential understanding of the futility of materialism as a means to true peace.

I quote Sonmi-451 from the movie *Cloud Atlas* by David Mitchell when she says,

"Our lives are not our own, we are bound to others, past and present. And by each crime and every kindness, we birth our future."

To actualize means to become as you are. "Become as You Are" is the title of an Alan Watts book which I quite enjoy. To become as you are means to stop dividing your reality from the interdependence of the collective existential framework that is reality. Embrace the diversity. Embrace the fact that you are nothing outside of relationship. Inter-being is the only reality, whether we see it or not. As we see this, we move closer and closer to the source consciousness that is Self, or Brahman in Hindu texts. According to Mahayana Buddhism, or Tibetan Buddhism, this journey gets us nowhere unless we are able to assist others. That is the role of the bodhisattva. As long as the majority of humanity is struggling to have their basic needs met or is being psychologically and sometimes physically forced into a development-minded architecture, perhaps to facilitate the return to the self-transcendent, it will be increasingly difficult to remain human amidst this division of the human race.

JOURNAL PROMPTS:

1. Why do you choose to give to another person? Are there specific things that you look for in order to unlock your generosity?
2. How do you feel when you give to another person? What sort of feelings or sensations come up when you do this? How do you feel when you do not give to a person in need yet you have resources to give? What sort of feelings or sensations come up when you do this?
3. When you look back on your life's journey from the point you are at now, list a few people and circumstances that you are grateful for that helped to guide you where you are today.
4. How has your comfort taken away from helping others? Do you think that one must reach a state of comfort in order to assist others in their lives?

ACTIVITIES:

1. Seek out experiences that make you question how much you need and how much you don't need. This may be accomplished by leaving your comfort zone and interacting with people who have a different way of life than you.
2. Find a local organization whom you can volunteer with, whether that be an animal shelter, environmental group or food kitchen.
3. Practice giving to others without the thought or inkling of expecting something back in return. This is the spirit of gift. See how that makes you feel.
4. Attempt to conduct two random acts of kindness daily to complete strangers. See how that makes you feel.

Journal Prompt #1:

Why do you choose to give to another person? Are there specific things that you look for in order to unlock your generosity?

Journal Prompt #2:

How do you feel when you give to another person? What sort of feelings or sensations come up when you do this?

How do you feel when you do not give to a person in need yet you have resources to give? What sort of feelings or sensations come up when you do this?

Journal Prompt #3:

When you look back on your life's journey from the point you are at now, name a few people and circumstances that you are grateful for that helped to guide you where you are today.

Journal Prompt #4:

How has your comfort taken away from helping others? Do you think that one must reach a state of comfort in order to assist others in their lives?

CHAPTER NINE

Entheogens: A Shortcut into Self-Transcendence

"Psychedelics are illegal not because a loving government is concerned that you might jump out of a third story window [but] because they dissolve opinion structure and culturally laid down models of behavior and information processing."
—Terrence McKenna

"The man who comes back through the Door in the Wall will never be quite the same as the man who went out. He will be wiser but less sure, happier but less self-satisfied, humbler in acknowledging his ignorance yet better equipped to understand the relationship of words to things, of systematic reasoning to the unfathomable mystery which it tries, forever vainly, to comprehend"
—Aldous Huxley, *The Doors of Perception*

At this point in time we all have probably heard of, and perhaps consumed, LSD and mushrooms, ketamine, MDMA, and many other psychotropic and psychedelic compounds. The term psychedelic comes from the Greek for "mind-manifesting." This term was popularized by Humphry Osmond, a British psychiatrist working in Canada in the 1950s. In a letter to Aldous Huxley, he wrote, "To fathom hell or soar angelic / Just take a pinch of psychedelic." Osmond had introduced Huxley to mescaline, and Huxley went on to write *The Doors of Perception* about his psychedelic experience.[47]

Plant medicines have become a major industry with the re-emergence of international seekers of Ayahuasca, San Pedro, Bufo, Kambo, Peyote and others. Indigenous people are the carriers of the medicine, but as of now it has stemmed out far and wide beyond their hands. It is now being held by people who have been trained by traditional shamans as well as by people who don't have deep training but see an opportunity to capitalize on the sacred; similar to Yoga. These are the self-proclaimed shamans. These plant medicines are wisdom carriers in themselves, and they are assisting the collective re-emergence of wisdom and memory from past traditions in a new context. Wisdom has no expiration date.

Many people have been working behind the scenes for many years to understand the implications and significance of these medicines. In the Western world, back in the day, Aldous Huxley wrote about his experiments with mescaline which preceded Timothy Leary and Richard Alpert, the late Ram Dass, with their movements from Harvard to the world. One of the catalyzers of this space was Albert Hofmann, a Swiss chemist known best for being the first to synthesize, ingest, and learn of the psychedelic effects of LSD, lysergic acid diethylamide. Hofmann was also the first to isolate, synthesize, and name the principal psychedelic mushroom compounds psilocybin and psilocin.[48] Neem Karoli Baba, otherwise known as Maharaji, who was Ram Dass's guru, frequently called LSD "yogi medicine", helping the western seekers move beyond their egoic limitations and blockages.

Many states in the U.S.A. and entire countries like Canada have witnessed the legalization of cannabis. Now, some cities like Oakland and Denver are moving onto the decriminalization of psilocybin. Rick Doblin and MAPS (the Multidisciplinary Association for Psychedelic Studies) are making waves in MDMA and LSD clinical trials. Paul Stamets is a pioneering mycologist who is changing many people's minds about the fungi kingdom. Michael Pollan's book *How to Change Your Mind* included some of the history and proponents of the movement as well as his own personal experiences and how they have helped him thrive. I suggest reading that book for more details on psychedelics and their history.

Throughout all of this, one thing has held true; these compounds are medicines when used in the right doses, set, and setting. And, poisons when used in others. They have been used as rites of passage and offered insight into unseen realms of the invisible and realms of consciousness for millennia. These substances are medicines because they show us states of being that are part of existence itself beyond our often self-imposed dimensional limitations. In other words, these states within the experience reveal the multi-dimensionality of our seemingly limited and identified perceptions. We can see fractal light patterns and the utter beauty of a mango tree and forget the language that we use to label them. These states induce healing through internal vision. Complexities and patterns become so simple to fix. Deep emotional traumas are released from the accumulated energy locales of our physical bodies. Spirits or invisible entities speak to us, such as Grandmother Aya or Grandfather San Pedro. We re-enter a time of innocence, a time of Eden. Conversely, we can re-enter times of hell. These times help to illuminate unkind actions or the mistreatment of others. All of it, so vivid, so clear, so undeniably true. All of these states are contained within ourselves.

THE WORLD-WIDE-MIND

These medicines act as experiential gateways to expand our minds, literally, into other realms or dimensions of consciousness. When I say expand, I am not talking about a conceptual word. Expansion is actually happening because the mind is not anchored within the physical brain. I have had many personal experiences and continue to do so where I intuitively understand that our brains are just tuning forks, or antennae. When certain experiences have left me overwhelmed, I have felt like 'my' mind was expanding out of my time-space locus visually like the roots of a mycelium network. I was able to see other people's thoughts, feel their emotions, and feel compassion for some of their life events that they hadn't revealed to me. This feeling of a thought-semantic-network similar to a mycelial network or a tree-root network is how I have envisioned the centrifugal expansion of the mind.

A seemingly good model with which to compare this experience, outside of a mycelial network, is the Internet. If you've ever seen a visual representation of the Internet, it looks very similar to the human brain, with lines criss crossing it, and nodes of focused light to which the lines are linked. For those who don't know how the Internet actually works, it is as follows:

The internet is the lifeline through which works a packet routing network works in accordance with the Internet Protocol (IP), the Transport Control Protocol (TCP) and other protocols. A protocol is a communication method, which, as in humans, is composed of language and social structures. These protocols structure how computers should communicate. A packet is fragmented pieces of a message being delivered through the network, like words being fragmented pieces in a sentence. You speak individual words, but their integrated product is a complete thought or sentence. The framework of this network is built from two pieces, servers. The machines that provide services to other machines are servers. And the machines that are used to connect to those services are clients. There are Web servers, e-mail servers, FTP servers and so on serving the needs of Internet users all over the world. When you are online, you are sitting on a client's machine (laptop) and accessing a specific website's server. The server's communication is constructed by its attachment to the physical framework of the internet itself.[49]

You and I may not directly connect physically, similarly to the geographical separation of servers and the clients, but we are connected via an entity, which we can call consciousness, or the Self. Breath is an entity that we can witness in all beings, from trees, to animals to ourselves. All energy is essentially just information. The information is delivered from the source, or as we will call it here, the World-Wide-Mind, through the connective network and manifests in a diversity of form. The forms take shape depending on the geographical location of the beings, which results in different physical traits, languages, species, cultures, DNA expression, and foods. Food is also just information. It receives the information of light through photons and waves, transmutes it into form, and we utilize that transmuted form to gain nutrition. All information delivery and reception is designated through this line, and without it, the receptors would cease to exist as well. Can we really get to the point without a defined language to accept that information is being delivered to us via all sources and all objects in our physical and invisible realities? From the imagery of a tree to the sound of a passing car to a voice in the wind, everything is always communicating with us. Whether or not we have tuned ourselves to be able to absorb the information is a different story. That's part of the journey.

What happens when we take psychedelics and plant medicines in the correct manner is that we are able to directly access the connective-line, which hosts an infinite amount of information. This information comes in our systems via wisdom and realizations of the intricacy, interconnectedness, and mystery of life. These plant medicines and the compounds within them help our antennae to be tuned into a different information channel or frequency, which enables us to receive different informational downloads that we seemed to not have permissions (Internet term) to gain beforehand. As we expand beyond our limited framework and protocol, we are literally expanding our access to the vast information and intelligence flow that exists and that invisibly connects us all. As we expand our access, our own minds are literally expanding beyond our time-space locus, which is designated by direct experience.

MORPHIC RESONANCE

Rupert Sheldrake, an English author and researcher in the field of parapsychology has proposed that the mind is extended in time and space. One of his main discoveries is of morphic resonance. Morphic resonance is a process of memory inheritance from a self-organizing system to a future system. It looks at laws of nature such as instincts in animals as habits learned and passed down through memory. He has discovered that memory doesn't need to be stored inside the brain, but rather the brain acts as a receiver for past influences of the species. Morphic resonance is therefore tapping into the phenomena of individualized memory and life now altering the collective memory of the future.

According to Sheldrake,

"We've all been brought up with the 17th century Cartesian view that our minds are located inside our brains. In this view, our minds are completely portable and can be carried around wherever we go, packaged as they are inside our skulls. Our minds, therefore, are essentially private entities associated with the physiology of each of our nervous tissues. This idea of the contracted mind, a mind which is not only rooted in the brain but actually located in the brain, is an idea that is so pervasive in our culture that most of us acquire it at an early age. It is not just a philosophical theory (although, of course, it is that); it is an integral part of the materialistic view of reality."

He goes on to state,

" ... our minds are extended in both space and time with other people's minds, and with the group mind or cultural mind by way of their connection to the collective unconscious. Insofar as we tune into archetypal fields or patterns which other people have had, which other social groups have had, and which our own social group has had in the past, our minds are much broader than the "things" inside our brains. They extend out into the past and into social groupings to which we are linked, either by ancestry or by cultural transmissions. Thus, our minds are extended in time, and 't believe they are also extended in space."[50]

In connection to the world-wide-mind, and in practice, morphic resonance is one possible reason why we experience visions while taking plant medicines. When many people consume Ayahuasca, for instance, they receive visions of a black jaguar. This vision comes to them despite them never having seen a black jaguar, and despite their geographical location being in Amsterdam. By applying these concepts, we begin to understand that the plants used in Ayahuasca itself carry memory, and we are ingesting their memory, or morphic resonance. These plants, originating in the Amazon rainforest, have witnessed and experienced this jaguar in their energetic field. When we ingest the plant itself, its informational field is delivered into a digestible form for us to witness and perceive. The information is translated into visuals, and we see a jaguar.

Normally, humans limit themselves to an understanding that

they are merely three-dimensional beings. This is completely false and is a limitation to enable functionality. Let us consider the human eye, which can typically detect wavelengths only from 380 to 700 nanometers.[51] The cone-shaped cells in our eyes act as receivers, or as prisms for this light. As the full spectrum of visible light travels through a prism, the wavelengths separate into the colors of the rainbow because each color is a different wavelength. Violet has the shortest wavelength, at around 380 nanometers, and red has the longest wavelength, at around 700 nanometers. If we are able to witness these colors in full form outside of our limitations of the nanometers of perception, we move into depths of sight that are multi-dimensional in themselves, such as fractals and time.

ENTHEOGENS AND THE RELATIVITY OF TIME

Over the past few years I have begun to intuitively understand substances and their effects on my perceptions pertaining to their influence on the relativity of time. Time is experienced subjectively within each and every one of us based on our thoughts, our conditions, our language. The field of study of time perception is a multi-disciplinary one, bringing together psychology, cognitive linguistics, and neuroscience. It refers to the subjective experience of time, which is measured by a person's perception of the duration of the indefinite and unfolding of events. This is limiting because it only studies humans; I believe that other beings also have unique experiences of time which are not being studied as of yet.

In our day to day lives, we experience time in different ways. Pre-coffee, post-coffee, without stress, with stress, pre-cannabis, post-cannabis. Our thoughts are designated by the experience of mind phenomena created by an internal or external stimulus. Just as for some, coffee has the ability to increase productivity and information processing, entheogens have the ability to alter our perception of time in accordance with our minds so that we witness and interact with information on different wavelengths. Why do you think it is when you consume LSD or cannabis, things in your visual perception seem to take on a different glow, a certain newness? Why does music suddenly become more fascinating and evoke a tangible feeling in the body?

I believe that the depth of the field is changing, enabling us to tap into subtler frequencies in the fields of time and space. As we alter the depth of our perception of time, the world itself changes. I believe that these plants are communicating with our antennae in a way that alters the very makeup of the relativity of time. And with this quickening or slowing of time itself, the depth and breadth of the information that we are capable of receiving also changes in visual, audible and other sensory-consciousness fields.

Plant medicines are not needed to induce these alterations in our perception of time and space, but they certainly provide a short-cut toward the understanding that if time and space are relative, perhaps everything that we see or know is only a fraction of the ultimate Truth of its multidimensional nature. We begin to experience the many different realms of consciousness that are just barely outside of our normal functionality based on our conditioning and forms of identity.

PITFALLS

That said, why is it so important to have experiences that expand our constructs of time and space? Having tasted the existential truth of multi-dimensionality, we begin to tap into the truth of inter-being and inter-connectivity through entheogens. One begins to understand on a deeper, subtler level that we are not separate from the wholeness of the Earth, our peers, our direct or indirect environment, and ultimately consciousness and existence itself. If we have an experience of this depth or gravity, not knowledge or conceptuality but an actual experience, our entire world changes. We begin to see ourselves as a part of something larger, part of a culture, part of a species, part of a planet, part of a consciousness, part of existence. Inevitably we become more inquisitive about the world that we were operating in, probably not accepting things at face value as much as we did prior. This leads to doing research and perhaps not taking things like happiness for granted. Things we've been told to be our whole life begin to crumble. Like Frank Zappa said,

> "If you end up with a boring, miserable life because you listened to your mom, your dad, your teacher, your priest, or some guy on television telling you how to do your shit, then you deserve it."

While all of these aspects are beautiful and necessary for the expansion of consciousness, I've observed two main pitfalls pertaining to these experiences. The first one is an over-identification with your own individuality from the experience. This can be viewed as a messianic type of issue. The second is a lack of integration of the experience into a pragmatic life-way. Both of these are extremely detrimental to the actual demolition project of enlightenment and connectivity, and are obstacles to these very powerful and sacred experiences that I find most readily in many spiritual communities.

The over-identification with your own individuality from the experience is not exclusive to plant medicines. However, the hierarchical viewpoints built upon ego that can come from a deep experience can create the illusion that one has a spiritual advantage over others. This separation and division is at the root of the issues themselves! The juxtaposition of righteousness and entitlement that stems from the identification with one's individuality, especially after a spiritual experience, can be toxic and is of the main proponents of the continuation of the culture in which we live.

Ram Dass has a beautiful story about this messianic phenomenon and his brother. He states,

> "I have a brother who is in a mental hospital, he thinks he is Christ. Well that's groovy, I am Christ also, but he doesn't think I'm Christ, he just thinks he's Christ. Because it happened to him and he took his ego with him, so he says "like I'm special" and when I say to him:
>
> "Sure man, you're Christ, I'm Christ too," and he says "You don't understand." And so when he's out he steals cars and things like that because he needs them, because he's Christ, it's alright. So they lock him up. And he says, "I don't know," he said to me, "I'm a responsible member of society, I go to church, me they put in a mental hospital. You, you got a beard, you wear a dress, you, you're out free." Sure, because as far as I'm concerned we're all God, that's the difference. That's the difference. And if you really think another guy is God he doesn't lock you up. Funny about that."

If you are God, everyone is God. It's not just you. This is where the over-identification can come into play and hinder deeper, subtler connection. In the monasteries in Nepal, we used to prostrate to Gautama Buddha around 4:45AM. What most people didn't realize is that we are all potential Buddhas, and therefore, we are really prostrating to our own Buddha-Nature potentiality. You are not the only one; we are all potentiality and on our own karmically-customized journeys.

Second, a lack of integration of the experience into a pragmatic life-way has often been overlooked as an important part of the process of deep entheogen work. It has actually started to become a specialization of so-called integration specialists, who attempt to assist those who are confused with shattered or lost identities to gather their pieces back up in a world that no longer makes sense to them. Without the integration of the information and wisdom collected from another field into the typical field of day-to-day life, things can become confusing, hard to bear and understand; basically hard to function within.

This is where the traditional eldering structure set up in indigenous communities after a right of passage assists in the processing and assimilation of the teachings with an application in the direct cultural environment. The *yamas* can also come in here with how we function within our deeper truths amidst societal constructs. The superficiality of our cultural life often becomes so difficult to comprehend that many keep going back to plant medicines to create more depth. This builds a reliance upon the medicine itself, which can become a poison. Paracelsus, a Swiss physician and German Renaissance philosopher, roughly states,

> "All things are poisons, for there is nothing without poisonous qualities. It is only the dose which makes a thing poison."

If we begin to dose ourselves too much with medicines, looking for healing or answers because we have not been able to integrate the wisdom in our day-to-day lives, it becomes a dangerous situation which can affect people dearly. We are back into a state of accumulation, trying to get back to that state where we currently are not. Taking time to rest and to reflect on these situations is key. Share time with nature, connect with your body in exercise and meditation and write down thoughts, feelings and emotions. These techniques over-time can assist in the comprehension and connecting of the dots between the inner planes of reality and the outer structure of society.

In summary, by working with entheogens and plant medicines, we begin to see everything as deeply interconnected. This exposes the cultural fallacy of over-individualization and people being praised for it. The reward and punishment system that is our cultural model is exposed as a societal condition. We recognize that this conditioned response, like Pavlov's dogs salivating at a bell, is moving against the deeper states of inter-being that must come to fruition in order for humanity to survive on this planet. We are Earthlings over any belief system, over any quarrel. We must, if anything, identify ourselves as part of a greater whole in which we can play a unique part and embrace the diversity within, but not see ourselves as separate from the system of consciousness itself. Entheogens' capacity to help us transcend our constructs of mind, space and time offer us a short-cut into these multidimensional levels of inter-being and interconnectedness.

JOURNAL PROMPTS:

1. Have you ever experimented with plant medicines? If so, what were some of the effects?
2. How were you able to integrate the experience with plant medicine into your day-to-day life?
3. After your experience, was there a long-lasting impact? Or did it fade away? Why do you think that this is?
4. Do you find yourself looking at your experience and feeling superior to others because you have had an experience and they haven't? Do you feel that the experience has created more connection or more division in your life?

Journal Prompt #1:

Have you ever experimented with plant medicines? If so, what were some of the effects?

Journal Prompt #2:

How were you able to integrate the experience with plant medicine into your day-to-day life?

Journal Prompt#3:

After your experience, was there a long-lasting impact? Or did it fade away? Why do you think that this is?

Journal Prompt #4:

Do you find yourself looking at your experience and feeling superior to others because you have had an experience and they haven't? Do you feel that the experience has created more connection or more division in your life?

CHAPTER TEN

Indigenous Worldview and Sacred Interconnectedness

"This we know; The earth does not belong to man; man belongs to the earth. This we know, all things are connected like the blood which unites one family. All things are connected."
—Chief Si'ahl, Duwamish Tribe

"And while I stood there I saw more than I can tell and I understood more than I saw; for I was seeing in a sacred manner the shapes of all things in the spirit, and the shape of all shapes as they must live together like one being."
—Heňáka Sápa or Black Elk, written down by John G.
   Neihardt, Black Elk Speaks

The people who were the most connected with the Earth are now the ones who have been the most oppressed, marginalized and silenced. The planned genocide of the indigenous peoples across the planet was rooted in one fact; that they were the protectors, propagators, and stewards of the land, and saw everything as intertwined on a familial and spiritual level. This holistic worldview stood in the way of the exploitative model of economic expansion that was coming in fast from Europe.

This literal interconnectedness is expressed in the varied

spoken languages, which merge concepts of land and spirit, and the practices and principles that encapsulated their world views. These understandings prevented them from ever over-harvesting, over-killing, harvesting out of season or taking anything out of turn or balance with the Earth. Certain groups of Europeans, who sought greener pastures for expanding their lives, saw this worldview as the biggest obstacle of them all. The colonialist mentality funded by the crown via the Catholic Church operated on the exploitative paradigm of separation. The indigenous people operated on a regenerative paradigm of interconnectedness. As these worldviews clashed, the colonialists, who had more weapons and barbaric tendencies, won. The framework of genocide and slavery is what the modern United States of America is built upon, and it is called civilization. Welcome to the land of the free and the home of the brave.

This entire worldview of resource exploitation rather than resource regeneration is the key difference. This shift leaves us where we are today. This worldview of exploitation was reinforced with the horrific and brutal conquest of the vast prairies, coastal areas, mountains, and forests of the Americas, Australia, Europe Africa and the South Pacific. Missionaries then converted indigenous people to Catholicism by force. They were coerced to have European-American style haircuts and forbidden to speak their languages. They had their spiritual belief systems ridiculed. Their names were replaced by European names to try to 'civilize' and 'Christianize' them. They were wrangled into reservations off the beaten paths on lands that were often not even their own. As this happened, the culture which was rooted in the language and traditions of interconnectedness with the land began to dissipate. Missionaries attempted to educate this worldview out of them and bring them into a Euro-American culture via government structures like the formation of the Bureau of Indian Affairs. In the Americas this created Native

American boarding schools, also known as Indian Residential Schools, which were usually harsh and sometimes deadly for the young children who were separated from their families and the worldview lineage.[52]

Reformers attempting to 'civilize' Native Americans into American culture promoted the Civilization Fund Act, which 'stimulated civilization processes.' This terminology asserts the illusion of superiority that the colonizers exhibited toward the Native people. The Europeans, who showed their truly barbaric practices and ways of life, viewed themselves as messengers of God.

John Trudell, one of the prominent voices of the American Indian Movement, states this fallacy of claiming civilization clearly when he says,

"The Great Lie is that this is civilization. It's not civilized. It has literally been the most blood-thirsty brutalizing system ever imposed upon this planet. [...] Or if it does represent civilization, and that is truly what civilization is, then the Great Lie is that civilization is good for us."[53]

In Australia, the Stolen Generation refers to the time period between 1910 and 1970 when, depending on region, 1 in 3 indigenous Australian children were forcibly taken from their families and communities with the goal of obliterating their worldview and requiring cultural assimilation.[54] What actually happened, according to a 2019 study by the Australian Institute of Health and Welfare (AIHW), was that children living in households with members of the Stolen Generation were more likely to "experience a range of adverse outcomes," including poor health (especially mental health), truancy, and poverty. These were by-products of a violent ripping apart of a worldview by intentional generational fracturing and segregation. The aim was to erase interconnected worldviews and subjugate entire cultures and peoples. It is a tactic of psychological warfare and genocide. It still continues today, as we are taught about Native peoples in brief as anecdotes of our history, rather than the framework of our land and toponymy. The legacy of the diverse range of Native American tribes and cultures existed for thousands of years prior to the white man's arrival with intricacies, follies, and beauty like any other culture, just like you and me. In the Southeastern Woodlands area of the U.S.A., at least one hundred tribes, such as the Chickasaw, Chakchiuma, Natchez, Calusa, Catawba, Opelousas and Machapunga, lived together, all with differing structures, languages and ways of life. How many of only this handful have you ever heard of? States like Massachusetts, Kansas, Missouri, Mississippi, all are named for various bands or tribes whom resided in the areas. The disconnection of language from meaning is one of the main aspects of the ripping apart of a connected worldview.

Fast forward to now. The human-centric worldview of exploitation has spread like wildfire. The separate self and its desire to maximize individual interest reigns supreme in every interaction and transaction in which we participate. We have lost the understanding of sacredness because of the commoditization of the profane belief system based on division. If we truly live by the worldview of interconnectedness and truly understand and view the world and reality in these terms, how could we ever attempt to murder an entire continent of people who lived here for tens of thousands of years? How could we kill hundreds of thousands of animals for their skins and their meat? How could we mine the Earth until we are looking at an uninhabitable landscape permanently scarred by destruction? How could we cut down unfathomable swaths of rainforests and ecosystems to plant monocrop soy for cattle? It is not all historical, it is still happening today.

If we truly could feel, rather than intellectualize this, we could not bear the thought of harming the external world in these ways. In fact, it would be quite the opposite. We would understand, that the more we harm the external world we harm ourselves. And we harm ourselves because we destroy the environment with our every transaction and ambition. Inevitably, the more destruction of the external aspects of our self occurs, the closer it gets to what we view as the individual. We are all proliferators of this destructive mindset, whether we deny it or not.

Black Elk states,

"There can never be peace between nations until there is first known that true peace which is within the souls of men."

FROM SACRED INTERCONNECTEDNESS TO PROFANE SEPARATION

The quote at the beginning of the chapter from Chief Si'ahl encapsulates this world view of interconnectedness. This world view is consistent, within its cultural specificities, with my experience in connecting with indigenous peoples around the world, from the Larrakia people in Northern Territory of Australia, to the Native Hawai'ians in Hawai'i, from the Tlingit people in Southeast Alaska to the Ewe people in Ghana. The primary worldview of the sacred, of interconnectedness, and of the way of life that stems from this, connects them all. The grand mystery of life is sacred. Although we assume we know what will come next, we can never predict the future. Each breath is a gift. An attitude of sacredness enables us to cherish these moments and revel in the immense cosmic design and in our ability to participate and witness the majesty.

Chief Luther Standing Bear sums it up with his statement,

"Kinship with all creatures of the earth, sky, and water was a real and active principle. In the animal and bird world there existed a brotherly feeling that kept us safe among them . . . The animals had rights—the right of man's protection, the right to live, the right to multiply, the right to freedom, and the right to man's indebtedness. This concept of life and its relations filled us with the joy and mystery of living; it gave us reverence for all life; it made a place for all things in the scheme of existence with equal importance to all."

This deep understanding separates the prime worldview difference. The indigenous people of the world sought the harmony of a species with its surroundings, the acceptance and the protection of this diversity, while others sought the dominance of surroundings by brute force. Hence the war on the wilderness and the domestication of nature which exists to this very day. We fear the wilderness because we cannot control it.

Joni Mitchell sings about it in 'Big Yellow Taxi.' This is, at least in the direct circles that I find myself within, the consensus thought. Indigenous people have long looked out at our current world, economic OS and seen destruction. We see development. I can't help but feel that an urgent and ominous crisis is happening every day as this attitude continues to spread. Long ago, with the onslaught of colonialism, this sickness of greed came into North America from far away and chopped down the trees, brought disease that sickened and murdered millions, dumped poisonous substances into the creeks and water sources, shot bullets and exploded bombs and tried to hide toxic waste underground or in rivers. These criminal perpetrators then walked away from it all, and continue to do so to this very day with legal frameworks for protection. Even after all of the land was taken and the various indigenous tribes were forced onto small swaths of reservation land, promises have been revoked and corporations go after resources on these lands. The Dakota Access Pipeline on Standing Rock Reservation is but one example that numbers in the hundreds and perhaps more.

With this separate worldview, we have made the sacred profane, and the profane sacred. As a species, we have attempted to wipe away millions of lives and tens of thousands of years of culture, wisdom, and evolution connected to the land, native plants and animals on the connected American continent and others.

Even the story we are told of the name America is false, and comes from a colonizer. This story is not the true origin of the name. Most of us were taught that the name of the continents of North and South America came from Amerigo Vespucci, a Florentine merchant who traveled during the so-called Age of Discovery. I was taught what feels to me more likely to be the real origin of the name while traveling through Central America. This same origin is called an alternative theory online. The origin of the name I was told, states that the name America came from the word Amaruca, "Land of the Plumed Serpents." Quetzalcoatl, the chief god of the Maya is the feathered serpent that looks like the morning glory vine that provided a psychedelic sacrament. In Peru, this god is called Amaru, as in Túpac Amaru, the last Sapa Inca defender killed by the Spaniards in Vilcabamba, Peru.[55] The tribes of the Aymara and the Quechua still exist in Peru today.

If we don't even know where we live, what do we know? We've really settled into this collective conspiracy that we understand what is happening around us. Do you know whose traditional lands you are currently occupying?

We as a species have erased thousands of languages that have an understanding of interconnectedness far beyond our measly English one. In these languages, connection, purpose, and meaning were intertwined. We've omitted and twisted history, proliferating this monstrosity. We've misconstrued empires and kingdoms of value built upon a swamp of lies. This is what happened when Caesar 'accidentally' burned the Library of Alexandria. So much knowledge and experiential wisdom has been lost. So much peace and prosperity has been shattered and harmed. Our worldview has been fragmented by the disavowal of our brothers and sisters in humanity through our diverse cultural ancestors, all for the sake of greed, domination and control.

I wrote a poem back in 2014 called 'I-dolla-try.' Even the Catholics who are supposed to be abiding by the Bible seem to miss this one, "You shall have no other gods before me." This is expressed in the Bible in Exodus 20:3, Matthew 4:10, Luke 4:8 and elsewhere, e.g.: "Ye shall make you no idols nor graven image . . . " Maybe people interpret things too literally, but, tell me, don't we worship wealth in our society? Celebrities, athletes, tech giants. All of these become people's idols, literally. I was asked many times growing up, "Who's your idol?" and I always said Cal Ripken, Jr. because my Dad liked him and he was dedicated to the team. This question is very common for kids to be asked. Now, this idolatry extends to the social media world, with influencers. What do all of these people have in common? Some form of wealth. Why do we want it? Our desires are out of whack; we are conditioned to crave something that we have been taught is valuable. To accumulate wealth is to destroy the planet.

We build out these frameworks of role models. We begin to structure our own models of the world based on roles. Models of expectation, models of how to live. Our getting caught in the roles themselves separates us from our true nature. Our true nature is not encapsulated into one role or the other, but rather in the role-lessness. Without roles, we embrace humanity in all of it's varied forms and the fluidity between them.

RETURN TO INDIGENEITY

At long last, the indigenous people are beginning again to have the respect, acknowledgement, and attempted reconciliation that they deserve. The wisdom of the ages and the story holders are the ones who know the way forward. The Hopi Prophecy humbles us in its wisdom that this is not the first time this sort of Earthly calamity is happening in the human world. The Hopi tell us that this story has repeated itself many times for as far back as human memory reaches, and they have predicted where we will end up if we don't change course immediately.[56]

Thomas Banyacya, the late Hopi elder, relates in two timely talks from 1995, referring to a petroglyph on a rock near his home, these different worlds. He states that there were three previous human worlds that were destroyed when people became greedy, worshiped technology as a god, fought and hurt each other, and repeatedly forgot the ethical teachings they'd been given to honor the Earth as the source of life and sustenance. Three apocalypses inevitably ensued—first by fire, then by ice, then by flood. Noah's Ark floated through one book's collective memory to escape a similar greed-ending catastrophe. As we are all witnessing now, the future is visible in the now, the destruction and mass hysteria is upon us.[57]

One of the tools that is assisting in this shift back to wisdom are the plant medicines from the various medicine carriers, which we discussed in a prior chapter pertaining to entheogens. These tools will naturally strip away veils of separateness that one experiences in one's waking reality based on the worldview of exploitation and competition. People become more sensitive in that they sense more, and intuition rather than rote fact becomes more delicately tuned and utilized. Biologically this is said to be the cause of the blocking of the Default Mode Network (DMN). The DMN is the name given to a network in the brain that has been shown to be crucial in normal, everyday consciousness. The DMN is a loose connection of different brain areas and neuron groups that communicate together to help us function in the world. High activity in the DMN is linked to mental processes such as our awareness of ourselves, roughly the same as the ego, social thinking (understanding what other people are feeling), and thinking about the past or future. Depression is a common example of an over-active DMN. Meditation assists also with ameliorating mal-effects of the DMN.[58]

COLLABORATION INSTEAD OF COMPETITION

Not only was the indigenous worldview based on non-separateness of the environment, but it was based on the communal rather than the individual basis of thriving. Therefore, it was based on collaboration rather than competition. Lame Deer in Seeker of Vision says it best here, with some sarcasm thrown in. He states,

> "Before our white brothers came to civilize us we had no jails. Therefore, we had no criminals. You can't have criminals without a jail. We had no locks or keys, and so we had no thieves. If a man was so poor that he had no horse, tipi or blanket, someone gave him these things. We were too uncivilized to set much value on personal belongings. We wanted to have things only in order to give them away. We had no money, and therefore a man's worth couldn't be measured by it. We had no written law, no attorneys or politicians, therefore we couldn't cheat. We really were in a bad way before the white men came, and I don't know how we managed to get along without these basic things which, we are told, are absolutely necessary to make a civilized society."

Isn't it a tragicomedy how in the sake of civilized society, things become a lot less civilized? Yet these so-called 'savages' were caretakers of the planet and of each other in their specific tribes. Did you know that the Declaration of Independence calls Native American people savages?[59]

This systemic racism is in our country's founding documents! Yes, wars did occur between tribes over various means, but it wasn't to take another tribe's resources, it was to protect. The overarching view of society was based on community, peace, and stewardship of the planet. Winona LaDuke in her book 'The Militarization of Indian Country' states,

> "There is also a critical difference between warfare designed to kill en masse, and warfare designed to keep enemies at bay, as was the ancient custom of tribes. The greatest honor a warrior could achieve was to "count coup" on an enemy—touching his enemy without inflicting any bodily harm. Such an act was a demonstration of bravery and skill as opposed to the demonstration of immense force that are intrinsic to America's military prowess."[60]

Our European ancestors however could be viewed as nothing but savages and barbarians, coming in to rape and pillage villages, murder through deceit with small pox blankets, trounce natural habitats, and harm thousands upon thousands of innocent animals. In the modern day, as we 'civilized' people continue our expansion rapidly across all realms of the planet, rendering the wild spaces fewer and fewer, pushing into new habitats where animals have never seen the likes of humans all in the sake of development, there comes a time when we all must hit the pause button. Our war on the natural world must come to an end. Our war on each-other must come to an end. We must stop seeking dominion over everything and embrace that we in all of our human stages and patterns are just a part of it. In fact, this is where the way of the peaceful warrior comes in.

OGICHIDAA—THE DEFENDER OF THE PEOPLE

The great Lakota Chief and Holy Man Sitting Bull has described the peaceful warrior. The Ojibwe word for warrior, although more multi-dimensional in its meaning than in English, is Ogichidaa, or Ogichidaag, "those who defend the people." He states:

> "For us, warriors are not what you think of as warriors. The warrior is not someone who fights, because no one has the right to take another's life. The warrior, for us, is one who sacrifices himself for the good of others. His task is to take care of the elderly, the defenseless, those who cannot provide for themselves and above all, the children, the future of humanity."[61]

Are we ready to be warriors in this context? Can we begin to see how our value system disconnects us out of our roles as protectors of the sacred, the progenitors of life? Can we begin to extricate ourselves from our own individualized storylines in order to step into the role of local and global community? As we begin to see our unique predicament in this life, we begin to see how we can serve others. The more we embrace ourselves the less we have to fear. We begin to shift into the self-transcendence that Yoga describes, that Maslow describes, that the bodhisattva lives, and in doing so, we assist in the transformation of our world back into connectedness rather than division.

Can we regain the Eden that our ancestors were privy to only a few hundred years ago? Can we expand our worldview to see that nothing is separate from us? Can we look at our history books and what we have been taught by the victors of an attempted genocide? Only the victors write history, and one of my favorite yet tragically true African proverbs states, "Until the lion has a voice, stories of the hunt will always glorify the hunter." Are we willing to speak up for those who cannot speak up for themselves, in language, such as the millions of animals slaughtered every day? Are we willing to protect those who are in harm's way via large-scale development projects that will wreak havoc on the land such as Standing Rock or a trade-way through Lago Nicaragua? Are we capable of returning to a life centered on community efficiency, inter-community trade, and stewardship? We will see.

JOURNAL PROMPTS:

1. Which indigenous people were stewards of the land you are now living on? How many of the names that you see in this place you call home are taken from indigenous names?
2. In what ways have you cut off the sacred interconnectedness in your life? How could you regain that understanding of connection?
3. In what ways could you function as a peaceful warrior in your own local community? In the global community?
4. What do you view as sacred in your life? Do you view any parts of your life as a ceremony with reverence and gratitude?

Journal Prompt #1

Which indigenous people were stewards of the land you are now living on? How many of the names that you see in this place you call home are taken from indigenous names?

Journal Prompt #2

In what ways have you cut off the sacred interconnectedness in your life? How could you regain that understanding of connection?

Journal Prompt #3

In what ways could you function as a peaceful warrior in your own local community? In the global community?

Journal Prompt #4

What do you view as sacred in your life? Do you view any parts of your life as a ceremony with reverence and gratitude?

CHAPTER ELEVEN

New-Age Spiritual Materialism and Babylon

"Being a good spiritual practitioner can become what I call a compensatory identity that covers up and defends against an underlying deficient identity, where we feel badly about ourselves, not good enough, or basically lacking. Then, although we may be practicing diligently, our spiritual practice can be used in the service of denial and defense. And when spiritual practice is used to bypass our real-life human issues, it becomes compartmentalized in a separate zone of our life, and remains unintegrated with our overall functioning."
—John Welwood, Human Nature, Buddha Nature
  interview with Tina Fossella.

"The overriding theme in this spiritual supermarket was that there was something missing which could be provided by the products being sold. Nowhere was the notion evident that perhaps the real problem was that we had too much to begin with, and what we really needed was to let go."
—Venerable Kobutsu Malone, The Engaged Zen
  Foundation

We are in the time of the Internet, a time of identification and information. We gobble up information, we find new ways to get deeper into ourselves, we learn about other cultures, we grasp and we grasp and we grasp. But within our polarized world, amidst all of the amazing resources that exist, misidentification and misinformation are rampant; both which are forms of ignorance.

Throughout my varied current life experiences, there was a constant witnessing of myself unfolding into the generosity and vastness of the world and its inhabitants. There was also a witnessing of the true colors of many of the self-proclaimed highly-spiritual people around the world. From my observations of these communities, they seemed to be structured within a hierarchical structure resplendent with spiritual materialism, phoniness and manipulation in the name of spiritual realization. The community didn't feel communal, and people were really just into their own stories. I giggle when Pema Chödrön says something along the lines of, "when I see someone so smiley all the time I wonder, wow, what repressed anger they must have!"

We as humans in this society find ourselves in quite the conundrum. We are in the pickle of trying not to be unhappy and trying to be happy. First, we are stuck in always trying. As Yoda says, "Try not. Do. Or do not. There is no try." Even in our trying we are in a catch-22. Past our trying, we are still there. We can't be unhappy because no one wants to be around unhappy people. Yet we cannot be happy either because we will be judged as inauthentic, envy will arise in others who are not happy, and people will question us as to how and why we are happy. They'll believe it's inauthentic, thrusting us into doubt and defense. We are so stuck in the middle of not wanting to be something that we are and wanting to be something else that we're currently not, that we never actually are what we are.

The world of advertising puts us into an uphill battle to push against the created feelings of inadequacy. It is difficult to be how you are, imperfections and all. Society tells us it is just not enough. Our peers tell us it is just not enough. Our parents have told us that it just wasn't good enough. Alanis Morissette sings about it in her song 'Perfect'. So we keep trying to accumulate complexity and nuance trying to become more of something which will inflate our own self-worth. Why can't we be who we are? Hence the compensatory self-identity; we idealize ourselves into something that we want to be which is derived from our sense of inadequacy. It's hard not to suffer from this trend in our current world.

Advertising, fashion and new-age trends, including spirituality, the modern vernacular build feelings of defectiveness via buzzwords that become trendy and then die away. The inherent meaning of many of these words is lost, which enables the ultimate purpose to be lost as well. I walked into an intentional community in Pāhoa the other day, and people were drinking cacao, listening to Navajo Flute music, and waiting for sound healing. When I asked about a pen, they snapped at me and told me I wasn't allowed to use a pen. So much for the holier-than-thou spiritual image that they were trying to hold up, can't even use a pen! But it wasn't their fault; I ultimately came around the adverse confusion of feeling attacked to feeling compassion for them. We've all been hoodwinked into trying to be something we are not to fit into a collective unit, a safety net for our insecurities to hide in. As Venerable Kobatsu Malone states, this spiritual materialism game could

"... become an endless occupation, jumping from cosmic consciousness to crystal healing to channeling to pyramidology to energy vibrations, to out-of-body experiences, to déjà vu, to ESP, to Atlantis, to reincarnation to endless other "ologies" and "isms." Truly a never ending story.... always searching, trying to find something, anything, to fill the perceived need that something is missing."[62]

Our bastardization of language also helps to proliferate this camouflage of the Truth. One example is the word sustainable. It is plastered on almost anything now. Sustainable rubber Yoga mats, sustainable panti-liners. We buy them because the word makes us feel good about ourselves, like we are really doing something nifty. What sustainable really means in definition is that they conserve an ecological balance by avoiding the depletion of natural resources. In all of these products, sustainability is out of the question at scale, and probably in day to day operations as well in most businesses.

This concept, which is actually extremely important, is now just a marketing term, spun to appeal to the masses desire for purpose. Nothing is sustainable past a certain threshold, which is why the localized, seasonal economy is the best solution to true sustainability. Spirituality is also becoming a self-marketing term—a way to join a group that will practice the same trendy things with you so you don't feel alone. We keep accumulating and accumulating varied things looking to make us something that we are not. This accumulation only adds to our identity, which pulls us deeper into our own stories.

The more I kept traveling, it seemed to me that many people were still not getting it on the deepest levels of this understanding. They were bypassing their own hard realities and the suffering of others by inflating their imaginary castle and moat to protect themselves or escape their pasts with new forms of identity. Everyone was still experiencing aggression, both gross and subtle. Spiritual gurus were smoking cigarettes, drinking wine, and womanizing. Self-proclaimed Caucasian yoginis were marketing themselves in photo-shoots, dramatically holding indigenous drums and feathers during sunsets to bump up their retreat numbers. People were projecting that they were angelic beings while merely capitalizing on a trend by spinning the economic wheels of an evolving wellness industry. This list could continue, and it does.

We live in a world of charlatans who use marketing and escapism to mask their own inadequacy and loneliness. As of now, within the spiritual community and other communities as well, the problem is that there is so much irrelevance and conflicting information that we have no idea what to believe anymore. We just munch information rather than use critical thinking and discernment. Furthermore, since the Western world honors proof over intuition, science and rationality over experience and belief, whoever can foot the bill on the newest proof gets the business. They get to spread the newest information and spiritual services if they are self-serving.

In some of these new-age spiritual communities in which I lived, I noticed many seekers were still craving higher levels of realization while simultaneously being averse to those who did not share their viewpoints. A spiritual-hierarchical division was forming because of the split of desire; craving and aversion. The more we set our preferences up for these reactions per desire, the more we create division. This lack of acceptance of others therefore was merely altering their desire systems input and objects rather than the desire itself. They wanted to surround themselves with themselves, preach to their choir and sit in their own echo chamber. The craving and aversion was still there, but now it was targeted at a new group, anyone who wasn't them. There was still an enemy, and the enemy was someone who was not as spiritual. Maybe they didn't wear regenerative, biodynamic cotton clothing, or they didn't know what a malachite crystal was, or they hadn't read the Pleiadian Agenda. Whatever gave them spiritual-one-upmanship was the source of the division.

Through travel, I continually witnessed firsthand how climate, environment and social mechanisms were changing across the world. I realized that from many angles, we were living in a perilous time. No matter which way I turned, people were over-identifying with their own individuality at the expense of losing the holistic nature of their existence, simultaneously alienating others. Yes, we all are unique in our own ways, with or without striving, with or without disassociating from others who don't share our belief systems.

We do not need to *do* anything to be unique—nor do trees. But trees are still classified as plants. They don't test out different costumes and try to become fungi. A human is still a human within the classification of a culture, of a consciousness. The uniqueness of the individual is still encapsulated by the existential connectivity that we are all having a human experience. When this individual identification of 'I' becomes stronger than the overarching understanding that we are all humans who need love and don't want to suffer, separateness occurs on a massive level. This creates the underlying mecha-schism (yes, that's a new word) of any form of violence, ranging from envy and judgement, to racism to physical abuse to poverty and war. All are forms of a hierarchical structure of inequality that stems from the lack of true experiential understanding of our connectedness with one another.

HOSTAGES OF IGNORANCE

These side-effects stem entirely from ignorance. We are hostages of ignorance, as Thich Nhat Hahn would say. The omission of information, the spread of misinformation and the denial and deflection of hard truths create ignorance. These truths tap into our self-responsibility structure and rattle us. They make us look at the nuts and bolts. Ignorance, being multi-fold, led to suffering in the spiritual communities as well as other communities in which I found myself. I hypothesize that this is because many of the communities believe that they are better than others or they know the only way, which is false. This misidentification of better-ness because of their knowing is toxic and fleeting. As soon as there is a new way of knowing, we're all on it.

This is the commoditization of a human; turning them into a gradable rubric to fit into your own subjective value system built upon self-righteousness. Any form of this identification with the juxtaposition of human value is actually against the core values of spirituality. This misidentification in itself is an identification. It is a mask of grandeur which is causing more and more confusion and separation in the world by recreating this cycle through individualized networks of social media and lifestyle circles. These are cliques, and by their inherent nature, push others out by identifying themselves as whatever the others are not. It's a new-age spiritual popularity contest. As opposed to dying into identity-lessness, people are using spirituality as a way for them to improve their identification.

These spiritual enclaves are popping up more and more, and they are isolating those who are outside this circle by gating themselves in with ideology. Alongside the ideology comes a fashion. The 'Tuluminati' in Tulum, Mexico are one example, where an ideology of leading the new world order with love and spirituality comes with a side of $149 hats with feathers and talismans. Without the style, you may not be in the group, as you don't fit in. These so-called spiritual values that are preached often use phrases and difficult-to-comprehend-vocabulary that the common man can barely understand. If 'they' are unable to understand, there seems to be an impatience that this person isn't on a certain level, or isn't spiritual.

Let's make this clear, we do not need to do anything to be spiritual. We are Spirit. Each breath is a respiration: in comes the spirit, out goes the spirit. Inspiration is the entrance of spirit for movement, for art, writing, for song. We are all vessels for this energy without doing a thing. By just being here now, we are spiritual. Sri Ramana Maharshi expounds,

"Your duty is to be and not to be this or that. 'I am that I am' sums up the whole truth. The method is summed up in the words 'Be still'. What does stillness mean? It means destroy yourself. Because any form or shape is the cause for trouble. Give up the notion that 'I am so and so'. All that is required to realize the Self is to be still. What can be easier than that?"

New-age spiritualism is just another form of isolation and religion, one which is based in idealism. Idealism is extremely violent because it takes a goal or ambition rather than the present moment for the reality. This therefore separates protagonists from their ultimate goal which is oneness, via division and projection of the moment. How can you be one if you cast others out? Once again, we do not need to do anything to be one. It is supported by the unification theory of quantum scale and cosmological-sized objects that is being worked on by Nassim Harrmein and The Resonance Science Foundation. All we are doing is attempting to experientially understand this existential truth of interconnectedness through our journey of life. We do this by stripping away our models of identification and conditioning, not by creating more.

WHO IS THE CONTROLLER?

The intentions of all of these spiritual movements are mostly positive ones. They are a starting point into looking deeper. The goal is acceptance. At least people can love other people freely in their spiritual community, so it seems. Most intentional communities that I've lived on from Hawai'i to Rhode Island to Australia to Thailand seem to be struggling with a sense of control.

It comes from the question of whether people who give up their desire for control and desire can function within society.

Krishnamurti questions,

"Is there in daily existence a way of living in which every form of psychological control ceases to exist?—because control means effort, it means division between the controller and the controlled; I am angry, I must control my anger; I smoke, I must not smoke and I must resist smoking. We are saying there is something totally different and this may be misunderstood and may be rejected altogether because it is very common to say that all life is control—if you do not control you will become permissive, nonsensical, without meaning, therefore you must control. Religions, philosophies, teachers, your family, your mother, they all encourage you to control. We have never asked: Who is the controller?"

Are we in control to love unconditionally? Is reciprocity necessary in love? Aren't these communities looking for peace still as rife with competition, jealousy, and comparison as mainstream ones? Esoteric interests do not prevent communities from being competitive and controlling. No matter what, we will mostly likely never get rid of our neuroses, so, why keep trying? Just come together, like the Beatles said long ago. It can all be so easy.

Love your enemy. This simple phrase really sums up and encapsulates an essential spiritual truth. When you love your enemy, there is no longer an enemy. You merge. You don't hate them, you just love them and have empathy for them, and in turn, you are loving and having empathy for the part of yourself that they represent. This real empathy creates togetherness because you avow your disavowed parts. There must be no division or aversion from 'them' to 'us', no blame on 'them.' Blame is another form of control, another form of self-pity. We must accept and embrace it all, as you love and accept your friends. Can you love Trump? Maybe humanly it is hard, but on a spiritual realm of equanimity, he is perfect as is. He is just a dude burning off his karma by being what some have been conditioned by society and morals to consider a short-tempered, environmentally-inconsiderate, chauvinistic bigot. Others see him as the epitome of success and the American Dream. Tomato, tomahto. Whatever he is and whatever anybody else is, from culture to gender to race, the point is not to divide and separate us based on these traits. It is merely the flavor of something larger than ourselves, a species put here to find and cultivate wholeness, a collective forgetting into a total remembering.

Until the point of no aversion and no division between anything in our fields of existence, there can never be peace in the world. We are trying to control our environments; we are trying to control our lives. We can go live in an eco-community off-grid on Samoa, but there is still no peace in the world. There may be peace in our individual world, but someone is suffering somewhere. This is due to the internal violence and contradiction that all of us represent by our beings. It is fundamental in division and separation which is buried deep within our self-identification and desires. Many say the root of all evil is money. I disagree. The root of all evil is the ignorance of our true nature. This leads us to have an out-of-balance craving-desire to shelter and protect ourselves from the outside world which we view as dangerous and separate. This creates the greed to accumulate for security, in which fiat currency is a vehicle. Our ignorance of interconnectedness is the cornerstone of control in the archway of violence.

BABYLON—THE AGE OF CONFUSION

Many who listen to reggae have heard the world Babylon. Reggae is rooted in the Rastafari religious and social movement. Artists from Bob Marley to Ronnie Davis to Luciano sing about Babylon. For us to gain a better understanding of this term in our modern-day context, including in spiritual communities, it is necessary to know about ancient Babylon. Babylon was an ancient civilization around 5-6000 years ago in Mesopotamia, ruled by influential kings such as Hammurabi and Nebuchadnezzar. Remember the paraphrased law "an eye for an eye"? That's Hammurabi.

The popular use of the word "Babylon" in reggae music can be traced back to Marcus Garvey's teachings, which liken the African people in the West to the Jews who were exiled in Babylon. For Rastas, European colonialism and global capitalism are regarded as manifestations of Babylon, while police and soldiers are viewed as its means to enforce.[63]

If you look at the planet and how much suffering there is, it is completely unbalanced in places that are not white. With regards to Rastafarianism, Africa and parts of the Caribbean, including Jamaica, are still struggling to survive due to the physical and psychological slavery instituted by white overlords, the kings of Babylon. Slavery leads to racism and poverty.

The overlap of the Biblical stories containing the hardships of slavery acquires meaning in the Rastafarian movement, because there is an eventual emancipation from the hardship. Babylon is labeled as the enemy, the source of their oppression. The Rastas shed more light on the fact that oppression is in fact taking place. I was told once on a beach in Hawai'I, not the Ziggy song, by a Rasta that for him dreadlocks represent Jesus carrying the oppression of the world on his shoulders. This definitive Babylon name and system give oppression a conceptual target, and increase the unity of the people towards right-action.

The word Babylon is not an arbitrary word that is used to describe oppression. Babylon was one of the first cities ever, and it operated under a specific belief system. The modern definition of Babylon describes a type of mentality that is common across economic operating zones and countries. It functions around the materialistic nature of Ancient Babylon, which provides us with a sharp contrast to the ideologies of the Spirit, or Jah. Jah is a short form, the first syllable, of Yahweh, the personal name of God which the ancient Israelites used.

Rastafarian religion places high value on the natural world as something with which we should live in harmony, but not control. Babylon is contrarian to that belief system. For example, modern society values its members according to their wealth and ability to work in a "professional" setting. Babylon mentality sees daily life as utilitarian, but does not place importance on the experiential and mystical elements of living.

The Babylonians were solely concerned with the material aspect of living, and the way that they practiced religion mirrors this tendency. The first records of cuneiform can be traced back to about 5000 BC in Mesopotamia. This language was originally used for accounting purposes and continued to develop throughout the era in which Babylon stood. This transactional mentality governed their lives and extended into their religion.[64]

An 'aha!' moment for me regarding Babylon came in 2015 when my friend's mother from Toronto directed me to meet one of her colleagues in Boston, a man named Jim. Jim was an Aramaic scholar in his 90s who translated the original Bible in his small, cramped South-End Boston apartment; a one-bedroom stacked with dusty books, papers and jazz records. Jim and I enjoyed many conversations that night. In one of them, I asked him about reggae music and if he knew about Babylon, which is mentioned on many different tracks. He told me that he never made the connection from Rastafarianism to Aramaic, but that the word Babylon comes from the root word *Balal* which means "to confuse." When I found this out, I also began researching and found that the word Babel, as in the tower, also has its root in this word. The Tower of Babel is the origin myth about why people speak different languages. At the modern-day site of Shinar, or ancient Mesopotamia, people agreed to build a city and a tower tall enough to reach heaven. God, observing their city and tower, confounded their speech so that they could no longer understand each other, and scattered them around the world.

I then made the hypothesis, that there may be a connection here between this root *Balal* and Belial or Baalial. The prefix of the word, which is the Aramaic letter Beth or the Hebrew letter Bet, is the linguistic-connective tissue. This word Belial, is a term from the Tanakh, or Hebrew Bible, that signifies a sub-sect of people who are characterized as wicked or worthless. Edgar Cayce often discussed in his trance-psychic sessions about his definition of the sons of Belial which was centered around individuals focused on self-gratification. Another translation of this Belial or Baalial is "yoke-less". This word, yoke, brings us back to our definition of Yoga. If Yoga is 'to yoke or unite,' then Baalial, or Babylon, or Balal, is to separate.

Finally, what was happening on so many levels of our cross-cultural-belief system made sense: we've become confused as to who we are because of our belief in separation. Our desire to accumulate worth is contrarian to the fact that our worth is directly interconnected with the Self.

This is also represented by the Kali Yuga in Hindu cosmology. Hindus believe that human civilization degenerates spiritually during the Kali Yuga. Common attributes and consequences are spiritual bankruptcy, mindless hedonism, the breakdown of social structure, greed, materialism, unrestricted egotism, and mental and bodily afflictions and maladies. Hinduism often symbolically represents morality (*dharma*) as an Indian bull. In Satya Yuga, the first stage of development, the bull has four legs, but at each age morality is reduced by one quarter. By the age of Kali, morality is reduced to only a quarter of that of the golden age, so that the bull of Dharma has only one leg.[65]

We live in a world of smoke and mirrors, misinformation, separation, and confusion. It appears to be moving in the direction of more and more division based on fear-mongering, and cloaked in more and more hierarchy and transactional power. This confusion also arises in the spiritual realms as well with the creation of styles of healing, styles of Yoga, and belief systems. We are becoming more and more dependent on others to tell us how we should look, act, smell, heal, and talk.

Krishnamurti states in one of his talks from 1955 in London:

" . . . Being in a state of confusion, we want someone to get us out of that confusion. So we are always concerned with how to escape or avoid the state in which we are. In the process of avoiding that state, we are bound to create some kind of dependence, which becomes our authority. If we depend on another for our security, for our inward well-being, there arise out of that dependence innumerable problems, and then we try to solve those problems— the problems of attachment. But we never question, we never go into the problem of dependence itself."

The confusion is created by the strangeness of our world. We are so far removed from the way that human beings were evolving for tens of thousands of years, that our expression has plateaued on the disconnected platform of the natural world. We have no idea what to do or who to believe anymore. As we seek security within the confusion, we become dependent. With that dependence comes centralization of power. It can range from the government to a spiritual teacher, either one can become a tyrant.

Now, with our instant access to the world via the internet, we are discovering how much of what we have been told is not true. We've been told foods are good for us, but those foods cause cancer. We've been told that our pharmaceutical system can heal chronic conditions, but they're actually incentivized to keep us sick, creating continued income by patching the side effects of additional drugs. People are turning the sacred into trends to be capitalized on; spinning the wheel of fortune and grasping at it trying to commoditize it.

The *LA Times* published an article with Shaman Durek saying, "shamanism is red hot right now."[66] If this sentence doesn't sum up the confusion of the sacred and the profane, I'm not sure what does. As discussed in the article, Durek is a sixth-generation shaman of the Afro-Haitian tradition. You don't just become a shaman because you think it is cool. To quote the movie Fight Club, "sticking feathers up your butt does not make you a chicken."

Durek's points in the article are quite accurate, and echo some things we've discussed in this chapter, but these points are a process, not a goal. They are pathways, not a label. We've taken lineages of process and tried to streamline them with our goals of instant gratification and reward. The trend of using something such as shamanism, which is an ancient and purposeful pathway of interconnectedness and healing to increase your capital gains is not why you do it. Perhaps you would have never been able to do it in the lineages and cultures from which it arose unless it was cosmically written into your birth. The fruitful darkness of confusion can lead to clarity.

I believe this to be the part of Babylon in a cyclical view of time. We had to get lost again to find again what really mattered.

THE WAR AGAINST DIVISION

We live in a world that is governed by homogeneity. Even people have become commoditized. Our homogeneity has us looking for the differences between each-other rather than the similarities so we can feel unique. Numbers on screens are symbolic of life and death. In this age of technology, we want to honor our uniqueness and share our voice. This part of technology is beautiful. People are speaking out, people are sharing information about what they believe in, amazing artists, poets, and musicians have channels to spread their vibrations. Now that people have found their voices, we are finding out how systemic racism, classism, ageism, and ableism are. We are realizing with real eyes the scale of the psychological warfare against us.

The system's status quo has been maintained by those who look to optimize efficiency in generating capital, which has been viewed as economically important. Yet the U.S.A. now faces the highest levels of unemployment in its history and the stock market is at some of its highest value. Over 40 million Americans have filed for unemployment during the pandemic—a real jobless rate over 23.9%.[67] African-American men are constantly being marked as suspicious, man-handled, and killed by police in the name of protection. Peaceful protests are getting teargassed. We are at war, and the war is for our freedom. The war is for our bodily sovereignty and minds.

One of my favorite songs entitled 'The 4th Branch' by Immortal Technique talks about these juxtapositions and this psychological and physical warfare. This psychological war is built upon confusion and lies, where we pledge allegiance to the land of the free and home of the brave which was built upon genocide and slavery.

Despite the Declaration of Independence and the Constitution and the rights that they claim that we have, many are realizing that these documents have not been honored for millions of Americans, including the original inhabitants of our shared continent. These people, such as African-Americans and the indigenous peoples, have been forcibly silenced, forced into systemic racism and oppression with a legal framework as backing, and made to be complacent as the structures of psychological warfare proliferated by the media continue to sway and condition white people's minds out of realizing it.

There is a war against we the people. We the people are all people. We all stem from the same genetics. We are literally brothers and sisters. We are all the same despite our uniqueness, despite how much melanin we have in our skin, despite what language we speak, despite what kind of foods we enjoy. We are people, human beings. The word human could be viewed as hue-man, a spectrum of color expressed in humanity. Whether or not I am vegan and you eat meat, I cannot hate you. I am not at war against you. I love you and want you to be informed that you are part of a system that creates suffering. You are only the problem as long as you ignore the root of the problem. If you choose not to act, I am not affected. Do what you want. I can't change anyone anyway; it's up to the person. You can't force others awakenings; you can only share in a non-attached away. Perhaps they will receive the message where they are at. If I water my garden, your roses don't grow. But maybe you see mine grow and wonder what the deal is and begin to water yours.

We are at war with ignorance and complacency. It is not targeted at a group. We need to unite our groups, not divide them even more. And the more we protest, albeit peacefully at first, the more violence seems to come in and divide us. It is not the people against the cops. It is the people against the viral mindset of exploitation and racism, against sexism, ageism and classism. It is a war against the viral mindset of division and separation as a whole. The mindset exists within ourselves.

Only within this system that drives us apart and frames other groups of people as the enemy can something like homogeneity and privilege exist. The mindset of division is trumping the mindset of acceptance. We are unique and there are many world views that can live under this one atmospheric roof of Earth. Plenty of land, too. Ain't no need to try to suffocate the culture and uniqueness of any group of people in order to live happily and in harmony. We must collaborate, not compete.

THE PATRIARCHY

The patriarchy is a word that is often thrown around nowadays. Often times, what is stirred up results in similar sentiments to the feminist movements; where all men are harmful and they need to be removed so that a matriarchically-organized societal way can come in to smash the patriarchy. What ends up happening here is another massive polarization, pushing away something is creating its opposite stronghold. Grasping is the reaction of the systemic way of living when its identity is threatened. Similar to how many organizations just simply continue existing because they exist, the patriarchy, or, in this case, oppressive patrilineal leadership is just grasping at their positions of power and unwilling to relinquish. However, there is an important point that must arise which is perhaps why the patriarchy arose in the first place and how to not repeat the same mistakes which will enable it to remain in an oppressive state.

In my eyes, the patriarchy is a sub-sect of a culture that feared the power of women. They feared the power of women because of the power of the moon-time, or the bleeding, which is when a woman is at her most powerful, intuitive and spiritually potent. Not all masculine or male-based leadership is toxic and demeaning, many men worshipped the blood as powerful. It enabled women to detox emotionally and become angelic and light. Many indigenous cultures who operated in a patrilineal sense, revered women for their powers during this time and would look to them for visions and connectedness with the spirit world. However, the Church opposed paganism, and within this opposition came the structure and oppression. There is a reason why most people have heard of Eve but not Lilith.

The potential pragmatic shift lies in a few places. One example would be the decrease in mechanization of time that the patriarchal system forces upon women, which is structured into our economic OS. Women operate on cycles, in deep communion with Nature. To continually push them into a linearity in a monthly schedule that does not take into account the sacredness of the moon-time is oppressive. This goes hand in hand with disconnecting them from their immense power as women, as the carriers of life, as daughters of the Moon by forcing them into models of productivity that don't take into account cycles that men don't have. As this mechanization of time has unfolded, women have been forced into believing that their femininity is weakness, that menstruation is inconvenient, and there are emotions around shame and embarrassment. Suppression has taken place on a physical level and also on an emotional level of embracing womanhood as opposed to being societally forced to take on the characteristics of males. This has manifested into things like tampons, birth-control, Midol and the like, as symptoms of this suppression are now being suppressed.

Our society which operates on linear time, as opposed to understanding and embracing the importance of the cycles and connectedness to Nature that women have, have stifled and pushed away these times, forcing this natural flow into a model that limits their power. It could be so easy to introduce flexibility in women's schedules per month as well as provide resources for female community gatherings to learn more into this interconnection and sacredness of the moon-time. It requires an acceptance of our differences and a flexibility of understanding rather than a one-size-fits-all model. The more we appreciate differences and install adaptability into our models, the less we become a judge and the more we become an admirer of our uniqueness.

In this regard, as a man, I begin to have compassion for the patriarchal system itself as I see that it is really just fear. And fear is a conditioned response which the system itself is trapped in. The fear is based on a response to power. Personally, I feel that inherently, most women are much more powerful than men; women are at the mercy of the great mystery and are deeply connected to Nature. Those men who feared their feminine power attempted to siphon control to appear powerful amidst it all which resulted in a model that traps us in homogeneity once again.

The relinquishment of power is practicing non-attachment. Sometimes it takes you to release your limitation of what you think is power in order for the true power to come in. In our economic model, it requires small movements now that can begin with corporate policy to begin to decondition this fear of women into an embracing of their power and connectedness with Nature.

THE POINT OF PRIVILEGE

Over the course of time, privilege and entitlement have become drastic dividers in our society. As we've stated above, when the consensus narrative is driven towards a single race or single economic operating system, it automatically shuns or forces assimilation into a structure of hierarchy which limits other patterns of expression. Hence, the juxtaposition of the 'haves' and the 'have-nots.' The unwanted dependency. Even this language around 'having' is completely biased in terms of the societal stick and carrot system which naturally alienates those for whom the system was not created. As people blindly use their privilege to amass wealth rather than sharing it, the polarities increase, as do the natural reactions of humans on the opposite side of the pole. The very fact that there is a capability to amass such wealth as Jeff Bezos or Bill Gates is the inherent issue in the system. There is no threshold regulation.

Sometimes when I think about privilege, I think about karma.

A few worldviews believe that karma is the indicator for how and when you are reborn. The Bardo Thodol, or Tibetan Book of the Dead, highlights how to awaken through death. Original-ly composed by Padmasambhava, an important Indian master of the eighth century, the Tibetan Book of the Dead was con-cealed in Tibet until it was discovered in the fourteenth century by Karma Lingpa, a famous Tibetan *tertön*, discoverer of ancient texts. Describing in detail the characteristics and fantastic vi-sions of each stage beyond death, the book includes invocations to be read aloud to the dying person, to help his or her successful journey toward liberation.[68]

The journey of transition and eventual liberation from one life to another is guided by karma. Ram Dass says, "Your karma is your mind."

This mind is carried over from lifetime to lifetime. It can be viewed as imprints of specific neural pathways or habits that con-tinued in a life, with enough inertia to push its way through to the next one. The state or realm that this energy passes through is referred to as the Bardo, the transitory time-space-period after death and into another rebirth. Science helps us to understand how karma functions as energy transference.

There is a scientific law called the Law of Conservation of Mass, discovered by Antoine Lavoisier in 1785. In its most com-pact form, it states that matter is neither created nor destroyed. In 1842, Julius Robert Mayer discovered the Law of Conserva-tion of Energy. In its most compact form, it is now called the First Law of Thermodynamics: energy is neither created nor de-stroyed. Then, Albert Einstein announced his discovery of the equation $E = mc^2$ and, as a consequence, the two laws above were merged into the Law of Conservation of Mass-Energy: the total amount of mass and energy in the universe is constant.[69] We are not going anywhere. We are just transitioning between states of being and patterns of energy ad infinitum. When we realize we're not going anywhere and have been doing this for a long while, we can relax a bit!

As karma navigates from life to life, we choose our next incarnation based on the knots that we must detangle, the patterns that we must decondition, the wounds that we must mend. In a spiritually equanimous way, everything is perfect as it is. This is not easy to say if one comes from a war-torn family in Syria or a family of Central African refugees crossing the Mediterranean Sea with their sole possessions on their backs. It is easy to say from my desk in Hawai'i. Sometimes this indifference that karma seems to hold makes people shun the entire belief system. The phrase *suffering is grace* comes into play. If we can truly begin to feel that the wounds we experience are in fact the treasures which we seek, the entire process of hardship may turn into the movement towards connectedness and compassion.

Rather than shun it and create a disavowed fragmentary existence consisting of all of our current predicaments, why don't we utilize it for its function at the moment? What I mean by this is that we can use our incarnations, our karma, our privilege, whatever you want to call it, to help transcend ourselves and to assist our fellows in humanity. The entire point of karma, and therefore privilege, is to help others through the helping of yourself. To be a defender of the people. I see this as relatively plain and simple. This is part of the evolution of lifetimes; the bodhisattva, the Ogichidaag. The question is, how can you use your current incarnation toward healing yourself so that you can be a vessel to heal others and the planet? What are you doing with your privilege? Are you expressing gratitude for the circumstances that you have been dealt through these cosmic cards and your own actions to improve upon yourself and the world? If you're not doing something to this regard, you are not using your privilege for its purpose. You are throwing it back in the face of time without gratitude and appreciation.

The first step is to recognize it on a case-by-case basis. In my case, I am privileged because I am a Caucasian European-American who grew up in an upper-middle class family in the suburbs of Boston. I was blessed to not be in a violence-ridden neighborhood, I never went to bed hungry, and I always had some toys at Christmas. I was blessed to have an education and to learn to read at a very young age, with teachers who showed up to school and who cared as much as they could about the outcome of their students' pathway towards knowledge. I went to university in Boston and have family and friends who support me. I have gathered a skill-set that makes me useful for service. My body is healthy and I have learned how to care for my health and connect with the land. My appearance attracts people towards me physically, so that my voice and message may reach them. Analyzing privilege helps us understand why we are here, and teaches us that it is to be used for self-transcendence and selfless service. First, the service must be directed towards ourselves.

If you are not questioning everything you are being told, you are not honoring your privilege. If you are not leaning deeper into your human-ness and the diversity of worldviews to expand beyond the measly little ego that exists in your conditioned models, you are not honoring your privilege. If you are not using the internet or tools to discover the true histories that have been covered up by our media and governments, you are not honoring your privilege. If you are not dedicating some amount of your skills and income to species or people who are systematically oppressed, you are not honoring your privilege. If you are working day and night on 'problems,' but are not positively impacting those who need your efforts most, you are not honoring your privilege. If you are still creating waste in a world where you can easily sacrifice small levels of convenience to prevent plastic from getting into the oceans, you are not honoring your privilege. If you are not wearing your heart on your sleeve and attempting to rise up against the oppressors of our own brothers and sisters, you are not honoring your privilege.

By giving back, sharing awareness and information, and dismantling oppressive systems, we are doing a small part of honoring our privilege. In doing so, we are honoring and releasing our karma simultaneously. We are helping each-other walk toward collective liberation. Not until everyone's universal basic needs as human beings are met can we have authentic peace as a species. And even then, we must still overcome the conditions of racism and other ideologies that divide us. Not until we are all liberated to express the true Self can there truly be freedom. If we welcome one another and use this interconnectivity and togetherness not for violence and evil, which will create the same things that we don't want, but for peace, we are really getting somewhere.

In the next chapter, we will discuss some of the blind-spots of privilege and how systemic manipulation keeps many aspects of this privilege hidden in plain sight.

I'll end this chapter here with a quote from Mary Oliver:

"The world's otherness is antidote to confusion [and] standing within this otherness—the beauty and the mystery of the world, out in the fields or deep inside books—can re-dignify the worst-stung heart."

JOURNAL PROMPTS:

1. If you consider yourself a spiritual person, in which ways are you using your spirituality as an advantage over others?

2. Do you use any sort of spiritual attainments or experiences to make your identity stronger in your own spirituality?

3.   With all of the information that is circulating the internet and social media, how do you know what to believe? Do you think it is easy to know what is true and what is not?

4.   In what ways do you find that you are polarizing people

Journal Prompt #1:

If you consider yourself a spiritual person, in which ways are you using your spirituality as an advantage over others?

Journal Prompt #2:

Do you use any sort of spiritual attainments or experiences to make your identity stronger in your own spirituality?

Journal Prompt #3:

With all of the information that is circulating the internet and social media, how do you know what to believe? Do you think it is easy to know what is true and what is not?

Journal Prompt #4:

In what ways do you find that you are polarizing people who do not support the same ideologies, belief systems or thoughts as you do? How would you embrace them rather than divide?

CHAPTER TWELVE

The Blind Spots of Privilege

"Prejudice is a burden that confuses the past, threatens the future, and renders the present inaccessible."
—Maya Angelou

"There is no such thing as race. None. There is just a human race—scientifically, anthropologically."
—Toni Morrison

We live in an overtly racist world. We see it in our thoughts and in our workplaces, as well as in more covert places. Slavery is the very framework our country is built upon. It is implemented generationally. The histories that are taught are one-sided; the victors' history. Children are bombarded on many levels with racism from the adults who implement the societal structures. A covert example is the common ice cream truck song. It is actually from a song released in March 1916 by Columbia Records written by actor Harry C. Browne. The title of the song is "Nigger Love a Watermelon Ha! Ha! Ha!" It depicts black people as mindless beasts of burden greedily devouring slices of watermelon.[70] Talk about programming for children. It leeches into our consciousness throughout every single day.

I never really knew what racism was when I was growing up, but I did sense an overwhelming amount of segregation, or rather, absence of diversity in my hometown of Andover, Massachusetts. One member of our basketball team named Chris was black. Other than the difference in his skin color, I never really understood the systemic racism that he would face that still plagues our world today. And somehow, the privileged dominant culture as a whole still doesn't notice it or move against it in a way that the violent behavior of racism warrants. The fact is, we do not move or push against the oppressive nature of our system if it continually benefits us. We like our comfortability. From here, there continues a lack of care from the dominant culture pertaining to the continued segregation and lack of integration of mostly African-Americans and indigenous people in suburban America. There doesn't seem to be any rush for the privileged to change the circumstances of the oppressed. Somehow, and this is the one of the baselines of privilege, the discrimination and oppression feels distant.

This stems from a lack of historical awareness and research as well as the exclusionary and exclusive way that society has been forming and functioning. If we could begin to uncover the multi-layered, multi-generational reason why our reality looks the way it looks, we would question why what is happening seems to be perfectly fine for the average person of the dominant cultural model. It would be difficult for us to go on our merry way interacting with the world on these terms that benefit us alone. We all, and by we I mean mostly the Caucasian culture which is proliferated through capitalism, have blind spots to this very deeply rooted issue that plagues the world because it doesn't seem to affect us.

Many people enjoy not caring what others think; they call it giving zero fucks. It seems to be a pretty popular phrase nowadays. I prefer to give many fucks, and perhaps those who give many fucks can help guide all the dropped fucks from others back to their owners for them to look at and acknowledge. Only the dominant culture would ever create such a phrase as giving no fucks, they have the privilege to give none. We have the luxury to give no fucks and proclaim that everyone should care less about what others think. Mostly, when this no fucks phrase is thrown out, we're talking about clothing or the way you talk or dress, not the systemic oppression and violence that plagues the majority of segregated peoples in the world today. We should be giving plenty of fucks about how the system is harming our brothers and sisters and how we, as people, live with and proliferate unconsciously the conditioned systemic values of oppression. Self-analysis and systemic analysis are both important, and to really delve deep we need to take a step back and look at what is really happening.

In general, I have always felt very lucky. I also feel that I have been exposed to more than the average Caucasian person in relation to cultural exposure. I have traveled to over fifty countries in the past ten years and have lived in Sub-Saharan Africa, in Ghana and Cameroon, for close to two years cumulatively. I consider myself pretty well versed in various countries' cultures, from the varied foods to the music to the dances to the spiritualities and structures of the kingdoms. I have many African and African-American friends whom I consider brothers and sisters. However, I know that I can never fully understand the day-to-day reality that many members of our human family must face on gross and subtle levels. The question led me to believe that due to my lack of understanding experientially, I was potentially feeding into the blind spots of my own privilege.

ALL LIVES MATTER IS RACIST

The phrase 'All Lives Matter' has created a lot of controversy because it comes from a point of blindness from the privileged.

But why is this phrase inherently harmful?

Yes, of course all lives matter. The fact that we even have to validate that all lives matter is atrocious. No reasonable human could disagree with this statement. However, the more that people say this, the more they silence the voices of those attempting to stand up for the systemic oppression that rocks our country and our world every day. Using this phrase is dismissive of the efforts taken and the existing movements of BIPOC to stand up for their lack of equal rights. Although it appears as a unitive phrase, it is divisive in its applications. 'All Lives Matter' stems from the dominant culture's need to compensate for discomfort and ignorance therefore nullifying true vulnerability. The book White Fragility is an amazing resource for these sort of topics. We've never experienced automatic mistrust and foreboding just due to our skin color. We have a responsibility to break down these layers of abjuration.

According to professor David Theo Goldberg, "'All Lives Matter' reflects a view of racial dismissal, ignoring, and denial." This is not even including the demeaning vocabulary of the word 'matters' itself. Trying to get someone to just come to the table saying that their lives 'matter' is appalling. 'Matters' doesn't mean more important than his or her life or any white life, just simply that their lives matter, have worth, have substance. It is similar to the vocabulary used when African-Americans were fighting for civil rights. Civil rights are not even equal rights or human rights, just civility. And even then, the 'civilized' people opposed this civility, and thought that those fighting for these rights didn't deserve even the civil decency that these rights would enable.

Professor Goldberg goes on to state,

"The insistence that Black lives matter accordingly is necessary only because, unlike "all lives," in this society, black

lives are too often taken not to matter. Black lives are presumed too readily in the U.S. not to inhabit the universal .
..Black people are far too readily denied decent education
and employment, stopped and frisked, apprehended, incarcerated, criminalized, animalized, killed.

Black lives in America are the objects of social sus-
picion as their constitutive condition, their very being.
Blacks are presumed to be up to no good, to be no good.
Black lives are flippantly extinguished, not least by cops,
by state representatives, by law and order."[71]

To compound this statement, the hardest part of facing one
of the main blind spots of privilege and essentially racism is the
fact that you yourself might not be overtly racist. You may actually believe that 'Black Lives Matter'. This is a confusing part for
most people. "But I'm not racist!" you may say. And, this could
be true. You may genuinely care and act in accordance with your
belief that our brothers and sisters of a different perceived race
or skin color are loved and important and deserve equality and
freedom. However, the construct of racism doesn't need you to
be or not to be racist; we are a part of the equation by having
the same skin color and culture as the oppressor. We have to
embrace the poles that have been rendered by the ideological
sickness of racism.

Racism is a systemic virus that is functioning within a framework of polarized sides, which, like the yin and yang, are black
and white. If you're not white in this society, you are non-white.
Therefore, for all the white people reading this, if we are in a
room with anyone who isn't of Caucasian descent, we are going
to be automatically considered the colonizer and the oppressor
and they are the oppressed. The tough part is, that this is accurate; these are just the facts. All we can do is recognize the
multi-generational horror that people who look like us created,

and begin to look deeply into the vulnerable and fragile parts of ourselves in order to change, proliferate mindlessly and not re-create the same injustices. Maybe there should be a Racists Anonymous, too, in which the first step is recognizing that based on our skin color we have been conditioned to believe that racism was not a problem. Regardless of where we actually are, we have to embrace the polarities that are unfolding in order to merge them and find balance.

Can we accept, that without any attempt or fault of our own, we have been born into the blood of the colonizers, that within our genetic make-up is the multi-generational responsibility that we must take back and forgive? We must allow ourselves to attempt to feel the pain of those who have been harmed; this is quite the weighted realization to come to. Through the allowance of pain, the change-process comes. This change-process, starting with acknowledgement, is a step that we often dismiss because it pokes one of the core unspoken wounds of atrocity; and wounds being poked are not very comfortable. However, the core wounds guard the treasure of the Heart.

We all like to be comfortable, don't we? We don't like the finger pointed at us, we prefer it pointed at somebody else while we stay safe. This acknowledgement which leads us to beginning the process of forgiveness and reconciliation points the finger back at us to dismantle the oppressive thoughts and belief patterns. As we move through them, it becomes uncomfortable. When it does, we then try to validate the fact that we are not racist or privileged by recalling our actions in the past or with others in our network to prove that we are not racist. This won't help. We are all part of the problem and the solution, simultaneously. Once again, no exclusion. We must embrace it all.

This diversion of responsibility is an aspect of privilege. Privilege gives us the ability to lack responsibility. It provides the ability to take responsibility for only our individual action rather than the action of the whole group or a race of people. For example, if I, a white person, commit a crime, I will be blamed. I might get a warning or a ticket, or I might get arrested. This also depends on status, connections, and other nuances. Perhaps my parents may give me a stern talking-to, but by and large it would be my fault as an individual. I'd probably get off the hook without too much of a hassle unless it was a pretty bad crime. Moreover, my issue is not an issue with the entire white culture, perhaps I am just a bad egg. If an aptly labeled person of color (POC) commits a crime, they are grouped in with an entire sub-section of people who are pointed at as a race rather than as individuals. Also, even if a POC is innocent, they are far too often grouped into the entire racial construct, abused and incarcerated. This happens en masse and those incarcerated fuel one aspect of modern day slavery.

THE PRISON-INDUSTRIAL COMPLEX AND MODERN-DAY SLAVERY

Prisons are one of the modern-day functioning versions of slave labor. One of the reasons it functions in this way is due to the group-responsibility versus individual action. African-American and minority groups as opposed to the dominant culture of Caucasian-Americans are by and large forming the majority of the incarcerated. African-Americans make up 13% of the U.S.A.'s population, but account for 40% of the incarcerated population. That means that African-Americans are five times more likely to be imprisoned than white men. If you factor the Hispanic population into it, you add on 16% of the population and a 19% incarceration rate. In other words, 29% of the population has approximately 60% of the incarcerated humans.[72]

This is called penal labor and is explicitly allowed by the 13th Amendment of the United States Constitution. The US Constitution states,

"Neither slavery nor involuntary servitude, except as a punishment for crime whereof the party shall have been duly convicted, shall exist within the United States, or any place subject to their jurisdiction."[73]

This literally is a loophole built into the system that is being maximized for manipulative and oppressive efficiency of the economic OS. The government gives themselves the right, through a manipulation of the arm of the law, to over-incarcerate whomever they want, in this case it is the African-American and minority groups, in order to serve their means. When they do this, they then have the option of putting them into modern-day slavery, literally, based on their incarceration. BIPOC people's slavery blocks have been transmuted from the open markets to the prisons, as the white man crafts these laws to continue the atrocities our country was built upon.

Federal Prison Industries (UNICOR or FPI) is a wholly owned United States government corporation created in 1934 that uses penal labor from the Federal Bureau of Prisons (BOP) to produce goods and services. FPI is restricted to selling its products and services to federal government agencies, with some recent exceptions. Government agencies have pretty big budgets, and need a large workforce to fill that demand.[74]

Associate Editor of *Prison Legal News*, Alex Friedmann regards the prison labor system in the United States as part of a "confluence of similar interests" among corporations and politicians referring to the rise of a prison-industrial-complex. He stated, "This has been ongoing for decades, with prison privatization contributing to the escalation of incarceration rates in the U.S.A."[75]

For those of you who don't know, we can flesh out a few terms. The prison-industrial-complex is deeply connected with the military-industrial complex. The military industrial complex is an informal alliance between a nation's military and the defense industry that supplies it, seen together as a vested interest which influences public policy. Normally, a driving factor behind this relationship between the government and defense-minded corporations is that both sides benefit—one side from obtaining war weapons, and the other from being paid to supply them, and if I may add, the construction or development contracts afterwards, which includes massive swaths of natural resources for further development based on our exploitative models. The term is most often used in reference to the system behind the military, where it is most prevalent due to close links between defense contractors, the Pentagon and politicians and gained popularity after a warning on its detrimental effects in Eisenhower's farewell address on January 17, 1961.[76]

The prison-industrial-complex uses prison-building and expansion as a means of creating employment opportunities and using inmate labor. These are particularly harmful elements as they require a continual incarcerated populace to create economic benefits.

One of the main players in this complex is CoreCivic, formerly the Corrections Corporation of America (CCA), a company that owns and manages private prisons and detention centers and operates others on a concession basis. CoreCivic manages more than 65 state and federal correctional and detention facilities with a capacity of more than 90,000 beds in 19 states and the District of Columbia. The company's revenue in 2019 was more than $1.98 billion dollars.[77]

Those of us with privilege get to bask in this innocence of individuality and lack of responsibility with our actions. We are not monetized for free labor in prisons, nor are we numbers on a racism death tally. We avoid getting lumped into larger groups that are discriminated against whether or not we commit an action. The remainder of the populace who isn't the dominant culture does not have this luxury. And the government pays for it through sponsored penal labor. All of this stems from the illusion of race that we have been scientifically convinced exists, when it actually scientifically doesn't.

THE ILLUSION OF RACE

Elizabeth Kolbert, a staff writer at *National Geographic* and author of the book *The Sixth Extinction: An Unnatural History* wrote an article about DNA and race in the special issue of *National Geographic* focused on race. She discussed in the article how race is a made-up label which is not rooted in science whatsoever. She explains that the idea of race, which has been deemed false, may have originated with a man named Samuel Morton.

Morton was an 18th century Philadelphia physician and founder of the field of craniometry. He collected skulls from around the world and developed techniques for measuring them. Apparently he accepted skulls scavenged from battlefields and snatched from catacombs. Morton also published '*Crania Americana*' in 1839 while a professor at Penn Medical College, where he divided mankind into five distinct races. He ranked these so-called races by the volume of the braincase, which he supposed correlated with intellectual capacity.

Samuel Morton writes of the 'Ethiopian Race:' "Characterized by a black complexion . . . the negro is joyous, flexible and indolent: while the many nations which compose this race present a singular diversity of intellectual character of which the far extreme is the lowest grade of humanity." Right off the bat, reading this caption, you can tell he is just plain ignorant. We'll go with it for now for congruence.

This '*Crania Americana*' publication became the leading text on racial difference in the United States. Morton collected 867 human skulls during his lifetime, which were gifted to the Penn Museum. With his research, Morton labeled each skull according to ethnicity. This craniometry, which today would be called a pseudo-science, according to his claims showed that whites, or "Caucasians," were the most intelligent of the races. Morton then stated about the rankings: "East Asians— "Mongolian"— though "ingenious" and "susceptible of cultivation," were one step down. Next came Southeast Asians, followed by Native Americans. Blacks, or "Ethiopians," were at the bottom."[78]

These claims by Morton validate modern-day American ideas about slavery and genocide. The genocidal period had already started before these dates with the Spanish colonization during 1492–1832. Furthermore, a few decades before the Civil War, Morton's ideas were quickly utilized by the defenders of slavery to give them validation for their treachery and ignorance. Today, Morton is known as the father of scientific racism.

What we are trying to do now is decondition the belief system of racism as well as reconcile, if possible, what has happened within ourselves and those affected. Once a belief system turns into a deeply-ingrained habit by being set into place by neural pathways, it becomes harder to eradicate, especially if it is a collective habit reinforced by societal constructs. The roots of habit formation are not scientifically proven, so essentially we are collectively operating habitually based on a lie. This lie transforms our politics, our neighborhoods, and our sense of self.

To further this modern-day understanding that the science is not based in truth, at a White House ceremony in 2000, Craig Venter, a pioneer of DNA sequencing who is known for leading the first draft sequence of the human genome observed, "The concept of race has no genetic or scientific basis." Let's dig into this.

Genetic research has really exploded recently, with amazing discoveries of the genome and groups like the Human Genome Project (HGP), 23andme and Ancestry.com. Most of this research according to the genome has shown us that humans all originate from Africa, and we are very, very closely related. In reality, we are more closely related than all chimps. We all, accordingly, have the same collection of genes, outside of identical twins, but have slightly different versions of some of them.

Our collective human species, *Homo sapiens*, evolved in Africa. This is no longer under contention. The place and time of origin is still continually being discovered. Some suggest that anatomically modern human features began appearing as long as 300,000 years ago, and then for the next 200,000 years or so, *Homo sapiens* remained in Africa. Africa, being quite a large continent, enabled these subgroups to migrate to different parts of the continent and become isolated from one another—in effect founding new populations.

The article goes on to discuss two groups on the continent that represent some of the oldest branches of the human family tree. It discusses the Khoe-San, who now live in southern Africa and the pygmies of Central Africa. In fact, the word *pygmy* is also a racist term originating from Homer in Greek mythology, which describes a dwarfish people. The so-called pygmy humans are mostly made up of the the Twa subgroup; hunter gatherers of the Congo Basin. This subgroup mostly consists of the Baka people, the Bambenga, the Bambuti, and the Batwa.

To continue, the article shares that *Homo sapiens* species have evolved more between different subgroups in Africa than outside of the original mother continent. Despite our massive dispersion across the Earth, the majority of the genetic tweaks occurred on the African continent.

The article goes on to say:

"All non-Africans today, the genetics tells us, are descended from a few thousand humans who left Africa maybe 60,000 years ago. These migrants were most closely related to groups that today live in East Africa, including the

Hadza of Tanzania...Somewhere along the way, perhaps in the Middle East, the travelers met and had sex with another human species, the Neanderthals; farther east they encountered yet another, the Denisovans. It's believed that both species evolved in Eurasia from a hominin that had migrated out of Africa much earlier."[79]

Natural selection then became the precursor to evolutionary trait differences. We can call these genetic modifications, like putting on a coat in cold weather. The coat does not change our humanity; it is just an adaptation to the climate. For example, people began to live in high altitudes like the Ethiopian highlands or Tibet or the Andean mountains, and certain genetic mutations assisted in these geographical states.

Looped into this is the fact that since humans have been living on the African continent the longest, they also have the most genetic, and linguistic diversity of any continent. Around 2,000 languages exist on the African continent, split up into language families such as Lingala, Fon, Yoruba, Swahili, Sara, Gbaya, and more. This diversity extends to the amount of melanin in the skin as well as the people from the continent, differing from people in northern Africa, to East Africa as well as West and Central.

As we continue with the illusion of race, the final point of debunking pertains to DNA. DNA really proves that there is no race. What we view as race is only different tweaks in the gene structure itself, which relies on the environment for expression. The genome itself is the same, just like a song on the piano is still a song on the piano, but it sounds different. The piano is still the instrument, just as *Homo sapiens* are still the species. Race is really just expressional diversity. There are no different divisions in humans; we are all humans.

Of course, just because race is an illusion doesn't make it any less powerful in today's world. To a disturbing extent, race still determines people's perceptions, their opportunities, and their experiences. As we see when we fill out different forms such as unemployment forms or standardized tests, in the census, we choose our race from a list that reflects the history of the concept. Choices included "White," "Black," "American Indian," "Asian Indian," "Chinese," "Japanese," and "Samoan."

For such a skeptical, scientific culture that we live in, it seems quite ironic that one of the biggest things that govern how people can live and collaborate is not based on science. It's time we return to the understanding that these diversities of skin color are byproducts of the Earth's varied environments. They are the medicine of life, not the poison. Without this diversity, we would be trapped in the homogeneity that we so often try to escape.

RACIAL TOLERANCE

"In order to understand the brutality of American capitalism, you have to start on the plantation."
—Matthew Desmond

Today, racial tolerance means that we are *tolerating* those of a different or minority race, not Caucasian, to live in our presence and function in society with us. Tolerance appears as a kind word, but it is far from kind in its connotations. Tolerance means the ability or willingness to put up with something, in particular the existence of a group of people, a set of opinions, or a pattern of behavior with which one does not necessarily agree. We are automatically saying that because of someone's race, which we've just discovered is not real based on science in the last section, we *have* to put up with them. It's not even effortless, it is forced because of how upside down the system is. This creates an automatic racial-self-righteousness and a hierarchical scale, which is the same as racism. The phrase racial tolerance is violent and has no place in the ideological vocabulary of human beings who share this planet. So, despite what is being discussed, racial tolerance is really just self-righteousness.

When others attempt to give a dose of the medicine back to the dominant culture, it is gas-lighted and snuffed out by force. As a dominant culture, we don't like having all of our wrongs revisited upon us. We have become too comfortable in this distant world without repercussion of the barbarisms we have committed as Caucasian people.

RACISM, INFRASTRUCTURE DEVELOPMENT, AND LOW-ROAD CAPITALISM

Furthermore, racism is also factored into the infrastructural and civil engineering of urbanized landscapes.

As we all know, slavery and genocide coincided with the history of the U.S.A. Slave masters who were white were always fearfully trying to keep African-Americans at bay, socially and politically. Morton's models of craniometry validated these desires. Before the Civil War, white masters kept enslaved African-Americans at labor in their fields, but with the abolition of slavery, the relationship changed to how they would be enslaved. As opposed to literally enslaving them on their properties, whites wanted them out of sight and out of mind, not interfering with their day-to-day puritanical illusions of grandeur. When this happened, racism began to be implemented as engineered infrastructural planning, hence the presence of ghettos and segregation in the U.S.A.

At first the rule was obvious, like when the cities of Baltimore and Louisville enacted laws that mandated residential racial segregation. Kevin M. Kruse, an American history professor at Princeton University wrote an article on this systemic racism, stating that,

"Such laws were eventually invalidated by the Supreme

Court, but later measures achieved the same effect by subtler means. During the New Deal, federal agencies like the Home Owners' Loan Corporation and the Federal Housing Administration encouraged redlining practices that explicitly marked minority neighborhoods as risky investments and therefore discouraged bank loans, mortgages and insurance there. Other policies simply targeted black communities for isolation and demolition. The postwar programs for urban renewal, for instance, destroyed black neighborhoods and displaced their residents with such regularity that African-Americans came to believe, in James Baldwin's memorable phrase, that "urban renewal means Negro removal."

This intertwined history of infrastructure and racial inequality extended into the 1950s and 1960s with the creation of the Interstate highway system ... As in most American cities in the decades after the Second World War, the new highways in Atlanta—local expressways at first, then Interstates—were steered along routes that bulldozed "blighted" neighborhoods that housed its poorest residents, almost always racial minorities."[80]

As the economics of our newly minted country began to gather steam, they proliferated the model of what sociologist Joel Rogers calls "low-road capitalism." The difference between low-road capitalism and high-road capitalism is the following,

"In low road capitalism the key thing firms compete over is price. There is therefore constant pressure to reduce costs so that prices can be lower. In high road capitalism competition is primarily over efficient production of value, productivity measured not by volume per unit of input, but revenue per unit of input."[81]

When a capitalist society goes low, wages are depressed as businesses compete over the price, not the quality of goods. So-called unskilled workers are typically incentivized through punishments, not promotions. inequality reigns and poverty spreads. Worker rights basically get annihilated. This still exists today. This also leads to the massive juxtapositions of wealth that exist within our society. If raw material for an iPhone is going for pennies on the dollar, but the iPhone itself is selling for upwards of $750, where is all of the markup going? The massive low-road capitalistic model without barrier thresholds to ameliorate exploitation creates massive inequality, poverty and oppression worldwide.

According to a different article written by Matthew Desmond, a sociology professor at Princeton University: "...consider worker rights in different capitalist nations. In Iceland, 90 percent of wage and salaried workers belong to trade unions authorized to fight for living wages and fair working conditions. Thirty-four percent of Italian workers are unionized, as are 26 percent of Canadian workers. Only 10 percent of American wage and salaried workers carry union cards ... "

This same article goes on to state,

> "Slavery was undeniably a font of phenomenal wealth. By the eve of the Civil War, the Mississippi Valley was home to more millionaires per capita than anywhere else in the United States. Cotton grown and picked by enslaved workers was the nation's most valuable export. The combined value of enslaved people exceeded that of all the railroads and factories in the nation. New Orleans boasted a denser concentration of banking capital than New York City. What made the cotton economy boom in the United States, and not in all the other far-flung parts of the world with climates and soil suitable to the crop, was

our nation's unflinching willingness to use violence on nonwhite people and to exert its will on seemingly endless supplies of land and labor. Given the choice between modernity and barbarism, prosperity and poverty, lawfulness and cruelty, democracy and totalitarianism, America chose all of the above."[82]

We need look no further than the slave auction blocks to understand America's low road capitalistic approach which has taken away people's rights and how our value system has been structured. This is the foundation of our modern capitalistic system and the multi-generational wealth that arises from it.

ALLYSHIP—BEYOND THE POLARIZATION

One of the basic things that we can do is open our eyes and see that racism is everywhere, every day. Just as our value system influences the economy, and legislation impacts our day to day lives, view the undercurrents of how racism is affecting your daily life. A privilege of being white is the freedom to not deal with racism all the time. As we begin to notice who speaks and what is said we see how things are done and how they are described. Certain people may not be present when racist talk occurs or they become defensive or deflective. Bring your awareness to hidden words for race, and the implications of the patterns, comments and policies that are being expressed. You already notice the skin color of everyone you meet—now notice what difference it makes.

By beginning to notice who is the center of attention and who is the center of power, we begin to see how violence is blamed on people of color, and how power and privilege is the provincial state of white people. We then can see how racism is denied, minimized, and justified.

A next step would be to dig into the history of the oppressed. As discussed earlier, nothing is really changing except the terminology and methods; the base of racial division is intact. Racism is really just an extender that creates economic issues, sexism, and other forms of injustice, so we must look at the ripple effect of what is unfolding throughout the entirety of the system itself. By witnessing what is happening and beginning to understand the hundreds of years of this maltreatment and abuse, a fire should be stoked to take a stand against injustice. These things are not comfortable, and will bring up fears and feelings of inadequacy, indecision, helplessness, or fear of making mistakes. Like a bike ride, you have to keep moving. Indecision and inaction are decisions.

Like water in a jug, racism takes the shape of the societal container that it is in. There will be ups and downs in the struggle for justice and equality, but we are striving for equilibrium. Attacking people doesn't address the systemic nature of racism and inequality, so it is best to look to avoid the reactionary nature of most aspects of the 'us' versus 'them' mentality.

Martin Luther King, Jr. states:

> "Violence as a way of achieving racial justice is both impractical and immoral. It is impractical because it is a descending spiral ending in destruction for all. It is immoral because it seeks to humiliate the opponent rather than win his understanding; it seeks to annihilate rather than to convert. Violence is immoral because it thrives on hatred rather than love."

As more and more people support the leadership of people of color, we will all unite and work together to build support networks, and collaborate with established groups to do the work together. Last but not least, include your children in the educational and action-oriented movement; they are the next-generation of leaders who can lead without bias and oppression. At the end of the day, we are all humans, and we must rise together so that we can live in peace in the understanding that what binds here on Earth is much more mighty and profound than what separates us.

JOURNAL PROMPTS:

1. One of the blind spots of privilege is that it doesn't necessarily only make the dominant (Caucasian) culture superior—it normalizes it. Can you think of any ways that you've participated in normalizing this dominant culture at the expense of other cultures?

2. How do you deal with feedback or constructive criticism when it comes to viewpoints you believe, honor or have learned over the course of your life? Does it insist on your fears, or do you take the feedback and use it to grow and change? How can you begin to grow in this area of vulnerability?

3. Unlearning takes years. While in this process, how can you walk in love instead of judgement, so that you can learn and not become defensive and deflective which creates more polarization instead of unity?

4. How has your desire or attainment of comfort kept you from taking action in situations that may seem uncomfortable? You can also share about instances when you didn't let uncomfortability keep you from acting—how did you feel then? Was it as bad as you projected it to be?

Journal Prompt #1:

One of the blind spots of privilege is that it doesn't necessarily only make the dominant (Caucasian) culture superior—it normalizes it. Can you think of any ways that you've participated in normalizing this dominant culture at the expense of other cultures?

Journal Prompt #2:

How do you deal with feedback or constructive criticism when it comes to viewpoints you believe, honor or have learned over the course of your life? Does it insist on your fears, or do you take the feedback and use it to grow and change? How can you begin to grow in this area of vulnerability?

Journal Prompt #3:

Unlearning takes years. While in this process, how can you walk in love instead of judgement, so that you can learn and not become defensive and deflective which creates more polarization instead of unity?

Journal Prompt #4:

How has your desire or attainment of comfort kept you from taking action in situations that may seem uncomfortable? You can also share about instances when you didn't let uncomfortability keep you from acting—how did you feel then? Was it as bad as you projected it to be?

The Return to Nature

"Look deep into nature, and then you will understand everything better."
—Albert Einstein

"Adopt the pace of Nature. Her secret is patience."
—Ralph Waldo Emerson

I'd like to start off first with a story of a beautiful community that I have lived on for many months. On the Big Island of Hawai'i, when you turn off the main road onto South Point Road, you journey down the slopes of Mauna Loa. Weaving through the rolling hills, you feel like you are on another island, the ocean a blue expanse in front of you. The community-land is hidden off a tiny, sparsely paved road which links to gravel and dirt filled with peridot stones. To find it, you must weave like a lilikoi vine. You find yourself tucked away in what feels like a dream. This property is designed so that the beauty and bounty of nature is all around you, blooming like the iris flowers on the pathways. The Hawai'ian name of the community can be broken down into four sections that represent 'a peaceful oasis for the transformation of the sacred light.'

When you wake up in the morning, fruit is on the ground. Depending on the season, there will be noni fruit, lemons, starfruit, Surinam cherries, grapefruits and tangerines waiting to be swooped up and eaten. Throughout the day, papayas ripen and lilikoi shine, beckoning you to bite into their juicy interior. Once you spend some time with the land, or the 'Āina, as it's referred to in Hawai'i, you immediately recognize that it takes mindfulness to tend to it and to build a healthy relationship with it. If you don't do your part, nature notifies you that you are not caring for it or that your intention is off. I've heard from some people up in the tablelands of Oregon and Idaho say that some root vegetables strangle themselves from a lack of human presence for harvesting. The plants become lonely and kill themselves. We often forget that we are merely a part of Nature, and that Nature is a part of us. We are intricately linked for our own survival. Trees breathe in carbon dioxide and we breathe in oxygen. Where's the separation? The process of forgetting and remembering our connection to the land comes in and out like breath. As long as our breath reminds us of our connection to the Earth, we are working our way back in.

Speaking of work, the steward of this particular community doesn't enjoy using the word 'work.' She prefers to use the word 'dance.' This relates to the Sanskrit word *Lila* or the divine play and *Nataraja*, or the depiction of the divine, dancing Shiva. We don't work with a table saw, we dance with it. She reasons that in our society, work has the negative connotation of duty. A lot of people segment their lives into work and not work. The separation of what we are working on versus what our passion is is quite often very deep. We can become so specialized that our mind has a hard time thinking creatively outside of our work that consumes us. Anything else outside of this work becomes a hobby, if you have time to focus on it and energy to pursue it. Oftentimes, work takes up so much of our lives that we are left unhealthy, drained and bereft of inspiration for the living of our life. If you have found your passion, perhaps the passion can be turned into such a grind and a chore when it is attached to work that it becomes dull or tedious. Such is the transactionary state of being revolving around currency and having to work to survive. This working to survive is another veil that has been pulled over our eyes. I wonder what it would be like if instead of work: life balance, there was life: work balance? A simple shift in the order of the phrases may result in a drastic measure of the recognition that life comes first.

When living in nature, everything becomes very simple. These constructs begin to fade away. The only currency that is truly of value is that which provides life; that comes from the Earth in many different patterned forms of rainwater, soil, air and light, fruits and vegetables, animals and fungi. All of these substances are converted into ourselves through processes of consumption. Converted light makes up our inputs. The sunlight comes down and is transformed into the physical structure of food through photosynthesis which executes its function on the substrate of soil and air. The medium of which we breathe, or our physical body's metabolism of energy is also a part of the interconnectedness of the quantum vacuum, which was discussed before in the chapter about Yoga. Any other material needs that have been added on top of these sustenance needs are completely fabricated out of desire and are not necessary in the scheme of our thriving as humans. When we truly are minimalists, we begin to minimize anything superfluous towards the cultivation of a deeper relationship with ourselves. It may be a style of architecture and a nice buzzword that is floating around, but true minimalism is returning back to the Earth and living in commune with it.

When in certain places, especially Hawai'i for me, the land is so alive and vibrant that I feel like I am being watched. This property has the same feel—that of a thousand eyes are watching you. The trees know what you are thinking, and respond accordingly. One of the temporary conclusions that I came to while in the community was that I was basically walking around my own mind. If I had a fear of something, the land would point it out. If I wasn't mindful or got greedy, the land would notify me immediately. Nature is a perfect mirror. The land on the island is so vibrant with life force, or *mana* as they call it in Hawai'i, that you start to feel how much life force lies dormant within yourself. We are only learning what such life can create within us as it ripples through us on every level. And, like Nature, the more we can channel this life force without grasping onto it for our own selfish means, the more abundance will yield for everything interconnected with ourselves.

One thing is for sure, working and dancing with Nature guides us to decondition the stories that bind us. This happens through our labor with the land. We work with the land until there is no difference between where your hand ends and the soil begins. We dance with the land until the perceiver and perceived elide. The doing becomes a happening. This is the state of non-duality. When you are fully engaged with your task on the land, whether it be using a sickle saw to uproot guinea grass or to uncover an ancient Hawai'ian heiau that has been covered in strangle vines and wild asparagus thorns, the absorption into the natural environment around you at times can be so deep that you finally understand the existential interconnectivity and non-separateness that is inherent on planet Earth. This interconnectivity is a universal Truth. As we've seen in previous chapters, sometimes it is labeled the *Tao*, sometimes *Dhamma*, sometimes *Purusa*, sometimes the quantum vacuum. The sometimes will be endless, but the something is the same.

When we become fully merged in an act where the perceived receiver is outside of yourself and all you are is a vessel of service, the barrier between the two entities of subject and object begin to blur like the colors of the sky during the changing of light between dusk and dawn. A similar blurring of depth or dimensionality occurs for me when I ingest a medicine such as cannabis or psilocybin. The world doesn't change per se, but the profundity of perception increases and the veils on our eyes connected to the controlling conditions of thought begin to soften and come to a natural cessation. As this happens, the threads that form the veil slowly disconnect themselves from one another and the light of wisdom and interconnection can pass through.

NAVIGATING OUR MINDS THROUGH NATURE

While I was on this particular land, I would often find myself walking around in between trees or tasks and wondering, on an existential level, "where am I right now?" As I perceived the external world through my eyes, which rendered reflected imagery into my brain to be processed, recognized, and acted upon, I began to recognize that we only truly navigate our own minds. We are enclosed in our own self-made labyrinth. We know the way out and we hold the keys. We are the blocks we set up for ourselves. Like its origin in Ancient Greece, the labyrinth's function was to hold the Minotaur, the monster eventually killed by the hero Theseus. Daedalus, the creator of the labyrinth had so cunningly made the maze that he could barely escape it after he built it. This rings true for our own minds as well.

We have monsters like the Minotaur within us; parts of ourselves we don't like to show because of the fear of shame, rejection, or fallibility. We have blind spots, we have weaknesses.

Our minds are bombarded with pathways created through the plasticity of the brain. I have begun to view my brain like a vast mountain of various hiking trails. There are certain trails which I have trodden for the past thirty-years, and those trails are quite well-worn. Some of these trails may not be useful anymore for navigating the mountain, although at the time they served their purpose. As a hiker, I can begin to choose which trails I want to continually walk and which ones I don't. By choosing, or forging new trails for walking on the mountain, I allow the well-worn trails to rest, and through rest is re-growth. Flowers and trees and shrubs will pop up on these well-worn trails and Nature will take back over so that trail is no longer walked upon. It merges back with the forest. As I begin to view my habitual structures in this context, it becomes easier to understand how simple it really may be.

According to an article on the neuroscience of behavior change, neural pathways, composed of neurons connected by dendrites, are created in the brain based on our habits and behaviors. The number of dendrites increases with the frequency of a behavior. I picture these neural pathways as deep grooves or roads in our brain. Our brain cells communicate with each other via a process called "neuronal firing."

Psychologist Deann Ware, Ph.D., explains that when brain cells communicate frequently, the connection between them strengthens and "the messages that travel the same pathway in the brain over and over begin to transmit faster and faster." With enough repetition, these behaviors become automatic. Reading, driving, and riding a bike are examples of complicated behaviors that we do automatically because neural pathways have formed."[83]

This process of self-navigation through Nature is the true journey of awakening. We have the capability to rebuild our neural pathways each and every day. We can do it with belief and practice. Or, if we want some help, it has been proven scientifically that psilocybin has neuro-generative effects in the hippocampal regions as well as trace-fear conditioning.[84]

It is easy to fall into habits, but we have the potential, with our brain's amazing capacity for plasticity, to heal negative habit patterns and tread more compassionate pathways. Similar to our example earlier of walking new trails, enabling healing to occur. We have the capability to tread more fruitful pathways every single day. We use effort to move towards our effortlessness, yet to get on the path it requires a discipline of willingness. We walk these paths within our own Souls through the external world to help us unravel the internal world of this life and lives immemorial.

NATURE'S MIRROR

Seeing Nature as something to be beautified and stewarded is really the recognition that we are to be beautified and stewarded ourselves. Not in the superficial sense, but on the deepest levels that are capable of being fathomed by thought. As we begin to truly integrate the understanding that everything we do is a ceremony and the ceremony is in fact leading us back through ourselves, we become our own altar, our own temple, our own forest. We begin to exhibit pure selfless intention of action like Nature. Nature gives selflessly, with no thoughts of reciprocity. We expand beyond the body and the ego-centric identification of "I." Nature becomes the altar on which our relationship to others, human and non-human, unfolds. The altar is the Earth, our connection with Nature and the gratitude to be invoked through the purest relation there is. The altar of Nature allows us to begin to love ourselves. The altar is every moment, passing by like clouds in the sky, perfectly imperfect and ever changing. Beauty exists because of the impermanence of all things in Nature, and to embrace the fleeting immaculate conception of every moment as new is to fully embrace the immense and awesome mystery of life. As we tap into this moment by moment unfolding in presence, we experience innocence. Nature helps usher in these feelings of child-like wonder, which is the pathway back home.

The famed New Age author and artist José Argüelles, who

organized the Harmonic Convergence in 1987, writes of the Mayan discussion about a new evolution of humans directly in communion with the land as it was before. These humans expand beyond this Earthly realm into other realms. Harmonic Convergence was the world's first synchronized global peace meditation. Through our connection with Nature, we become multi-dimensional and begin to understand language that does not come through in words.

The word multidimensional can often be viewed in a little bit of a 'woo-woo' sense. However, dimensions do not necessarily only refer to science fiction novels. The word dimension is multi-dimensional as well. As human beings, we are multidimensional, or multi-faceted. Things are operating on many different layers, visible and invisible. Through specific situations, we witness our expression. While in Nature, the platform of expression is brought back into a hoop. The hoop is the cycle of our relationship with an integral dimension of ourselves, which is the natural world. The seasons to plant, when the rain comes, the season to harvest and spread seed simultaneously to make sure that next year there are more plants than this year. Co-creating and regenerating the land is our chance to co-create and regenerate ourselves. We need not look any further in front of our own noses than the ground on which we walk. The way back home is the return back to cooperation with the land and the worldview to protect it as we would our own family.

The disconnect that exists can easily begin to be mended. It is as simple as digging your hands into the soil. If you haven't ever planted a seed and tended it so it may grow and become a plant or a tree, I highly suggest participating in that process. It is identical to the processes of our own humanity. On the physical level, from the seed or ovum meeting the sperm, we were loved and nurtured inside the dark and warm and moist area of the womb, like plants in soil. From here, we could begin to form in the process of germination. As we emerged into the light, we needed nutrients and those to watch over us carefully so that no parasites, animals or bugs came and tried to harm us. And slowly but surely, we grow. We grow to the point where hopefully we can yield fruit to others and from there spread our own seeds on the same land from which we have sprung. On a psychological level, an idea, thought or a belief is a seed. We water it in the depths of our mind, over and over we turn it like a coin on a gambler's fingertips. These ideas eventually, if watered enough, begin to take root. Once they've taken root, they begin to grow from a thought into an idea into a belief. These beliefs may not always be the sweet and succulent banana-kind that you want in your mind-garden of Eden. They may be the weeds, or the strangle vines.

If you've ever inspected weeds or strangle vines, they look peculiarly like the plants, so it becomes hard to differentiate what is edible from what is predatory. They are so tricky in fact, that they may look, smell and appear identical to other plants; a brilliant survival tactic of the weeds. It begs the question, if we view our minds as a garden, what weeds are we allowing to grow? What weeds are growing that we don't recognize as weeds? Are we allowing bad habits, conditions or harmful belief systems take root in the fertile soil? Are these weeds strangling out the trees that should be yielding fruit? What people in our life are like weeds? The ones who take and take yet yield nothing in return that assists with our growth; in fact, they stunt it. You can begin to get pretty deep into the mind-garden while you're out there in silence with the Earth. She shows us what is inside.

My first journey deep into the mind-garden was at Mouna Farm on the island of O'ahu in 2013. For the first month when I arrived on the farm, I had to weed six hours a day for a month. By the time the first two weeks were over, a lot of internal baggage and patterns were coming up. Thoughts of "What am I doing? This is stupid." to "Is this really necessary? I have a college education." Self-judgements, judgments of others, conditioned response over conditioned response arose. Slowly, I began to view the places where I was weeding in the garden as parts of my own mind. Every time I pulled out a weed, I would pull out a toxic thought pattern. Every time I would beautify an area, I would feel more beautified myself. I was weeding out my own karmic seeds. This was my first deep experience into the experiential mirror that Nature provides. Now, seven years later, I have my PhD in weeding. Through pick-axing the roots out of large clumps and sickling away the excess to be burned, as long as you get to the roots, the weeds disappear forever.

SIMPLE LIVING, HIGH THINKING

Bill Mollison, the Australian researcher who helped to spread the theory and practice of permaculture states,

> "The greatest change we need to make is from consumption to production, even if on a small scale, in our own gardens. If only 10% of us do this, there is enough for everyone. Hence the futility of revolutionaries who have no gardens, who depend on the very system they attack, and who produce words and bullets, not food and shelter."

The more we collaborate with Nature and provide for her, the more she will provide for us. It is quite beautiful, and simple. The common mantra at Mouna Farm, where I began my Hawai'i journey in 2013, coined by the owner Sooriya Kumar, was "simple living, high thinking." This four-worded mantra is one of the keys to unlocking our woes.

Essentially, if I could sum it up, it would be to move away from materialism as well as the thoughts that create materialism. Move away from a reward and punishment lifestyle based on a value system that operates on maximizing self-interest and accumulating. Move away from this concept of linear time. Nature operates on cycles, and so do we. Nature is a constantly unfolding process, and so are we. The more and more we move away from levels of linear thinking the less and less we need to rely on other things to allocate our worth to. Therefore, the less you have that takes up your energy through thought or upkeep, the more you become. Your energy is being brought back in from the external world; a reclamation of power. The tether to mainstream society becomes looser and looser, until materials cannot fulfill any such desire you have. This is simple living. Simplicity is how you can maximize the expression of life through yourself.

As we simplify our lives, we truly begin to see how food sovereignty is the way towards decolonizing our minds. Seeds carry memory. The land carries memory. As we begin to see the abundance that the natural world provides, we decolonize our thought process to witness the reasons why we are attached to an economic system that requires us to work to live. As we do this, it becomes simpler and simpler to identify what steps must be taken to extricate yourself from that system. The basic substance of our survival depends on our understanding of cycles in relation with Nature. The cycle of the seasons, the cycle of food growth, the cycle of animals. This is the Hoop, in which humans are an integral part. The commune or union of humans in the cycles of Nature is key in our reclamation of power. The toiling away the hours in order to fill your time with distraction and superfluous material and identified thought forms will fall away as Nature is brought to the forefront. The merging of the technological systems of now with the wisdom of the land of indigenous traditions is a large part of the continued evolution in the consciousness of humanity.

High thinking comes in accordance with self-transcendence which is discussed earlier. The high thinking can be viewed as taking a zoom-out moment, a shift in vantage point. Imagine flying high above the land into the atmosphere and taking a glance down at Earth. The less you need, the more you can now dedicate towards others. Others are just extensions of ourselves, just as certain plants in the forest are extensions of the forest itself. As we become less and less attached from materialism, we move into a different direction. The direction of *vairagya*; or non-attachment. This is the complete equanimity or even-keel attitude of possessions of any kind, mental or physical.

When you are equanimous about these possessions, you avoid any accumulation as a whole. It is better to just give with no expectation of reciprocity or return then to hold onto something for safe keeping. Nature doesn't accumulate. Put down what you're carrying; you've been holding that weight too long. Compost your own identification into the fertile soil of the divine. When we relinquish the weight of our own image of what we think we are, it's like removing the emotional weight of a dumbbell off your back. It is a relief to no longer carry around the patterns that never served us in the first place! It is a long journey, but there is no better companion to go on the trek back to our own responsibility and power than with nature.

I wrote a short poem called 'Links' that follows us through our journey into equanimity.

> objectivity is the link to equanimity
> equanimity is the link to non-attachment
> non-attachment is the link to acceptance
> acceptance is the link to compassion
> compassion is the link to love
> love is the link to joy
> joy is the link to innocence
> innocence is the link to eternity

JOURNAL PROMPTS:

1. Describe your most significant experience with nature. Remember to weave in the sights, sounds, smells and other sensory details of the experience. Did it have a positive or negative effect on your relationship with the natural world? Did the experience change you as a person?

2. Imagine that one day you went out for a walk and the trees began to speak to you. What do you think they would say about their relationship to humans and how would you respond? Do you think it would change the way you interact with the natural world?

3. When is the last time you simply sat in nature and observed? What was your experience like? Why do you think it is so difficult to just sit and be, without doing anything? How does this difficulty to just sit and observe hinder our expression in life?

4. What similarities do you see between humans and the natural cycles of Nature? How does the way that we treat Nature describe how we treat ourselves as humans and other species? In what ways do our current models of the world honor these methods?

ACTIVITIES:

1. Begin to notice the different types of trees, shrubs and plant life around where you live. Is any of it edible? Perhaps you can learn to identify the types of nature around where you live.

2. Spend 15 minutes in Nature everyday just sitting and observing. No cell phone, no added on stimulation.

3. Look into your own communities and see if there are any projects that may be initiated to benefit the community as

a whole in regards to Nature, preservation or the like.

4. Research local food producers and farms. If you have space, maybe you can even begin to grow some of your own food!

Journal Prompt #1:

Describe your most significant experience with nature. Remember to weave in the sights, sounds, smells and other sensory details of the experience. Did it have a positive or negative effect on your relationship with the natural world? Did the experience change you as a person?

Journal Prompt #2:

Imagine that one day you went out for a walk and the trees began to speak to you. What do you think they would say about their relationship to humans and how would you respond? Do you think it would change the way you interact with the natural world?

Journal Prompt #3:

When is the last time you simply sat in nature and observed? What was your experience like? Why do you think it is so difficult to just sit and be, without doing anything? How does this difficulty to just sit and observe hinder our expression in life?

Journal Prompt #4:

What similarities do you see between humans and the natural cycles of Nature? Do you think we are a part of Nature or the controllers of it? In what ways do our current models of the world honor one or the other?

CHAPTER FOURTEEN

Equanimity is the Key:
A Lesson from Vipassana

"Service is how you deal with suffering; it awakens intense emotions. Your heart will break and you have to let it. But, you've cultivated another plane of reality that notices it and allows it—a plane of equanimity."
—Ram Dass

"You always own the option of having no opinion. There is never any need to get worked up or to trouble your soul about things you can't control. These things are not asking to be judged by you. Leave them alone."
—Marcus Aurelius, Meditations

If any of you reading this have completed a Vipassana meditation, you will be familiar with the term equanimity. In Buddhism, it is one of the four sublime attitudes, and corresponds with neither a thought nor an emotion. Rather, it is the steady, conscious realization of reality's transience. It is the ground for wisdom and freedom, and the protector of compassion and love. By embracing equanimity, you embrace the constancy of change without clinging to how it moves or how you move within it.

Throughout the Vipassana meditation, which I cannot recommend highly enough, you move deeper and deeper through the bodily sensations, watching them rise and fall away as objective phenomena. The goal, if you can call it a goal, of the meditation technique is to become completely equanimous with the sensations themselves; cultivating a space of non-reaction. Essentially, you begin to extricate yourself from the sensations as subjective by being able to view them and whatever is triggered through them as constantly changing and impermanent. The word in Pali, the language of Gautama Buddha, is *anicca*. *Anicca*, as mentioned in the chapter about Yoga, means changing. By understanding the nature of change, we begin to unravel our own sense of the 'I' as a separate entity and move deeper into a space of observation. As our quantum molecular structure is buzzing around in particles and waves that are constantly changing, which one of those molecules is 'I?' We are never the same 'I' as we were ten minutes ago, or even ten seconds ago. The discontinuity is so rapid and seamless that we assume continuity. Without this continuity, we would have no way to understand what we view as ourselves or time, hence the purpose of us building storylines. But according to physics, we are new every moment, and all of these storylines merge into one continuous, all inclusive storyline of consciousness.

One day, when I started to think about the rapid discontinuity that we are a part of, I intuited what the sound *Aum* may be. In my theory, if the rising and passing away of phenomena on a quantum level is so rapid that it appears continuous, perhaps it appears like a sound to our senses. The sound of *Aum* may be the sound of change.

We are so bombarded with change in this world. Because of this uncertainty, we seek security, and security is reliant on dependence or attachment. To this regard, Krishnamurti states:

"So long as there is attachment, dependence, there must

be exclusion. The dependence on nationality, identification with a particular group, with a particular race, with a particular person or belief, obviously separates. So it may be that the mind is constantly seeking exclusion, as a separate entity, and is avoiding a deeper issue which is actually separative—the self-enclosing process of its own thinking, which breeds loneliness."

As he states above, we formulate belief systems, prejudices, and judgments which separate us and them. We attach to outcomes based on these belief systems, and if these outcomes are not met, we are outraged—oftentimes rightfully so. But our outrage very often only creates more division, which doesn't get to the end result we are hoping for.

EQUANIMITY AND CONSCIOUS RESISTANCE

Conscious resistance is necessary and rises out of informed belief systems. If we attach to something changing based on our expectation models of how we want it to change, we will always be unsatisfied, as our needs may never actually be met. Equanimity solves for this. It is one of the keys to accepting reality as it is rather than clinging to our expectations for it. This does not mean indifference, nor does it mean inaction. However, if we are attached to how we want things to be and they end up differently than how we expected, then suffering arises. A part of conscious resistance is resisting falling into trap to our attachments.

We can try to lay our judgments and opinions of righteousness upon it, our own stories we overlay on top of it that create our subjective and collective realities. Spiraling together in Coriolis, we are connected in the vacuum of our own minds. Our expected outcomes are delusions. Imperfections are illusions. In fact, imperfections are natural in being human and are of the utmost importance to accept. Without equanimity, we can never have peace. We must love our people, not hate the enemy. We must reallocate the attention we channel as intention towards feelings of togetherness and compassion rather than creating division through violence and expectation.

This is part of *ahimsa*. Many of you may be aware of Mahatma Gandhi. His practice of *ahimsa* and *satyagraha* during Britain's Salt Act of 1882 is one of the prime examples of equanimity and non-violence in peaceful protestation and action. For some historical context, The Salt Act prohibited Indians from collecting or selling salt, a staple in their diet. Indian citizens were forced to buy the vital mineral from their British rulers, who, in addition to exercising a monopoly over the manufacture and sale of salt, also charged a heavy salt tax. Gandhi declared resistance to British salt policies to be the unifying theme for his new campaign of "satyagraha," or mass civil disobedience, and marched with thousands of Indians from his religious retreat near Ahmedabad to the Arabian Sea coast, a distance of some 240 miles. The march resulted in the arrest of nearly 60,000 people, including Gandhi himself. India was finally granted its independence in 1947. His equanimity didn't render him indifferent or passionless, but it enabled the re-programming of the hatred of the enemy British into a non-attached outcome centered around compassion for the people. That's equanimity in action.[85]

This understanding of non-reactivity, or equanimity, was one of my take-aways from the Vipassana meditation that I participated in while on Aotearoa, or New Zealand, on the North Island at Dhamma Medini.

S.N Goenke states:

"Any moment in which one does not generate a new saṅkhārā, one of the old ones will arise on the surface of the mind, and along with it a sensation will start within the body. If one remains equanimous, it passes away and another old reaction arises in its place. One continues to remain equanimous to physical sensations and the old saṅkhārā continue to arise and pass away, one after another. If out of ignorance one reacts to sensations, then one multiplies the saṅkhārā, multiplies one's misery. But if one develops wisdom and does not react to sensations, then one after another the saṅkhārā are eradicated, misery is eradicated."[86]

To take it to a deeper level, while in silence at the Vipassana, I realized that I must be equanimous with my own equanimity. Meaning that if somehow I were to notice myself getting caught up in a judgment or a labeling of something based on a pattern, I would allow the reaction of me judging myself to pass as well. We must be non-judging of our own self-judgments. The more that I react to myself the more I will react to others. Embracing imperfection and recollecting the disavowed parts of ourselves are part of the holistic journey. We must be equal; inclusive and accepting through the concentric circles of our own unfolding, as much as we do with our own practice of equanimity. A flower does not judge itself as it blooms. It just blooms, in its own time, in its own way. The judgments are the blocks that we experience.

Our preferences, and our heavy investment in them are fuel for the torturous emotions that we experience and the continued agitated nature of our world. Can we be accepting of things that don't fit our levels of expectation, comfort, result or style? Can we be accepting of people who commit horrendous acts toward other humans because of their lack of awareness? Can we embrace the people who hurt us most? Can we overcome anger, hatred, bigotry and systemic oppression and be the more mature humans who re-funnel that misplaced energy into love and compassion for our human species? Can we accept our diversity and differences and dance with our sameness?

NON-ATTACHMENT AND EMOTIONAL CHARGE

By accepting things as objective phenomena without possession of them, we forge a way forward to eliminate the charge behind the preferences; the likes, dislikes, emotions and opinions. I must clarify that eliminating the charge does not mean eliminating passion. Rather, eliminating the charge is eliminating the attachment to someone or something receiving your opinion with open arms. If they oppose it, can you remain level-headed and composed, without becoming righteous? When we have a charge around these aspects of our mind, we are just digging our heels into our own identification with ourselves. Instead of becoming reactive to the outside world as an attacker on our peace, enable yourself to accept the world as it is. The quote below sums up equanimity:

> "Where would I find enough leather
> To cover the entire surface of the earth?
> But with leather soles beneath my feet,
> It's as if the whole world has been covered."
> —Śāntideva

As we relinquish our preferences, we relinquish our emotional charge. We slowly overcome the foes of hatred that result from separating us and them based on our preferences. We move from exclusivity to inclusivity. When we stop trying to create a world that is built around our cravings for something, or our aversions to something else, the wall of preconceptions around our identity that give birth to oppression, prejudice, and wars crumble down. The less we attach to these phenomena in our lives as the only way, the less we are swept away into reaction;

which is just a habitual response that replaces a sovereign action.

Sovereign action can only be birthed from the new moment. If you are not carrying any weight from the past moments in order to alter your new action, then you are free to act in accordance with Truth and alignment. Moving from recognition to de-escalation is as simple as sitting with the phenomena of discomfort or pleasure and letting these feelings slowly fade away. The feeling that arises is becoming comfortable with groundlessness. It only appears that we have control. From where do we derive our breath? All of a sudden, poof, it's gone, and so is life. Equanimity helps train us for the most important part of life; death. And due to our death-a-phobic culture, we are quite negligent and heedless in our reverence and preparation for death.

In the *Tao Te Ching*, Lao Tzu states the below, which is a beautiful understanding of equanimity for our modern times:

"Accept disgrace willingly.
Accept misfortune as the human condition.

What do you mean by "Accept disgrace willingly"?
Accept being unimportant.
Do not be concerned with loss and gain.
This is called "accepting disgrace willingly."

What do you mean by "Accept misfortune as the
  human condition"?
Misfortune comes from having a body.
Without a body, how could there be misfortune?

Surrender yourself humbly; then you can be trusted
  to care for all things.
Love the world as your own self; then you can truly
  care for all things."[87]

If we can really begin to drop into the space behind the right and the wrong, behind the reaction and the response, then we can find a place to rest. A true sign of growth is how quickly we can admit error. As we honor the empathetic and connective reality that as we love the world as ourselves and do unto others as we would have done onto us, we can truly care for all things. Equanimity provides this fertile space for us to create in the continuous unfolding of moments from a place of freshness, that is not dependent upon our trained reactions. The quicker that we can catch ourselves before we fall into the rut of a habitual response of defense or escalation which normally tries to utilize a reaction to buffer our own righteousness, we diffuse conflict and enter into a place of the reclamation of our own power. When there is no one else to blame, not even yourself, when all that is happening is unfolding in front of you and you do not possess or cling to any of it, you become a part of the infinite expanse that holds the space for absolute empowerment.

JOURNAL PROMPTS:

1. What things currently in your life do you attach possession to that are really out of your control? What is your reaction when these things do not turn out as planned?
2. What do you view the difference is between responsibility "to" something and responsibility "for" something? How, when we discern levels of responsibility for our own actions does that help to diffuse our reactivity?
3. How could practicing equanimity decrease the amount of polarization in our world today?
4. Why does our reactivity create violence? What do you think the best way for you is to decrease how reactive you are in your life in general?

Journal Prompt #1:

What things currently in your life do you attach possession to that are really out of your control? What is your reaction when these things do not turn out as planned?

Journal Prompt #2:

What do you view the difference is between responsibility "to" something and responsibility "for" something? How, when we discern levels of responsibility for our own actions does that help to diffuse our reactivity?

Journal Prompt #3:

How could practicing equanimity decrease the amount of polarization in our world today?

Journal Prompt #4:

Why does our reactivity create violence? What do you think the best way for you is to decrease how reactive you are in your life in general?

CHAPTER FIFTEEN

The Reclamation of Power: A Speech by John Trudell

"The day the power of love overrules the love of power; the world will know peace."
—Mahatma Gandhi

"Love is the people's power."
—Tupac Shakur

The following chapter is the "We Are Power" speech from Document 62 of the International Work Group of Indigenous Affairs (IWGIA). They are an independent international organization which supports indigenous peoples in their struggle against oppression. The speech was given by John Trudell, the Last National Chairman of the American Indian Movement, at the Black Hills International Survival Gathering on July 18, 1980. His words still ring true of what we still face today. I need not say more in this chapter than what he relayed 30 years ago. His words touch upon many of the facets of this reconnection with ourselves and the natural world, and the truth of our own power.

".... I would like to talk tonight in honor of all of us in the struggle who have lost our relations to the Spirit World. I would like to talk in honor of the wind, one of the natural elements. This is a survival gathering and one of the things I hope you all learn while you're here is…to appreciate the energy and power that the elements are, that of the sun, the rain and the wind. I hope you go away from here understanding that this is power, the only real, true power. This is the only real, true connection we will ever have to power, our relationship to Mother Earth.

We must not become confused. We must not become confused and deceived by their illusions. There is no such thing as military power. There is only military terrorism. There is no such thing as economic power. There is only the economic within these illusions so we will believe they hold power in their hands. But they do not. All they know how to do is act in a repressive, brutal way.

The power. We are a natural part of the earth. We are an extension of the earth; we are not separate from it. We are a part of it. The earth is our mother. The earth is a spirit, and we are an extension of that spirit. We are spirit. We are power. They want us to believe that we have to believe in them, that we have to assume these consumer identities and these political identities, these religious identities and these racial identities. They want to separate us from our power. They want to separate us from who we are. Genocide.

Genocide is just an intellectual way of saying murder because we live in a so-called "civilized", industrialized world. And because this world is allegedly civilized and allegedly has laws, they can't go out and call an act of murder, murder any more. They call it genocide to throw another illusion in our eyes. And they have limited our ability to see the necessity for our survival because they want us to believe that genocide just means physical extinction.

We must consider the spiritual genocide that they

commit against us: the spiritual genocide that white people have been victimized for thousands of years, the spiritual genocide that told them not to respect the earth—the spiritual genocide that told them not to respect the life that is the earth—but to pay all their tribute through the churches to god and even, that heaven would take care of them in the afterlife. They tried to take and suppress our natural identity, our natural spiritual connection to the earth.

We must move to the time when we truly understand our connection to real power because these people who deal with illusions and imitations, these men who have attempted to "improve upon nature", they want to keep us confused. They want to keep us confused with sexism and ageism, racism and class. They want to keep us in confusion so that we will continue to believe in one lie after another as they program them into our minds and into our society.

There is no hope for the American political system. The ruling class, the exploitative one percent who control world economics today, are not going to change under the existing political rules. They are going to lie to us and they are going to create the illusion of "changes", and they are going to push one face after another in front of us, making promises. We have to understand our role as a natural power. We have to understand that when our oppressor treats us this way and does these things to us, we allow him to do it so long as we accept his lies. As long as we make excuses for his lies, as long as we tolerate his brutality, then we allow him to mistreat us. We have been allowing it too long. That's genocide.

When I go around America and I see the bulk of the white people they do not feel oppressed. They feel powerless. When I go amongst my own people we do not feel powerless. We feel oppressed. We do not want to make the trade. We see the physical genocide they are attempting to inflict upon our lives and we understand the psychological genocide they have already inflicted upon their own people . . . that this is the trade-off they want us to make for survival, that we become subservient to them, that we no longer understand our real connection to power, our real connection to the earth.

Power. They can't stop the wind and they can't stop the rain. They can't stop the earthquake and the volcano and the tornado. They can't stop power. We are a spiritual connection to the earth. As individuals we have power and, collectively, we have the same power as the earthquake, the tornado, and the hurricanes. We have the potential. We have that connection.

We must be willing in our lifetime to deal with reality. It's not revolution we're after; it's liberation. We want to be free of a value system that's being imposed upon us. We do not want to participate in that value system, we don't want to change that value system. We want to remove it from our lives forever. Liberation. We want to be free. But, in order for us to be free, we have to assume our responsibilities as power, as individuals, as spirit, as people. We are going to have to work at it. We are going to have to be committed to it. We must never underestimate our enemy. Our enemy is committed against us 24 hours a day. They use 100% of their efforts to maintain their materialistic status-quo. 100% of their effort goes into deceiving us and manipulating us against each other. We have to devote our lives. We have to make our commitment. We have to follow a way of life that means we are going to resist forever.

In the 1980s, we have to start working more realistically with a resistance consciousness. A resistance, something we can pass on as strength to coming generations. A resistance where organizational egos do not get in the way, a resistance where the infiltrators and provocateurs and the liars and the betrayers and the traitors do not get in the way. We will not get our liberation if we do not seriously analyze the experiences of our own lifetimes. The other side, the enemy, has studied. they understand what we were up to in the 1960s. they understand what we wanted in the early '70s. They have studied us.

They create certain events, and they manipulate the economics, and they manipulate the circumstances because they want to smash us the same way they did in the '60s, so they can come in and smash our movements. We must become of a resistance consciousness. We must say that, "we will not allow you to smash us, even if it means that we have to deal with the part of you that you planted in me. We will not allow you to smash us. This is part of our obligation to the earth. Only by fulfilling our obligation to the earth can we fulfill our obligation to the people. Only by understanding our connection to the earth can we create a fair system that's going to be good to the people."

We must go beyond the arrogance of human rights. We must go beyond the ignorance of civil rights. We must step into the reality of natural rights because all the natural world has a right to existence. We are only a small part of it. There can be no trade-off. We are the people. We have the potential for power. We must not fool ourselves. We must not mislead ourselves. It takes more than good intentions. It takes commitment. It means that at some point in our lives we are going to have to decide that we have a way of life that we follow, and we are going to live that way of life, even when our enemies totally surround us, even when our enemies act against us with brutality and harshness, lies and bribes. We are going to have to stand with our way of life. That is the only solution there is for us. We cannot reach a point in our lives where we're going to sit back and say, "well, we'll make this compromise with the other side."

They have every intention that they are going to use the nuclearization of the world to colonize you all. There is a new Indian this time. The new Indian is white. They don't need you any more because they've got an entire potential world market with millions and millions of consumers. So, all the lies they've dangled in front of your faces, well, they're going to start pulling back on these lies a bit, and they're going to start slapping you all with a bit of reality: the reality that there are not political freedoms in America; the reality that there is not religious freedom in America. You all are going to have to deal with reality and stop making excuses for America.

We Indians are going to have to act as runners and messengers. We are going to have to run and act as teachers. We are going to have to talk to all the people who will listen to us about what we believe, what it is that we know to be right. We're going to have to find ways to become a communication of ourselves. They are afraid of us. We must always remember that every time they have to create a system built upon traitors coming in and betraying you, any time they have to build that system, it is because they understand they have a weakness. And if we persist in our struggle and become dedicated in our resistance…we will take them down through that weakness.

It doesn't matter how many jail cells they build. It doesn't matter how many racist judges, sexist judges, agist judges and class judges they have. It doesn't matter how many of their side they put into illusory positions of 'respectability'. It doesn't matter what they throw at us because we make the difference. We make the decision. We are power.

They deal in illusions, and that's all it is. We must not be afraid. We must never allow fear to be a part of our life. We must always deal with reality. They have been able to use the element of fear to control the masses of people through murder and making the rest of the people afraid of being murdered. But what good is it to live on this sacred place, what good is it to be here if we can't live with dignity and respect? We are here just for our own purposes any more than we are here for them.

We have to understand the implications of slavery and that America is a slave state. One way to understand this is that all of you grew up and left your homes to seek your independence, and immediately went into debt. And there went your independence. Slavery is slavery. Whether you are an indentured servant or in debt, or whether you are in chains, slavery is slavery. We have to evaluate our values. We have to start stepping away from the concepts they forced us to learn. We must share knowledge. We must not be drawn into their traps. Whatever we do, we must do as a resistance; whatever we do as people, whatever we do in the name of the people and the earth, we must do this with humility and with gratefulness for what we are and what we have. But we should not do it with pride.

Because John Wayne is proud, the Marines are proud. People flying B-52 bombers are proud. How are we doing to get our liberation if we take on their characteristics? It is time for us to think. We hate to think about the terminology we use, (but) we must think about the thoughts that go with the terminology.

We must make our resistance totally complete. There must be no last way, half way measures. We have to learn to put up and deal with the hard times just like we enjoy the good times. We have to learn and understand that hard times are necessary for the good times to be here. We have to learn and understand that all the struggle we will go through in our lives does not mean we are losing. We have to understand that they want us to be lazy in our minds and lazy in our spirits and lazy in our thinking. But the nature of the People of the Earth has always been of struggle. It has always been. As the indigenous people of the western hemisphere, we have learned to struggle and live because of the struggle of our living. We learned to live with harmony and respect for Mother Nature. We never forgot who we were...

We always had to struggle, so let's not fool ourselves and try to make ourselves quit what we believe just because it's going to get hard. Let's struggle for a purpose. Let's struggle for the freeing of the earth because only by freeing the earth, and those who would attack the earth, can we be free ourselves. It is the only way we can do it.

There have been many social revolutions in America. There have been many social organizations. There have been women's rights movements; there have been equal rights movements; there have been union movements. And look who's still controlling our lives. We've got to deal with that reality. The people have risen before. The people have spoken before. The people have tried before. But somewhere they did not pull it all together, the reason being that they always attempted to change the social conditions of America without addressing the issue of our relationship to the land. They cannot exploit economics without the land...

We must not take them on just on the fact that we are going to own the land ... our concern must be for the land as well as ourselves. If we do not use our minds to think of our coming generations, they will win their psychological genocide against us. We must not become discouraged. We must never quit ... if they stop us one way, then we must find another way. They are afraid of consistency.

They always throw issues at us to keep us jumping from one issue to another. They throw lies and illusions in front of us. We must learn from the Vietnam war. The white American people said they were against war. That's what the people said. Then they went and listened to their lying politicians, and their lying politicians said, "Okay, we will help you. We will declare peace." And so the lying politicians got the people to settle for withdrawal from Vietnam as being peace. And meanwhile my people were going through a war right here, right here on the Pine Ridge Reservation. And all that went unnoticed in the celebration over peace being declared the lie was sunk in, and the American people accepted the lie.

When the black people were struggling for what became civil rights, really they were talking about equality. The politicians stepped in and said, "We will help you all." And the black people settled for civil rights, which is only a part of life. Now the politicians come talking again: "We are going to help you with nuclear power." We've got to think about our past experience.

If we are going to consciously become power and use our power correctly ... we are going to have to find a way to communicate our thoughts and our resistance and our consciousness which will not accept the nuclearization of the earth, that this goes against everything we know and believe in, that this time we draw the line. We have to take the initiative. We can no longer afford to become and remain reactionary...we should work within our movements, but we must always remember these are parts of a total resistance. The resistance is the one thing at this point in our generation which can give life to the coming generations.

When we talk about the other side and energy, we can only place so much responsibility on the shoulders of the enemy. And we do have an enemy. We can call him Jimmy Carter or Ronald Reagan, or we can call it Trilateral Commission. We can call them anything we want, but we've got to come to the reality that they are the enemy because our friends and the people who love us would not do this to us. So they are the enemy. We have to deal with this reality: "the enemy." There must be this consciousness that goes into our minds and we will start to act accordingly. And we must know what responsibilities we must place upon the enemy, and what the responsibilities we must take upon ourselves. Because, when we talk about "the energy crisis," we must remember that we are energy...We are energy, so we must, if we are going to go out with the truth and spiritual connection behind us when we stand against our enemy—and we accuse the enemy of misusing energy, and we accuse him of abusing it—then we better think real hard about how we misuse it ourselves. Because we are energy. We have to deal with that.

We are energy, and its how we use ourselves that allows the enemy to misuse us. This resistance and this struggle for survival must total, absolutely complete. There are no half measures. They have interfered in our lives since the moment we were born. Look at America. You have to pay to be born, and you have to pay to be buried. That tells you a lot about our freedom. And if they've gotten it in our consciousness to accept that, then we've got a lot of work to do. We really do. But we have the ability to change it because we are a natural part of the earth. Because we are here. The earth did not put useless things here. We are a natural part of creation.

They have been attacking indigenous people, and they have been misusing white people and they want to push us all into a position where all we think about is ourselves. They want us to forget the earth, just like they used early Christianity to make the Christians forget the earth. They want to do it to all of us again, in this generation. They want to isolate us and call us names like "communist" or "anarchist" and "terrorist" and "criminal." They want to attack us. they want to use terrorism to intimidate us. We must build a resistance in our hearts that says we will not accept it; we will never accept it.

As to the indigenous peoples, I don't know how you all relate. But indigenous people, understanding power, we are the sprit. We are a natural part of the earth. And all our ancestors, and all our relations who have gone to the Spirit World, they are here with us. They have power. They will help us. They will help us to see, if we are willing to look. We are not separated from them because there is no place to go. This is our place, the earth. This is our mother. We will not go away from our mother.

No matter what they do to us, no matter how they strike at us, overtime they do it, we must continue. But we must never become reactionary. The one thing that has always bothered me about revolution is that every time I have met the revolutionaries they have acted simply out of hatred for the oppressor. What we must do is act out of love for our people. No matter what they ever do to us, we must always act out of love for the people and for the earth. We must never react out of hatred for those who have no sense."[88]

These last lines I believe to be the key. We must act out of love for our people and the Earth. No matter what happens, we cannot act out of hatred. The more we embrace this reclamation of our own power to love as opposed to hate, we meet in the fulcrum point of our human experience and begin the path towards de-polarizing our world and collaborating together on things that really matter for us as a whole.

Postscript

If we have been following closely what John Trudell is saying, he is guiding us into the reclamation of our own power. The same is true of the motive of this book. This book is really me writing to myself a synopsis of the last eight years of my life. In it, we explored how we can connect the dots cross-culturally and take our power back. John brings this back to the fact that everything that we have been taught, even the word civilization in general, is a lie. How can something called 'civilized' be the progenitor of barbarism and genocide in these ways?

We must not cower in the face of these deeply rooted systemic manipulations. We must face the storm head on and holistically. Through him and many others throughout time, these messages have been echoing. There are frameworks, pathways, and maps, through which one can begin to reclaim one's power and freedom, which is being threatened more and more every day.

The first step is to recognize that almost everything we have ever been told is probably a misconstrued version of the truth, if not an outright lie. We must recognize that fact to get to the point of constructing something that is actually of value. To get to the nuts and bolts you begin the process of accepting deconditioning. Unlearning. Then begins the demolition project. Like lava covering land and ocean to rebuild itself, destruction leads to creation.

From the onset of the demolition project, we can begin to take a look at our value system from an objective point of view. Individually and collectively. Our main conditioned value system is the framework for the continued destruction and exploitation of Earth as well as our disconnection from each other and the natural world. It is centered on the paradigm of separation. The separation is of ourselves from Spirit, and thereby the separation of ourselves from everybody else. Without this value system and economic OS in place, which blocks out the externalities of its mechanism, the planet would not be in its current situation, nor would animals or humans. The value system incentivizes greed and hoarding, and dis-incentivizes honesty with the lack of transparent structure, continued maltreatment of the populace on behalf of financial institutions and the like. The paradigm of ruthless competition over Earth-centric collaboration. This value system capitalizes on our untrained, reactionary desire system, which has formed us into a hedonistic society that craves continued accumulation and pleasure and averts suffering and hardship. This has rendered us mentally lazy, disconnected, and selfish. However, as we begin to look at this directly without looking away, we can view it as a collective forgetting. Once we recognize what we have collectively forgotten, it ushers in the time of collective remembering and a reassessment of value. Once you've recognized that you've strayed from the path, you're back on the path.

As we begin to introduce the experience and understand that all knowledge turns into wisdom through experience, we see why the experience economy is beginning to flourish. However, by continuing to fluff around on the paltry layers of experience because of our initiation into superficiality and fear of depth, we barely touch upon the depths of connection that the human experience enables. By seemingly failing to gain wisdom, we continually try to accumulate experiences thinking that quantity is king. This is a pitfall of our value system which only leads to our trying to accumulate experiences themselves, which builds attachments and buries us deeper into separation from the moment. Moments are in and of themselves wealth, but you cannot accumulate them; they are priceless and impermanent. With this motive validated by societal constructs, we accumulate superficial, cursory and fleeting information and never delve into the depths of our connectivity with the surrounding world because we try to grasp onto it. Consequently, we continually collect more and more things, adding to our complexity rather than returning to simplicity.

Ayurveda, the ancient science of life practiced in India, talks about how the first formation of disease in the human organism is the result of accumulation. We take this diagnostic model of the physical human organism and extrapolate it outward to the planetary being of Earth. By witnessing the fact that the existing operating system and value system bases itself on accumulation, we begin to understand why our world is very ill. Similar to how an Ayurvedic doctor would diagnose a patient and begin to see how they could stop accumulating foods that are throwing their bodily constitution out of equilibrium, we begin to diagnose our species as a whole to understand what is leading to this disease formation. In Ayurveda, if you are of a *pitta* constitution and are eating too many fermented or spicy foods, you will aggravate your bodily system and create disease. In the same way, if we continue to aggravate our individual bodies by accumulating ideologies and material things which are connected directly to our planetary body, we will suffer and potentially perish as a current species. We must recognize the process of accumulation and its detriment to come to a halt. Once we have stopped, we can pull back our vantage point in order to reverse the formation of disease. The opposite of accumulation is dispensation, which leads to fluidity and balance.

One of the ways to achieve this balance is to stop the worshipping of technology which has deepened our identifications with our individual selves. This reinforced identification has the enhanced ability to create a trigger for this accumulation. When we overuse the mechanism, the target of the trigger, which is our own self-identification and ego-centricity comes into play and creates competition, reactionary states and confusion. We begin to live deeply into comparative models. We become even more deeply divided from one another through the expression of our own self-identification, and the wound of separation grows deeper.

An original experiential path towards union or merging is then brought into the conversation. Yoga, which literally means to yoke together or union, is the experiential science that deconstructs the entire paradigm of separateness through dissolving your psychological identifications and conditionings. This is accomplished through observances, disciplines, physical practice, breathing regulation, and meditation. Yoga focuses on reconnecting us with the subtler parts of ourselves. Beginning with purification techniques, moving into the physical body with asana practice, and working our way through the breath, to the mind and beyond it to purer states of consciousness, Yoga is a map to use the duality in the natural world as a tool to merge with the constant change and through it to the immutable Self, or *Purusa*. This *anicca* or change, is the only constant in this dualistic reality. The resistance to change is attached to our stories we view as reality. The space that we cultivate by merging with the constancy of change is centered in the changeless. We enter back into a state of wonder. We return to a state of innocence which accepts it all in wonder.

From the discussion around Yoga, we are brought back into one of the documented inhibitors to our conscious evolution; food. Nutrition, in its root form comes from the nourishment that Nature provides for our survival. As our foods are more and more tampered with, we become more disconnected from the roots of nutrition, the roots of Nature and essentially, the roots of ourselves. As we are split from the roots, like in any endeavor, we stray further into confusion and sickness. By the introduction of GMOs, which are pesticide-resistant, and the abuse of the consumption of alcohol, coffee, and meat, we look into how our existing dietary system creates an unsettled mind. With an unsettled mind it becomes difficult to cultivate states of presence and acceptance, which continue us attached to the tetherball swings of our uncontrolled emotions. In Ayurveda, one looks to achieve a *sattvic* mind, one that is completely at peace and enables stillness. With the majority of our diets, we are fueling the *rajasic* mind, which is equated with aggression, and the *tamasic* mind, which is equated with inertia or laziness. In order for us to continue the journey into the reclamation of our self-responsibility, we must align our consumption of foods and other inputs with these *sattvic* living qualities. If we cannot do that, we do not have fertile soil for the complete transformation of our consciousness.

If we are able to take care of our diet and our physical needs, as discussed in Abraham Maslow's 'Pyramid of Hierarchies', we can begin to move towards a place of self-actualization. However, in Maslow's initial model, this self is actually still limited and selfish and does not take into account dependent arising. As we move up through the deficiency needs that are being met physiologically, we begin to see that in order for us to move beyond self-actualization, we must move into a space of self-transcendence. As we self-transcend, we are directionally aligned with the ultimate goal of Yoga, which is to dissolve the illusion of separateness by embracing the world within and beyond our-selves as connected. Only in self-transcendence is Maslow's pyr-amid complete, because the self, or the little 'I,' is transformed into the Self-actualization, or the 'merged I' of all sentient be-ings. When the Self, or the non-dual is reached, that is the point of true self-transcendence; and once that point is attained, you become a vessel for selflessly serving others. Hanuman encapsu-lates this energy within how he serves Rām.

Our world is one that loves instant gratification. This is one of the conditioned values that we must let come to a natural cessation. When we begin to uncover the fact that we are just a part of Nature, we begin to see that we follow similar cycles to nature. However, because of this desire to experience something directly and quickly, the use of psychedelics or entheogens has risen dramatically since the 1970s. The use of these magnificent compounds gives us a shortcut into self-transcendence. We ex-perience the multi-dimensionality of existence. They can show us how interconnected everything actually is. The use of entheo-gens bends the relativity of time, and we begin to understand the subtler layers of things, which envelops us in the great mys-tery of life. The only pitfall of using these substances is that they have the capability to strengthen your identification of your ego which leads to messianic complexes in separateness and hier-archical rank over others. In addition, if you lack the eldering structure to integrate wisdom that was glimpsed under their influence you may end up quite confused and lost within our disconnected societal constructs. The strongest takeaway from entheogens and plant medicines is the rapidity with which one can feel the subtlety, interconnectedness and the inter-being of existence that can be achieved without using these medicines. It can provide a glimpse into the promised land, of sacred inter-connectedness.

The indigenous peoples of the world have always held the

worldviews of sacred interconnectedness. Through many of their languages and relationships with the land, there was no framework for exploitation of themselves or others built in. The mountains and the rivers and the wind are their brothers and sisters. As we are but an extension of the land, if the land was exploited, so were we. If we didn't respect the land, we didn't respect ourselves. This holistic worldview gave them the inherited role of protectors, propagators, and stewards of the land itself, ushering in thousands of years of regeneration and the safety of plant and animal species alike. As our value system of exploitation attempts to continue its domination of Nature, its war and dominion on the wilderness, these indigenous protectors were violently murdered over hundreds of years in the largest continued attempted genocide the world has ever seen. The genocide was not only attempted physically, but also psychologically and spiritually. It is still continuing today overtly in places such as the Amazon, the Dakotas and across Australia. The return to this understanding of sacred interconnectedness with the land can be guided and facilitated by the wisdom keepers who never forgot who they were and their connection to the planet.

Despite the holistic worldview that we all are looking to connect to and our progress to the means, our society is still deeply divided. This division stems from confusion and informational irrelevance. For example, many new-age spiritual communities are becoming commoditized rather than embracing differences. Their members still want a certain idealized self-image, a compensatory identity that fits a new mold. This desire sparks division, and has been proliferated by misinformation and identification. Spirituality is based in divorcing ourselves from anything that creates more division. Spiritual communities often miss this point, setting up hierarchies and using trends to amass wealth and influence, which feeds into the entire Babylonian system, as it is referred to in reggae.

This Babylonian system is rooted in materialism and confusion. The Aramaic root of Babylon is *Balal* which means to confuse. From this confusion stems the fertile soil for systemic oppression, which wages war against the people in order to make them complicit in consumerism and feed into divisive belief systems that enable the perpetuity of power centralization. This renders the true power source, which is Nature and the connected populace, fragmented, and makes it easier to conquer. We must come back together to understand that we are not hating a physical enemy, but rather, a viral mindset of division and separation that is spread by ignorance and malice. We can be together without division and work collaboratively towards dismantling these conceptual frameworks that separate us from our power.

One of the most profound and simple ways to dismantle the value system and everything we cling to is through Nature. Nature is the gateway to responsibility and reclaiming the understanding of the world as our mirror, as a part of us is paramount in this return to our own power. By working and dancing with Nature, you begin to see many of the patterns that you live with, many of which you may not recognize in your day-to-day life. The care and intention that you put into the land, you get back in return. You will know when you are not fully engaged with the land, and if so, things can happen very quickly which bring you back to awareness. Nature is our true teacher. The trees have survived storms and they have learned to bend with the wind instead of fighting it. Their roots are strong and they yield fruits for humans and animals alike to share. The rocks in the rivers, continually polished by the flow of crisp water from the glaciers, become smooth over time. Our mind is the garden; we are the Earth. Our breath feeds the trees, which feed us oxygen. We are interconnected on every level. Without the harmonious orchestra of humanity and Nature, humanity does not survive.

In accordance with the harmony of Nature, we learn that similar to it, we must enter into a state of equanimity. Equanimity is the non-attachment to expectations, the acceptance of the reality as it is. Without always clinging to the fruits of our efforts and how we want the world to be, we are able to move fluidly within our reclamation of responsibility. We become responsible "to" things that bring us joy and passion, yet not responsible "for" the outcome. This split of possession from the end result of our efforts amidst a system that thrives on its own spiritual perfection frees us from the burdens of always thinking that we know what is best.

When we finally begin to experientially understand the interconnectivity with nature and each other through de-systemizing and de-conditioning our belief systems, we begin our collective path to the reclamation of power. As of now, we are complicit in giving our power away freely to a centralized system based on an economic ideology that strips us of the potential for us to be sovereign beings. The jewel of these trying times is the reclamation of power that has been stripped continuously as we demand more and more quantity and more and more novelty. We begin to stop diverting our responsibility to other parties to manage it or to rule it through an all-seeing eye, and we stop centralizing our needs and wants to an external source to be the custodian. These custodians are playing their own games, like the interest rates that the Fed charges the banks and then the banks charge you after they lend your money out. We reclaim our power. Now, with new technologies like blockchain, we can even begin to do so on a financial level. By working with Nature we can do it; growing our own food and catching our own rain water. Food and water security is true sovereignty because we no longer have to rely on our ideas of work to live. By dismantling the oppressive systems of beliefs like patriotism and religion, we can do it. We begin to understand that our conscious resistance can never surrender until these aspects of our world change. And our world changing depends on our own internal world changing. We stop resisting ourselves and our fears and surrender into our power. We connected humans are the power source. We are a part of Nature. Divided and separated, we crumble. Together, we are power.

But remember, the beginning of the journey towards awakening lies in the realization of that we do not really know anything.

Start again.

Dreams of 'The Dasoham Project'

"As long as you and I are in the illusion of duality we think we are different, then we will be in a social role of service. If we really know that we are really one being, then that social costume and persona drop away and we can meet somewhere beyond what we think ourselves to be. As Hanuman says, "When I don't know when the cloud is there I serve Rām, and when the cloud is lifted I am Rām."
—Ram Dass

"My game is to have the courage to live like it is only us."
—Ram Dass

The writing of this book throughout the last few months took place concurrently with an initiative in my mind called 'The Dasoham Project.' Dasoham means roughly, "I am (your) Servant" in Sanskrit. Historically this is related to Hanuman and Lord Rām, of the Hindu tradition. Hanuman is known as the perfect servant, and Rām is an incarnation of God.

The first thing we will break down is the term servant in this context.

Servant has a negative vernacular connotation in our society.

It normally refers to someone of a lower class who has a relationship with someone of a higher station, a master. The servant does whatever that master desires for labor. Servants can be treated badly, with the master trying to get as much out of them as possible, and for the cheapest cost.

However, in the context of spirituality, the servant is surrendering to the highest manifestation of cosmic order, and serving or surrendering their own being to this knowing and order, we can call this God or Consciousness or Divinity, is a route to union. In Hindu philosophy, it has been called karma Yoga, or the selfless action path; the path of surrender. Self in the phrase selfless means your egoic or conditioned self. The self that often manifests via attachment, desiring and grasping at life trying to preserve it. You are literally surrendering your own ego to your own pure potentiality in order to perform the harmonious works of the will of a higher, purer conscious order.

As Ram Dass had said in one of his many lectures, and I roughly paraphrase,

> " . . . the role of surrender doesn't mean that the outside-business-as-usual doesn't exist, it's about how conscious are the beings who're doing it. When they've (these people) have surrendered their ego they act in harmony with the universe. For this, all the impurity has to be burned out of the system, and that's the only work to do. I'm doing anything as a purification exercise on myself because all I have to offer to another being is my own purity, my own being, my state of existence. The less ego the more there is to offer. So, what're you really surrendering? You're surrendering a little hollow empty trip, that maybe goes on another 40 years . . . there is a surrender that's no surrender, into pure light."

In essence, Dasoham means 'Servant of the Divine Will', or 'That which Surrenders to God or Consciousness', and is the first step in the progression towards union in karma Yoga, or selfless action. This is not a religious concept trapped in dogmas, but rather an ancient scientific approach to merging with the consciousness that exists within and around us at every moment in time.

ADVAITA VEDANTA: PHILOSOPHICAL PROGRESSION OF DASOHAM TO HAM

In the progression through this servant-hood, Dasoham is the initial stage, which is in Duality (Dvaita) or, I am His* Servant. Here there are two personalities, "I" and "Him", which is still separate, therefore, not oneness. Therefore, in the second stage Da has to be given up. Visishtadvaita follows, which is known as The 'Soham' state. This is not oneness: it means "I am Him." Now, 'So' has to be given up. What is left then is 'Ham'. Ham is the Advaita state—I am I. Soham and Dasoham are both outlooks utilized for the cessation of the illusion that "I am the body." Eradication of the ego is the main aim of both these attitudes.

Dasoham is to remember always the Truth that the Absolute alone is the doer and the instigator, His will alone prevails, and that there is no "aham" ("I"ness) that separates me from Him. One who experiences the perfect Dasoham state also experiences "Soham."

*keep in mind that His (masculine) is representative of the Creator. Her, or Mother or Nature, is the manifestation of all else in the Universe other than the Creator. The Creator or Consciousness is given (male) and received/ manifest through Nature (female).

THE FIRST TRUE SERVICE PLATFORM

From this origin and process, the idea of The Dasoham Project arose. It would be the first true service platform, where service or surrender to or into yourself through another being exists for no cost at all. This is revolutionary because it is moving towards eliminating the transactional element from an interaction, a facet of the gift economy. It takes the doing, and moves it to being.

Instagram is the highlight reel of people's lives, so filtered and edited that you can almost feel the humanity being pulled out of it. People are now posting on Instagram about true vulnerability, about how this is not real life and the dangers of getting caught up in what can seem like the perfect life, while the poster truly has tears of a clown. We as humans hide behind our posts of perfection, just like our identities. Isn't it about time we come together regarding how we really feel? The emotions between the highlights are the journey itself. We can serve one another and make this world a more peaceful and united place by being truly honest with ourselves and others. Are you up for the challenge?

No more them, no more us. Compassion requires feeling all the feels; grief, pity, pain, suffering, hope, joy and sadness. At the same time, equanimity of mind is seeing that it is all a dance that's quite perfect. What karmic predicament other beings are caught in, that's their incarnation. We can look at things in different ways. To quote Ram Dass, "Is that other being their action or are they caught in a web of where their action is a result?"

We can break down our political, religious, gender, financial, and racial boundaries by serving one another authentically and genuinely from the Heart, without requiring reciprocity.

How much is your time worth, what are they trying to get from me, are they trying to hustle me, what about my margin, is all dissolved. As long as this world remains in a transactional and therefore exploitative mechanism there can never be peace and there will always be rich and poor, suffering and everything that comes in duality. Maybe this is just part and parcel of being a human being. However, if a system is broken, that's when we can look at ways to mend it, and to mend it, you don't use the same approach as last time. Einstein calls that insanity. We seem to be trapped in this duality, because for true peace to be in a setting such as ours there must be a comparative measure of un-peace, which is war, turmoil and unrest. The essence of transaction is impermanence, and the essence of impermanence is duality, which is expressed through Nature, *Prakrti*, which is Consciousness, *Purusa*, in manifest form.

Current society, put another way eloquently by Ram Dass, is the way it is because:

> "…we got so frightened that the fear led to greed and the greed led to separateness and the separateness led to protecting the king of the mountain and that led to immense suffering of other people which led to terrorism and violence and that threatens the establishment and the games go on and on until you see what needs to be done to have a change to stop all of that."

Nature, being pure sacrifice requires a receiver for its sacrifice to be noticed and accepted. Music is not music if there is no one labeling it or listening to it calling it music, it is just sound happening. Even if a musician is listening to his or her own music, that is listening, and therefore the dual loop is complete. Therefore, this idea of the servant and the one being served is the portal into escaping duality through duality itself. That is the reason why Nature has been manifest in the first place.

Therefore, the practical goal of The Dasoham Project is to see if we can merge with the experience of the other in a context that lacks transactionality. This contract is clear from the get-go. We can call it the gift of giving yourself. We are just beings sharing our vulnerabilities, which someone will receive. We can share what we have acquired through a transaction prior, with-

364 THE AGE OF SEPARATION

out any transaction in the moment. We give what we can and the rest goes. We meet in the middle of our human Hearts and then hopefully enter into our spiritual Hearts beyond our own identifications which provide the veil in which we are caught in. As we see our own shared quandary on this planet, our feelings and karmic conditioning is chipped away as we see what is happening. And over time, like water polishing a stone, it all becomes smooth.

People can always try to make themselves feel good by volunteering, but that's not in the essence of service, that is in the essence of ego-boosting, like someone going to an orphanage under the guise of helping when really they are looking for external validation. It doesn't kill the whole intention or action while there or the happiness you brought to the children, but it does decrease the authenticity of your action which means you are trapped in a moment outside of the present one.

True service is karma Yoga, which is serving the Divine, which is everything and everybody, including you. That level of service is therefore unitive because you are serving yourself.

When this level of karma Yoga is practiced on a small level, then this compassionate action, rooted in the right action via the Truth emanating from your Heart, ripples out into every single interaction that you experience day to day, moment to moment. The recognition of yourself in another is the recognition that the other is you. Once you recognize this, how can you steal from somebody? How can you discriminate or exercise bigotry and racism? The violence train, hurtling at the speed of sound, for perhaps the first time in your life, begins to squeeze on the brakes and the system will eventually come to a halt. No matter what operating systems you are working within, they all are exposed for what they are: identifications of a limited existence, because they are something limited to your 'own' ego or "I" state, which gains strength in a collective ego setting through its personal locus of control. To expand beyond that is grace; to move beyond your "I" is enlightenment.

The evolution of serving one person, or being served in this non-attached way, moves you forward to seeing everyone as someone to be served. This service to another is the route to your own happiness, as true happiness and joy comes from the experience of togetherness and authentic interconnectedness. For joy and peace to come, we must move beyond the polarization. Beyond the separation.

Glossary

'Āina – Hawai'ian word for 'the land', or 'spirit of the land'. Traditionally, the concept goes back to times of mythos, and is illustrated in the creation chants of the Kumulipo. This chant emphasizes the connection between the spirit, land and the people. In everyday practice, it embodies a deep passion for the land, working with the land as is often demonstrated in songs, hula, talking-story and lifestyle practices such as farming.

Adaptogenic – Qualities of a select group of some mushrooms and some herbs that support the body's natural ability to heal and deal with various stressors. They are called thus because of their ability to adapt their function according to the specific needs of the body. This may be physical, chemical or biological needs. Some common adaptogens are ashwagandha, ginseng or schisandra berry.

Anuloma Viloma – 'alternate nostril breathing', a form of pranayama that is often practiced before seated meditation or asana practice. Its purpose is to stimulate the nadis or energy channels that run throughout the body.

Ayurveda – Ayurveda is one of the oldest life sciences known to humans. Transcribed in Sanskrit, the roots of its name lie in the two words: 'Aayus,' which means life and 'Veda,' which means science or knowledge. Dhanvantari is the Hindu god of medicine and an avatar of Lord Mahavishnu. He is mentioned in the Puranas as the god of Ayurveda. It uses the elemental energetic makeup of the universe to uphold our biological health, prevent disease and heal ailments.

Balal – the Aramaic root of the words Babylon and Babel. The meaning is 'to confuse', which correlates directly with our current state of being. We have become confused with the media and the superfluous amount of information irrelevance. We've become confused in our relation to Nature and with other people. This confusion renders us in a time and place where we don't know who to trust, even if we should trust ourselves. Therefore, we come disconnected or confused to who we really are, or what we really are. We become unyoked, or separate from our divine nature. This correlates directly with the Kali Yuga, which is mentioned earlier in the book and here in the glossary.

Citta – the mind is called the *citta* in Yoga. *Citta* is the sum total of three factors. The flow of traditional thought goes from A-C and is referenced in the *The Yoga Sūtras of Patanjali.*

1. Manas – desiring part of the mind;
2. Buddhi – intellect or discernment;
3. Ahamkara – ego or 'I'

Civilization – by definition, the stage of human social and cultural development and organization that is considered most advanced, or any complex society characterized by urban development, social stratification, a form of government and symbolic systems of communication such as writing. We often connect the word civilized with civilization, which means that we consider civilization to be civilized. What John Trudell exposes is that our current civilization is the most barbaric and violent, oppressive and environmentally destructive force that the planet has ever seen. Yet, we continue to operate on levels of superficial respectability while causing extreme and sometimes irreversible harm to our only shared home. John Trudell calls civilization, "The Great Lie". He states, "The Great Lie is that this is civilization. It's not civilized. It has literally been the most blood-thirsty brutalizing system ever imposed upon this planet. [...] Or if it does represent civilization, and that is truly what civilization is, then the Great Lie is that civilization is good for us."

Commoditization – normally used in a business context, this process removes the individual, unique characteristics and brand identity so that the product becomes interchangeable with other products of the same type. In a human context, as we are conditioned into respectability and placement amidst a turning economic wheel, we are removing the uniqueness of our beings and becoming a homogenous, disconnected society that assists the proliferation and continuation of our economic OS.

Darshan – Sanskrit translation to roughly 'viewing'. It is normally correlated with an opportunity or occasion of seeing a holy person or the image of a deity.

Dependent arising – sometimes referred to as Pratītyasamutpāda, it is also the state of inter-being. For example, an apple does not arise only from the seed, it also requires soil, water, sunshine, fertilizer, etc. The apple tree in turn has many effects. It gives rise to many apples, and those many apples each contain many seeds, and each of these seeds in turn can become the source for another apple tree which will give rise to more apples. In this way, we are all tied intricately together and within this interconnected framework, which are reliant on certain things to exist, certain nodes of potentiality, and if these were not present then we also would not be here today. It is an understanding of the interconnectedness of our realities.

Ecocidal – by definition, this relates to criminalized human activity that violates the principles of environmental justice. Since the environment does not have a voice that many seem to understand nor really care about, corporations have continually implemented varieties of ecocide on different levels of severity to maintain our economy which operates on an extractive paradigm. Essentially, most actions that we take are ecocidal, from purchasing plastic, to eating cookies with palm oil in them, we just don't see the direct repercussions as we are far removed from specific parts of the supply chain.

Four Noble Truths – The first noble truth is that life is suffering in the realms of samsara. The second noble truth is that the arising of this suffering is from thirst or desire, attachment, clinging. The third noble truth is there is a cessation of suffering if you are able to let go of your clinging and desirous thirst. The fourth noble truth is the pathway to do this, also known as the Eightfold path.

GMO – According to the Non-GMO project website

"A GMO, or genetically modified organism, is a plant, animal, microorganism or other organism whose genetic makeup has been modified in a laboratory using genetic engineering or transgenic technology. This creates combinations of plant, animal, bacterial, and virus genes that do not occur in nature or through traditional crossbreeding methods. Genetic modification affects many of the products we consume on a daily basis . . . "

Heiau – an ancient Hawai'ian temple or sacred site.

Impermanence – this principle forms the framework for the Buddha's teaching, having been the initial insight that impelled him to leave the palace in search of a path to enlightenment. Impermanence, in the Buddhist view, encompasses the sum of conditioned existence, ranging in scale from the macro to the micro. This impermanence relates to the immense dimensions evolving and disintegrating in repetitive cycles throughout beginning-less time, our inescapable mortality and the condition of being bound to aging, sickness, and death, of possessing a body that is subject to disintegration, as well as the radical impermanence uncovered only by sustained attention to experience in its living immediacy: the fact that all the constituents of our being, bodily and mental, are in constant process, arising and passing away in rapid succession from moment to moment without any persistent underlying substance.

Indigeneity – According to LaDonna Harris, Founder and President of Americans for Indian Opportunity, "Indigeneity assumes a spiritual interconnectedness between all creations, their right to exist and the value of their contributions to the larger whole. At the core of Indigenous thinking is that coexistence relies on the ability of all peoples' and living things' voices be heard and heard equally."[89]

Kalāpa – is a term in Buddhism that refers to the smallest units of physical matter said to be about 1/46,656th the size of a particle of dust from a wheel of chariot. In contemporary Buddhist meditation practice, the observation and analysis of kalāpas is a type of Vipassana practice that aims to allow direct observation of impermanence and non-self.

Kali Yuga – in Hindu cosmology. Hindus believe that human civilization degenerates spiritually during the Kali Yuga Common attributes and consequences are spiritual bankruptcy, mindless hedonism, the breakdown of social structure, greed, materialism, unrestricted egotism, and mental and bodily afflictions and maladies. Hinduism often symbolically represents morality (*dharma*) as an Indian bull. In Satya Yuga, the first stage of development, the bull has four legs, but at each age morality is reduced by one quarter. By the age of Kali, morality is reduced to only a quarter of that of the golden age, so that the bull of Dharma has only one leg.

Kapala Bhati – this is another form of pranayama. It is

roughly translated as 'skull breaking'. The technique consists of alternating short, explosive exhales and natural inhales. Exhales are generated by powerful contractions of the lower belly close to the diaphragm, which push air out of the lungs. Inhales are responses to the release of this contraction, which sucks air back into the lungs.

Kuleana – a Hawaiian value and practice which is loosely translated to mean "responsibility." The word kuleana refers to a reciprocal relationship between the person who is responsible, and the thing which they are responsible for. For example, Hawaiians have a kuleana to our land: to care for it and to respect it, and in return, our land has the kuleana to feed, shelter, and clothe us, through this relationship we maintain balance within society and with our natural environment.

Lilikoi – Hawai'ian word for passion fruit.

Mahāyāna Buddhism – translated roughly to 'great vehicle', this is also known as Tibetan Buddhism. One of the main focal points of Mahāyāna refers to the path of the Bodhisattva, which is the seeking complete enlightenment for the benefit of all sentient beings.

Ogichidaa – The Ojibwe word for warrior, although more multi-dimensional in its meaning than in English, is Ogichidaa, or Ogichidaag, "those who defend the people." He states:

> "For us, warriors are not what you think of as warriors. The warrior is not someone who fights, because no one has the right to take another's life. The warrior, for us, is one who sacrifices himself for the good of others. His task is to take care of the elderly, the defenseless, those who cannot provide for themselves and above all, the children, the future of humanity."

Organic – According to The Department for Agriculture

and Rural Affairs (DEFRA) in the UK, they state that:

"Organic food is the product of a farming system which avoids the use of man-made fertilisers, pesticides; growth regulators and livestock feed additives. Irradiation and the use of genetically modified organisms (GMOs) or products produced from or by GMOs are generally prohibited by organic legislation.

Organic agriculture is a systems approach to production that is working towards environmentally, socially and economically sustainable production. Instead, the agricultural systems rely on crop rotation, animal and plant manures, some hand weeding and biological pest control".

Ouroboros – This is the symbol on the front of the book itself. In brief, the Ouroboros is a Greek word meaning "tail devourer," and is one of the oldest alchemical and mystical symbols in the world. It can be perceived as a snake that is enveloping or eating itself, where the tail appears to disappear but really moves into the inside of the snake. This can be likened to the inner domain or reality, the invisible nature, vanishing from view but still existing. It can also be seen to symbolize the cyclic Nature of the Universe: creation out of destruction, Life out of Death. It eats its own tail to sustain its life, in an eternal cycle of renewal. Carl Jung states,

"the alchemists, who in their own way knew more about the nature of the individuation process than we moderns do, expressed this paradox through the symbol of the Ouroboros, the snake that eats its own tail.

The Ouroboros has been said to have a meaning of infinity or wholeness. In the age-old image of the Ouroboros lies the thought of devouring oneself and turning oneself into a circulatory process, for it was clear to the more astute alchemists that the prima materia of the art was man himself.

The Ouroboros is a dramatic symbol for the integration and assimilation of the opposite, i.e. of the shadow. This 'feed-back' process is at the same time a symbol of immortality, since it is said of the Ouroboros that he slays himself and brings himself to life, fertilizes himself and gives birth to himself. He symbolizes the One, who proceeds from the clash of opposites, and he therefore constitutes the secret of the prima materia which [...] unquestionably stems from man's unconscious."[90]

Permaculture – Bill Mollison, the Tasmanian son of a fisherman who first coined the term 1978, defined permaculture as

"The conscious design and maintenance of agriculturally productive systems which have the diversity, stability, and resilience of natural ecosystems. It is the harmonious integration of the landscape with people providing their food, energy, shelter and other material and non-material needs in a sustainable way."[91]

Prana – life force energy. It is also the energetic makeup of the subtler level of being beyond the physical body, called the *pranic* sheath. This dimension of reality is subtler and vaster than the physical one.

Sādhanā – daily spiritual practice. In direct translation it could be viewed as a discipline to attain desired knowledge or a goal. Sadhguru describes it as, "Everything can be sādhanā. The way you eat, the way you sit, the way you stand, the way you breathe, the way you conduct your body, mind and your energies and emotions ... " If I could go a step further, beyond well-being, the goal is liberation or freedom and through developing a daily practice that may integrate with how our existing society functions, you develop a pathway towards self-transcendence that is assimilated into your day-to-day reality.

Saṅkhārā – The formations aggregate is an umbrella term that includes all volitional, emotive, and intellectual aspects of mental life. And consciousness which is the fifth aggregate, is the basic awareness of an object indispensable to all cognition.

Satsang – is a Sanskrit word which roughly means to associate with true people, or to be in the company of true people. We can call this a spiritual community or fellows on a similar, true spiritual path.

Sūtra – this is the Sanskrit word for 'thread'. This is what the sūtras of Patanjali in accordance with Yoga represent; the bare minimum fiber that individual teachers in accordance with accurate lineage can add on their beads of personal experience and wisdom. They are the connective lineage of Truth in Yoga, the guiding principles of which to navigate the experiential science of union.

Tefillin – sometimes known as phylacteries, they are a set of small black leather boxes containing scrolls of parchment inscribed with verses from the Torah. Tefillin is worn by observant adult Jews during weekday morning prayers.

Teleology – by definition it is the explanation of phenomena in terms of the purpose they serve rather than of the cause by which they arise. For example, a teleological explanation of why spoons have a circular, bowl-like shape is that this design helps humans eat certain foods; scooping food to help humans eat is what spoons are for. In the context of this book, Alan Watts refers to the teleological trap of the mind. The mind's teleological trap is when the mind acknowledges that whenever there is effort in anything you create to escape the process, it cannot be the source to which you are looking to return. This is because that thing you are creating, that imagined freedom-state, cannot be created by the effort of the mind-based system because it is a thought. Thoughts are merely a bi-product within the fabric of consciousness, which it is not meta to. If you can think it, you can know for sure that it is not that.

Toponymy – by definition it is the study of place names, their origins, meanings, use and typology.

Ujjayi – this is another form of pranayama. It is created by gently constricting the opening of the throat to create some resistance to the passage of air. Gently pulling the breath in on inhalation and gently pushing the breath out on exhalation against this resistance creates a well-modulated and soothing sound—something like the sound of ocean waves rolling in and out.

Vairāgya – the root meaning of vairāgya is to be uncoloured. In essence, you can live amidst the world yet you are not tethered or attached to it. This roughly translates as dispassion, detachment, or renunciation. However, I view dispassion as quite a cutting word as it may bring up thoughts of indifference and complacency. This is not the case. This state normally coincides with a particular renunciation from the pains and pleasures in the temporary material world. So, in our modern context, as opposed to the renunciation of everything, a true practitioner will become detached from the reactionary nature to the external world itself, so that the external world has no power over you. You can still participate in the world and use right-action in regards to social and environmental justice, for example, yet you are not thrown into suffering if your expectations or models of how you wanted something to look or happen do not come to pass. In this fluidity and innocence, the moment-by-moment consciousness has no need to attach to anything, no grasping and no pushing away. It is purely there and by being there it acts in accordance with natural law.

Vritti – Within the *citta*, there are the *vrittis*, which are mind modifications. The five *vrittis* are as follows:

1. Pramāna – correct or right knowledge
2. Viparyaya – misconception, or incorrect knowledge
3. Vikalpa – verbal delusion or imagination
4. Nidra – sleep
5. Smrti – memory

Wu-wei – in Chinese—non-doing or 'doing nothing'. This concept is key to the noblest kind of action according to the philosophy of Taoism—and is at the heart of what it means to follow (Tao) or The Way. A common quote pertaining to this is, "The Way never acts yet nothing is left undone."

It doesn't mean not acting, but rather it means effortless action, or actionless action. It is closely connected to the reverence for the natural world and its spontaneous and inevitable processes, its fluidity amidst change. It involves letting go of ideals that we may otherwise try to force too violently onto things, it follows a path of least-resistance without trying to follow a path of least-resistance. Normally, feelings of self-transcendence and a loss of self-centeredness arises which has the potential to release an energy that is normally held back by an overly aggressive, willful style of thinking.

Notes

1   Lisciotto, Carmelo for the Holocaust Education & Archive Research Team
    (H.E.A.R.T.), (2007), *Joseph Goebbels, "The Poison Dwarf"*, Retrieved from:
    http://www.holocaustresearchproject.org/holoprelude/goebbels.html
2   Cision Contributor, (2018, January 22). *Are Declining Attention Spans Killing
    Your Content Marketing Strategy?* Retrieved from: https://www.cision.com/
    us/2018/01/declining-attention-killing-content-marketing-strategy/
3   Oxford Poverty & Human Development Initiative, (2008), *Bhutan's Gross
    National Happiness Index*, Retrieved from: https://ophi.org.uk/policy/national-
    policy/gross-national-happiness-index/
4   Cornell, Carolina, (2018, July 2), *The Patient Advocacy Groups that Accept the
    Most Big Pharma Money*, Retrieved from: https://www.classaction.com/news/
    patient-advocacy-groups-big-pharma/
5   Postman, Neil, (1985), *Amusing Ourselves to Death: Public Discourse in the Age
    of Show Business*, New York, N.Y., U.S.A.: Penguin Books
6   Built-In, *Blockchain* 101, Retrieved from: https://builtin.com/blockchain
7   Irfan, Umair, (2019, November 18), *Brazil's Amazon rainforest destruction is at
    its highest rate in more than a decade*, Retrieved from: https://www.vox.com/
    science-and-health/2019/11/18/20970604/amazon-rainforest-2019-brazil-
    burning-deforestation-bolsonaro
8   University of Maryland. (2019, June 19). "U.S. beekeepers lost over 40 percent
    of colonies last year, highest winter losses ever recorded: Results point to a need
    for increased research, extension, and best management practices." *ScienceDaily*.
    Retrieved from: www.sciencedaily.com/releases/2019/06/190619142532.htm

9   Lytkowski, Juliana. (2020, April 19). *Curbing America's Trash Production: Statistics and Solutions.* Retrieved from: https://www.dumpsters.com/blog/us-trash-production#:~:text=The%20average%20American%20consumer%20produces,6%2C570%20pounds%20per%20family

10   Cleary, Thomas. (1998, September, 1). *The Sutra of Hui-neng, Grand Master of Zen.* Shambhala Dragon Editions

11   HuffPost, (2012, July 12), *American Yoga: How Many People Practice Yoga in the United States?,* Retrieved from: https://www.huffpost.com/entry/american-yoga_n_2251360

12   Goenke, S.N., Day 5 *Discourse,* Retrieved from: https://www.dhamma.org/en/os/10-day/summaries/day5

13   Goenke, S.N., Day 6 *Discourse,* Retrieved from: https://www.dhamma.org/en/os/10-day/summaries/day6

14   Goenke, S.N., Day 6 *Discourse,* Retrieved from: https://www.dhamma.org/en/os/10-day/summaries/day6

15   Satchitananda, Sri Swami, (2012, September 14), *The Yoga Sūtras of Patanjali,* U.S.A, Integral Yoga Publications

16   *Political History.* Retrieved from: https://www.hawaiiankingdom.org/political-history.shtml

17   Sen, Paul. (2007, July 25). *Tiny finding that opened new frontier.* Retrieved from: http://news.bbc.co.uk/2/hi/science/nature/6914175.stm

18   Youssef, Elyane. (2016, December 21). *The Rumi Poem We All Should Read.* Retrieved from: https://www.elephantjournal.com/2016/12/the-rumi-poem-we-should-all-read/

19   Non-GMO Project. *What is a GMO?* Retrived from: https://www.nongmoproject.org/gmo-facts/what-is-gmo/

20   History.com Editors. (2011, August 2). *Agent Orange.* Retrieved from: https://www.history.com/topics/vietnam-war/agent-orange-1

21   Lewin, Jo. *What does organic mean?* Retrieved from: (https://www.bbcgoodfood.com/howto/guide/organic

22   Gal, David, "Let Hunger Be Your Guide? Being Hungry Before a Meal is Associated with Healthier Levels of Post-Meal Blood Glucose." (December 18, 2015). *Journal of the Association for Consumer Research,* 1:1, 2016, Forthcoming, Retrieved from: https://ssrn.com/abstract=2705592

23   Freund, Daisy. (2011, August 25). *How Animal Welfare Leads to Better Meat: A Lesson from Spain.* Retrieved from: https://www.theatlantic.com/health/archive/2011/08/how-animal-welfare-leads-to-better-meat-a-lesson-from-spain/244127/

24 Theobald JL, Spoelhof R, Pallasch EM, Mycyk MB. "The Beef Jerky Blues: Methemoglobinemia From Home Cured Meat." *Pediatr Emerg Care.* 2018;34(7):e122-e123. doi:10.1097/PEC.0000000000000917. Retrieved from: https://pubmed.ncbi.nlm.nih.gov/27749634/

25 Marquez, Emily. (2018, August 2). *In the U.S. and the world, pesticide use is up.* Retrieved from: http://www.panna.org/blog/us-and-world-pesticide-use

26 Toland Frith, Katherine, Mueller, Barbara. (2010, March 31). *Advertising and Societies: Global Issues, Second Edition.* U.S.A. Peter Lang Inc., International Academic Publishers

27 Rachdaoui, Nadia, and Dipak K Sarkar. "Effects of alcohol on the endocrine system." *Endocrinology and metabolism clinics of North America* vol. 42,3 (2013): 593-615. doi:10.1016/j.ecl.2013.05.008. Retrieved from: https://www.ncbi.nlm.nih.gov/pmc/articles/PMC3767933/

28 Kuakini Health System. *Caffeine: America's Most Popular Drug.* Retrieved from: https://www.kuakini.org/wps/portal/public/Health-Wellness/Health-Info-Tips/Miscellaneous/Caffeine—America-s-Most-Popular-Drug

29 Tajima, Yutaka. "Coffee-induced Hypokalaemia." *Clinical medicine insights.* Case reports vol. 3 (2010): 9-13. doi:10.4137/ccrep.s4329. Retrieved from: https://www.ncbi.nlm.nih.gov/pmc/articles/PMC3046007/

30 Arrotta, Madison, Pranin Organic. *How Caffeine is Robbing Your Adrenals.* Retrieved from: https://csnn.ca/vancouver/blog/caffeine-adrenal-connection/

31 Morse, Dr. Robert. *Dr Robert Morse's Adrenal Gland Herbal Formula.* Retrieved from: https://www.ourbotanicals.com/product/adrenal-glands-tincture/

32 Gilmartin, Marieke R et al. "Prefrontal cortical regulation of fear learning." *Trends in neurosciences* vol. 37,8 (2014): 455-64. doi:10.1016/j.tins.2014.05.004. Retrieved from: https://www.ncbi.nlm.nih.gov/pmc/articles/PMC4119830/

33 Anxiety and Depression Association of America. *Facts & Statistics.* Retrieved from: https://adaa.org/about-adaa/press-room/facts-statistics

34 Pan, An & Sun, Qi & Bernstein, Adam & Schulze, Matthias & Manson, JoAnn & Willett, Walter & Hu, Frank. (2011). "Red meat consumption and risk of type 2 diabetes: 3 Cohorts of US adults and an ppdated meta-analysis." *The American journal of clinical nutrition.* 94. 1088-96. 10.3945/ajcn.111.018978. Retrieved from: https://www.researchgate.net/publication/51562202_Red_meat_consumption_and_risk_of_type_2_diabetes_3_Cohorts_of_US_adults_and_an_ppdated_meta-analysis

35 David Pimentel, Marcia Pimentel, "Sustainability of meat-based and plant-based diets and the environment." *The American Journal of Clinical Nutrition*, Volume 78, Issue 3, September 2003, Pages 660S–663S, https://doi.org/10.1093/ajcn/78.3.660S

36 Loria, Joe. (2020, February 4). *Factory Farming is Killing Our Planet: Here's How*. Retrieved from: https://www.worldanimalprotection.us/blogs/factory-farming-killing-our-planet

37 Williams, Adrian C, and Lisa J Hill. "Meat and Nicotinamide: A Causal Role in Human Evolution, History, and Demographics." *International journal of tryptophan research* : IJTR vol. 10 1178646917704661. 2 May. 2017, doi:10.1177/1178646917704661. Retrieved from: https://www.ncbi.nlm.nih.gov/pmc/articles/PMC5417583/

38 Specia, Megan. (2019, June 24). *Saudi Arabia Granted Women the Right to Drive. A Year on, It's Still Complicated*. Retrieved from: https://www.nytimes.com/2019/06/24/world/middleeast/saudi-driving-ban-anniversary.html

39 Saleem RA, Othman N, Fattah FH, Hazim L, Adnan B. "Female genital mutilation in Iraqi Kurdistan: description and associated factors." *Women Health*. 2013;53(6):537-551. doi:10.1080/03630242.2013.815681. Retrieved from: https://pubmed.ncbi.nlm.nih.gov/23937728/

40 Koltko-Rivera, Mark E., Review of General Psychology (2006), Vol. 10, *Rediscovering the Later Version of Maslow's Hierarchy of Needs: Self-Transcendence and Opportunities for Theory, Research, and Unification*. Retrieved from: https://www.simplypsychology.org/maslow(2).pdf

41 McLeod, Saul. (2020, March 20). *Maslow's Hierarchy of Needs*. Image Retrieved from: https://www.simplypsychology.org/maslow.html

42 The World Bank. (2018, September 19). *Decline of Extreme World Poverty Continues but Has Slowed: World Bank*. Retrieved from: https://www.worldbank.org/en/news/press-release/2018/09/19/decline-of-global-extreme-poverty-continues-but-has-slowed-world-bank

43 Maslow, A. H. (1943). "A theory of human motivation." *Psychological Review*, 50(4), 370–396. https://doi.org/10.1037/h0054346

44 Merchant, Brian. (2017, June 20). *The One Device: The Secret History of the iPhone*. Retrieved from: https://www.theguardian.com/technology/2017/jun/18/foxconn-life-death-forbidden-city-longhua-suicide-apple-iphone-brian-merchant-one-device-extract

45 Koltko-Rivera, Mark E., Review of General Psychology (2006), Vol. 10, *Rediscovering the Later Version of Maslow's Hierarchy of Needs: Self-Transcendence and Opportunities for Theory, Research, and Unification*. Retrieved from: https://www.simplypsychology.org/maslow(2).pdf

46 Koltko-Rivera, Mark E., Review of General Psychology (2006), Vol. 10, *Rediscovering the Later Version of Maslow's Hierarchy of Needs: Self-Transcendence and Opportunities for Theory, Research, and Unification*. Retrieved from: https://www.simplypsychology.org/maslow(2).pdf

47 Tanne, Janice Hopkins. "Humphry Osmond." BMJ : *British Medical Journal* vol. 328,7441 (2004): 713. Retrieved from: https://www.ncbi.nlm.nih.gov/pmc/articles/PMC381240/

48 Biello, David. (2008, April 30). *Albert Hofmann, Inventor of LSD, Embarks on Final Trip*. Retrieved from: https://www.scientificamerican.com/article/inventor-of-lsd-embarks-on-final-trip/

49 Shuler, Rus. (1998). *How Does the Internet Work?* https://web.stanford.edu/class/msande91si/www-spr04/readings/week1/InternetWhitepaper.htm

50 Sheldrake, Rupert. (Spring 1988), *Psychological Perspectives*, 19(1) 64-78. Retrieved from: https://www.sheldrake.org/research/morphic-resonance/part-iii-extended-mind-power-prayer-morphic-resonance-and-the-collective-unconscious

51 National Aeronautics and Space Administration, Science Mission Directorate. (2010). *Visible Light*. Retrieved from NASA Science website: http://science.nasa.gov/ems/09_visiblelight

52 Davis, Julie. "American Indian Boarding School Experiences: Recent Studies from Native Perspectives." *OAH Magazine of History*, Volume 15, Issue 2, Winter 2001, Pages 20–22. Retrieved from: https://doi.org/10.1093/maghis/15.2.20

53 Kupfer, David. (2015, December 11). *Remembering John Trudell, Voice of the American Indian Movement*. Retrieved from: https://progressive.org/dispatches/remembering-john-trudell-voice-american-indian-movement/

54 Behrendt, Larissa. 2012. *Indigenous Australia for Dummies*. Wiley Publishing Australia PTY LTD, Milton, Australia

55 Walker, Charles. Fall 2014. *Peru: Reflections of Tupac Amaru*. Retrieved from: https://clas.berkeley.edu/research/peru-reflections-tupac-amaru

56 Waters, Frank. (1977, June 30). *Book of the Hopi*. U.S.A., Penguin Books

57 McLeod, Toby. (2020, April 4). *Hopi Prophecy—A Timeless Warning*. Retrieved from: https://sacredland.org/hopi-prophecy/

58 Garrison, Kathleen A et al. "Meditation leads to reduced default mode network activity beyond an active task." *Cognitive, affective & behavioral neuroscience* vol. 15,3 (2015): 712-20. doi:10.3758/s13415-015-0358-3. Retrieved from: https://www.ncbi.nlm.nih.gov/pmc/articles/PMC4529365/

59 In Congress. (1776, July 4). *Declaration of Independence: A Transcription.* Retrieved from: https://www.archives.gov/founding-docs/declaration-transcript#:~:text=He%20has%20excited%20domestic%20insurrections, all%20ages%2C%20sexes%20and%20conditions

60 LaDuke, Winona. (2013, March 1). *The Militarization of Indian Country.* Makwa Enewed; 2nd edition

61 LaDuke, Winona. (2013, March 1). *The Militarization of Indian Country.* Makwa Enewed; 2nd edition

62 Malone, Kobatsu. (2010). *Narcissism and Spiritual Materialism: The New Age Legacy.* Retrieved from: http://www.engaged-zen.org/articles/Kobutsu-New_Age_Legacy.html

63 Edmonds, Ennis B. (2012). *Rastafari: A Very Short Introduction.* Oxford: Oxford University Press

64 Schmandt-Besserat, Denise. (1996). *When Writing Came About.* The University of Texas Press. Retrieved from: https://sites.utexas.edu/dsb/tokens/from-accounting-to-writing/

65 Kitsikis, Dimitri. (1985). *L'Orocc, dans l'âge de Kali,* France, Naaman.

66 Fulmer, Melinda. (2019, December 20). *Why shamanism is red hot right now: 12 things you need to know.* Retrieved from: https://www.latimes.com/lifestyle/story/2019-12-20/shaman-durek-guru-to-the-stars

67 Lambert, Lance. (2020 May 28). *Over 40 million Americans have filed for unemployment during the pandemic—real jobless rate over 23.9%.* Retrieved from: https://fortune.com/2020/05/28/us-unemployment-rate-numbers-claims-this-week-total-job-losses-may-28-2020-benefits-claims-job-losses/

68 Simmons, Nancy & Guarisco, Elio. (2013, March 12). *The Tibetan Book of the Dead: Awakening Upon Dying.* U.S.A., Penguin Random House.

69 Chem. Eng. News 1994, 72, 37, 38–45. (1994, September 12). *Antoine Lavoisier & the Conservation of Matter.* Retrieved from: https://doi.org/10.1021/cen-v072n037.p038

70 Johnson III, Theodore R., (2014, May 11). *Recall That Ice Cream Truck Song? We Have Unpleasant News For You.* Retreived from: https://www.npr.org/sections/codeswitch/2014/05/11/310708342/recall-that-ice-cream-truck-song-we-have-unpleasant-news-for-you

71 Goldberg, David Theo. (2015, September 25). *Why "Black Lives Matter" Because All Lives Don't Matter in America*. Retrieved from: https:// www.huffpost.com/entry/why-black-lives-matter_b_8191424

72 Sakala, Leah. (2014, May 28). *Breaking Down Mass Incarceration in the 2010 Census: State-by-State Incarceration Rates by Race/Ethnicity*. Retrieved from: https://www.prisonpolicy.org/reports/rates.html

73 The U.S. National Archives and Records Administration. *13th Amendment to the U.S. Constitution: Abolition of Slavery*. Retrieved from: https://www. archives.gov/historical-docs/13th-amendment

74 Federal Bureau of Prisons. *Program Details*. Retrieved from: https://www.bop. gov/inmates/custody_and_care/unicor_about.jsp

75 Sloan, Bob & Elk, Mike. (2011, August 1). *The Hidden History of ALEC and Prison Labor*. Retrieved from: https://www.thenation.com/article/archive/hidden-history-alec-and-prison-labor/

76 Eisenhower, Dwight D. (1961). *Transcript of President Dwight D. Eisenhower's Farewell Address*. Retrieved from: https://www.ourdocuments.gov/doc.php? flash=false&doc=90&page=transcript

77 Core Civic, Inc. (2020, February 12). *CoreCivic Reports Fourth Quarter and Full Year 2019 Financial Results*. Retrieved from: https://www.globenewswire.com/ news-release/2020/02/12/1984157/0/en/CoreCivic-Reports-Fourth-Quarter-and-Full-Year-2019-Financial-Results.html

78 Kolbert, Elizabeth. (2018, March 12). *There's No Scientific Basis for Race— It's a Made-Up Label*. Retrieved from: https://www.nationalgeographic.com/ magazine/2018/04/race-genetics-science-africa/

79 Ibid.

80 Kruse, Kevin M. (2019, August 14). *What does a traffic jam in Atlanta have to do with segregation? A lot*. Retrieved from: https://www.nytimes.com/ interactive/2019/08/14/magazine/traffic-atlanta-segregation.html?mtrref= undefined&gwh=DA8972C77E6DA148BEAA2BA8C8F2B7BF&gwt= pay&assetType=REGIWALL

81 Rogers, Joel. (2009 August). *High Road Capitalism*. Retrieved from: https:// www.ssc.wisc.edu/~wright/ContemporaryAmericanSociety/Chapter%209%20 --%20high%20road%20capitalism%20--%20Norton%20August.pdf

82 Desmond, Matthew. (2019, August 14). *In order to understand the brutality of American capitalism, you have to start on the plantation*. Retrieved from: https://www.nytimes.com/interactive/2019/08/14/magazine/traffic-atlanta-segregation.html

83 Fit4D. (2017, August 8). *The Neuroscience of Behavior Change*. https://
    healthtransformer.co/the-neuroscience-of-behavior-change-bcb567fa83c1

84 Catlow BJ, Song S, Paredes DA, Kirstein CL, Sanchez-Ramos J. "Effects of
    psilocybin on hippocampal neurogenesis and extinction of trace fear condition-
    ing." *Exp Brain Res*. 2013;228(4):481-491. doi:10.1007/s00221-013-3579-0.
    Retrieved from: https://pubmed.ncbi.nlm.nih.gov/23727882/

85 History.com Editors. (2010, June 10). *Salt March*. Retrieved from: https://
    www.history.com/topics/india/salt-march

86 Goenke, S.N., *Day 5 Discourse*, Retrieved from: https://www.dhamma.org/en/
    os/10-day/summaries/day5

87 Feng, Gia-Fu & English, Jane, (1972), *Lao Tsu - Tao Te Ching, Chapter 13*,
    Wildwood House 1991. Retrieved from: https://www.wussu.com/laotzu/
    laotzu13.html

88 Churchill, Ward, (1988 December). IWGIA Document Number 62: *Critical
    Issues in Native North America*. Retrieved from: https://www.iwgia.org/
    images/publications//0100_62_critical_issues_in_native_North_America.pdf

89 Harris, La & Wasilewski, Jacqueline. (2004). "Indigeneity, an alternative world-
    view: Four R's (Relationship, Responsibility, Reciprocity, Redistribution) vs.
    two P's (power and profit). Sharing the journey towards conscious evolution."
    Systems Research and Behavioral Science. 21. 489 - 503. 10.1002/sres.631.
    Retrieved from: https://www.researchgate.net/publication/227931327_
    Indigeneity_an_alternative_worldview_Four_R's_Relationship_Responsibility_
    Reciprocity_Redistribution_vs_two_P's_power_and_profit_Sharing_the_
    journey_towards_conscious_evolution/citation/download

90 Jung, C.G. (2014, March 1). *Collected Works of C.G. Jung, Volume 14:
    Mysterium Coniunctionis 2nd edition*. U.S.A., Princeton University Press

91 Barth, Brian. (2016, April 19). Permaculture: *You've Heard of It, But What
    the Heck Is It?* Retrieved from: https://modernfarmer.com/2016/04/
    permaculture/

About the Author

RYAN J. KEMP is an author, poet and universal thinker who frequently writes about philosophy, psychology, consciousness and spirituality. He has worked in, lived in, and traveled to over forty-five countries in the past eight years working on global issues such as food waste, women's education equality and energy independence. Ryan is also a certified YTT-200 hour Ashtanga Yoga teacher and an Ayurvedic dietician and masseuse. His other three books include: *Returning Home: A Collection of Poems From Around the World* and two children's books titled: *My Day With the Monk* and *A Walk in the Park: A Tale of Impermanence*.

He currently resides on the Big Island of Hawai'i.